Shri Sai Satcharitra:
The Wonderful Life and Teachings of Shirdi Sai Baba

by Hemadpant
(Govind Raghunath Dabholkar)
Original English Translation by N. V. Gunaji
this edition Edited by Evan Rofheart

Published by:
Enlightenment Press
2016
New York City

Sri Sai Baba

Preface to the this Edition
by Evan Rofheart

Who was Shirdi Sai Baba? Baba lived all his adult life in Shirdi, a small village in India. To the unknowing, He seemed a simple beggar, dressed in torn clothes, having no need for any material item. Claiming neither the Hindu nor Muslim religion, nor any religion. He lived in an abandoned Mosque with no roof and everyday took his food from a few people, making his rounds with his begging bowl, door to door.

What really was happening; He was burning the karmas of everyone who came to Him, in the dhuni (Divine Fire) Baba kept burning at all times. Healing and giving guidance on every level. Hundreds of thousands of miracles are attributed to Him in His life and they have multiplied now after His Mahasamadhi. Baba left His physical form in 1918, but his Divine Energy and Intention and Power is always available and at work in the world.

The Shri Sai Satcharitra is a discourse based on experiences Baba's devotees had with Him during His life on earth. It is said that Shirdi Sai Baba caused it to be written through Shri Anna Saheb Dabholkar - Hemadpant - by giving inner motivation to him. Baba had clearly told him: "I Myself write my own life. Hearing My stories and teachings will create faith in devotees' hearts and they will easily get self-realization and bliss...." (Shri Sai Satcharitra, Chapter 2)

Antonio Rigopoulos, in the prologue to his book, 'The Life and Teachings of Sai Baba of Shirdi', says that "...millions of people revere and worship Him as a God, an avatar, and as a teacher of tolerance and mutual harmony between Hinduism and Islam". Rigopoulos believes that Baba's "... ever-expanding fame is due, in the first place, to his alleged powers as a miracle worker and a healer." "Besides this fundamental characteristic of the saint of Shirdi, his personality remains, overall, enigmatic and obscure. His birthplace and religious affiliation are a mystery to all, and today people still debate whether he was a Hindu or a Muslim." "What is certain is that a young ascetic identified by the villagers as a Muslim, reached the hamlet of Shirdi one day in the last century (i.e. in the 19th century); that he was attributed the name of Sai Baba; and that he lived in the village (in Ahmednagar district of the State of Maharashtra) till the end of his days, dwelling in a dilapidated mosque."

"He was of unpredictable moods - loving, harsh, humorous, abusive! But he had spiritual charisma whether he was speaking in parables or observing prolonged silences. "Sai Baba's whole persona, his movements, words and glances conveyed a tangible and immediate experience of the sacred. "The holy preceptor by the word lighted a lamp; thereby was shattered darkness of the temple of the self; and the unique chamber of jewels was thrown up".

Zarine Taraporevala, writing in the preface to her translation of this book, "Sree Sai Samartha Satcharita", writes, "The people of Shirdi worshipped Sai as their God. He dwelt in Shirdi as the embodiment of pure Existence, Knowledge and Bliss - the Sadguru, who was King of Kings! King of Yogis! Absolute Brahman! While eating, drinking, working in their backyards and fields, doing various household chores, they always remembered Sai and sang of His Glory." Explaining how this book came to be, she writes, "It occurred to Govindrao Raghunath Dabholkar to present Baba's legendary life, while he was intermittently living in Shirdi from 1910 to 1916, after he witnessed Baba grinding wheat and then having the flour thrown on the village border limits to cast out cholera. This incident was the inspiration for "Sree Sai Samartha Satcharita" for Dabholkar, as he contemplated Baba's grinding, almost every day, not of the wheat, but sins and the mental and physical afflictions and miseries of his devotees."

"Dabholkar's poetic work runs into fifty-three chapters, modeled on the 'Eknathi Bhagvat', containing more than nine thousand ovis or verses. Every chapter is a mixture of philosophy, anecdotes and teachings. His book is akin to the Vedas for Sai's devotees." To many people, The Divine Truth imparted by this book is even greater than the knowledge contained in the Vedas and the Gita, because all the characters and events in it are real and authentic and have been recorded in detail by many devotees.

To Baba all religions were One, and it is hoped that all readers of this kindle version of the Shri Sai Satcharita, will come to know and experience their own Universal Truth.

~ Om Sai Ram ~

Note for this Edition

I have attempted to remain true to N.V. Gunaji's original English translation. While some of the sentence structure and references may be slightly obscure for the Western reader, what is clear is that since the original English translation by N.V. Gunaji was published, that it has in its unaltered state, been a core component of the spread of knowledge and devotion to Shirdi Sai Baba in the English speaking world. To help the reader with some of the obscure words and references in the Satcharitra, I have added a Glossary at the end. Note also that "Rs." throughout the text is the symbol for rupees, in the same way that "$" is the symbol for dollars. ~ E.R.

Chapter I

Salutations -- The Story of Grinding Wheat and Its Philosophical Significance.

According to the ancient and revered custom, Hemadpant begins the work, Sai Satcharitra, with various salutations.

First, he makes obeisance to the God Ganesha to remove all obstacles and make the work a success and says that Shri Sai is the God Ganesha.

Then, to the Goddess Saraswati to inspire him to write out the work and says that Shri Sai is one with this Goddess and that He is Himself singing His own life.

Then, to the Gods; Brahma, Vishnu and Shiva - the Creating, Preserving and Destroying Deities respectively; and says that Sainath is one with them and He as the great Teacher, will carry us across the River of Worldly Existence.

Then, to his tutelary Deity Narayan Adinath who manifested himself in Konkan - the land reclaimed by Parashurama, (Rama in the Hindi version) from the sea; and to the Adi (Original) Purusha of the family.

Then, to the Bharadwaja Muni, into whose gotra (clan) he was born and also to various Rishis, Yagyavalakya, Bhrigu, Parashara, Narad, Vedavyasa, Sanak, Sanandan, Sanatkumar, Shuka. Shounak, Vishwamitra, Vasistha, Valmiki, Vamadeva, Jaimini, Vaishampayan, Nava Yogindra etc., and also modern Saints such as Nivritti, Jnanadev, Sopan, Muktabai, Janardan, Ekanath, Namdev, Tukaram, Kanha, and Narahari etc..

Then, to his grandfather Sadashiv, father Raghunath, his mother, who left him in his infancy, to his paternal aunt, who brought him up, and to his loving elder brother.

Then, to the readers and prays them to give their whole and undivided attention to his work.

And lastly, to his Guru Shri Sainath - an Incarnation of Shri Dattatreya, Who is his sole Refuge and Who will make him realize that Brahman is the Reality and the world an illusion; and incidentally, to all the Beings in whom the Lord God dwells.

After describing in brief the various modes of devotion according to Parashara, Vyasa and Shandilya etc.., the author goes on to relate the following story:

It was sometime after 1910 that I went one fine morning, to the Masjid in Shirdi for getting a darshan of Sai Baba. I was wonder struck to see the following phenomenon. After washing His mouth and face, Sai Baba began to make preparations for grinding wheat. He spread a sack on the floor; and thereon set a hand- mill. He took some quantity of wheat in a winnowing fan, and then drawing up the sleeves of His Kafni (robe); and taking hold of the peg of the hand-mill, started grinding the wheat by putting a few handfuls of wheat in the upper opening of the mill and rotated it.

I thought 'What business Baba had with the grinding of wheat, when He possessed nothing and stored nothing, and as He lived on alms!' Some people who had come there thought likewise, but none had the courage to ask Baba what He was doing. Immediately, this news of Baba's grinding wheat spread into the village, and at once men and women ran to the Masjid and flocked there to see Baba's act. Four bold women, from the crowd, forced their way up and pushing Baba aside, took forcibly the peg or handle into their hands, and, singing Baba's Leelas, started grinding. At first Baba was enraged, but on seeing the women's love and devotion, He was much pleased and began to smile. While they were grinding, they began to think that Baba had no house, no property, no children, none to look after, and He lived on alms, He did not require any wheat-flour for making bread or roti, what will He do with this big quantity of flour? Perhaps as Baba is very kind, He will distribute the flour amongst us. Thinking in this way while singing, they finished the grinding and after putting the hand-mill aside, they divided the flour into four portions and began to remove them one per head. Baba, Who was calm and quiet up till now, got wild and started abusing them saying, "Ladies, are you gone mad? Whose father's property are you looting away? Have I borrowed any wheat from you, so that you can safely take the flour? Now please do this. Take the flour and throw it on the village border limits." On hearing this, the women felt abashed and whispering amongst themselves, went away to the outskirts of the village and spread the flour as directed by Baba.

I asked the Shirdi people - "What was this that Baba did?" They replied that as the Cholera Epidemic was spreading in the village and this was Baba's remedy against the same; it was not wheat that was ground but the Cholera itself was ground to pieces and pushed out of the village. From this time onward, the Cholera Epidemic subsided and the people of the village were happy. I was much pleased to know all this; but at the same time my curiosity was also aroused. I began to ask myself - What earthly connection was there between wheat flour and Cholera? What was the casual relation between the two? How to reconcile them? The incident seems to be inexplicable. I should write something on this and sing to my heart's content Baba's sweet Leelas.

Thinking in this way about this Leela, my heart was filled with joy and I was thus inspired to write Baba's Life - The Satcharita. And as we know, with Baba's grace and blessing this work was successfully accomplished.

Philosophical Significance of Grinding

Apart from the meaning which the people of Shirdi put on this incident of grinding wheat, there is, we think, a philosophical significance too. Sai Baba lived in Shirdi for about sixty years and during this long period, He did the business of grinding almost every day - not, however, the wheat alone; but the sins, the mental and physical afflictions and the miseries of His innumerable devotees. The two stones of His mill consisted of Karma and Bhakti, the former being the lower and the latter the upper one. The handle with which Baba worked the mill consisted of Jnana. It was the firm conviction of Baba that Knowledge or Self-realization is not possible, unless there is the prior act of grinding of all our impulses, desires, and sins; and of the three Gunas, viz... Sattva, Raja and Tama; and the Ahamkara, which is so subtle and therefore so difficult to be got rid of.

This reminds us of a similar story of Kabir who seeing a woman grinding corn said to his Guru, Nipathiranjana, "I am weeping because I feel the agony of being crushed in this wheel of worldly existence like the corn in the hand-mill." Nipathiranjana replied, "Do not be afraid; hold fast to the handle of knowledge of this mill, as I do, and do not wander far away from the same but turn inward to the Center, and you are sure to be saved."

Bow to Shri Sai -- Peace be to all

Chapter II

Object of Writing the Work - Incapacity and Boldness in the
Undertaking - Hot Discussion - Conferring Significant and
Prophetic Title of Hemadpant - Necessity of a Guru

In the last Chapter, the author mentioned in the original
Marathi book that he would state the reason that led him to
undertake the work, and the persons qualified to read the
same and such other points. Now in this chapter, he starts to
tell the same.

Object of Writing the Work

In the first chapter, I described Sai Baba's miracle of checking
and destroying the epidemic of Cholera by grinding wheat and
throwing the flour, on the outskirts of the village. I heard other
miracles of Sai Baba to my great delight, and this delight burst
forth into this poetic work. I also thought, that the description of
these grand miracles of Sai Baba would be interesting, and
instructive to His devotees; and would remove their sins, and so I
began to write the sacred life and teachings of Sai Baba. The life
of the saint is neither logical nor dialectical. It shows us the true
and great path.

Incapacity and Boldness in Undertaking the Work

Hemadpant thought that he was not a fit person to undertake
the work. He said, "I do not know the life of my intimate friend
nor do I know my own mind, then how can I write the life of a
saint or describe the nature of Incarnations, which even the Vedas
were unable to do? One must be a saint himself, before he could
know other saints, then how can I describe their glory? To write
the life of a saint is the most difficult, though one may as well
measure the depth of the water of the seven seas or enclose the
sky with cloth-trappings. I knew, that this was the most
venturesome undertaking, which might expose me to ridicule. I,
therefore, invoked Sai Baba's grace.

5

The premier poet-saint of Maharashtra, Shri Jnaneshwar Maharaj, has stated that the Lord loves those who write the lives of saints; and the saints also have a peculiar method of their own of getting the service, which the devotees long for, successfully accomplished. The saints inspire the work; the devotee becomes only an indirect cause or instrument to achieve the end. For instance, in 1700 Shaka year, the poet Mahipati aspired to write the lives of saints. Saints inspired him, and got the work done; so also in 1800 Shaka year, Das Ganu's service was accepted.

The former wrote four works - Bhakta Vijaya, Santa Vijaya, Bhakta Leelamrit and Santa Kathamrit, while the latter wrote two - "Bhakta Leelamrit and Santa Kathamrit", in which the lives of modern Saints were described. In chapters 31, 32 & 33 of Bhakta Leelamrit and in chapter 57 of Santa Kathamrit, the sweet life and teachings of Sai Baba are very well depicted. These have been separately published in Sai Leela Magazine, Nos. 11 and 12, Vol.17; the readers are advised to read these chapters. So also Sai Baba's wonderful Leelas are described in a small decent book named Shri Sainath Bhajana Mala by Mrs. Savitribai Raghunath Tendulkar of Bandra. Das-Ganu Maharaj also has composed various sweet poems on Sai Baba. A devotee named Amidas Bhavani Mehta, has also published some stories of Sri Baba in Gujarathi; some Nos. of Sainath Prabha, a magazine published by Dakshina Bhiksha Sanstha of Shirdi, are also published. Then the question of objection comes in, that while so many works regarding Sai Baba are extant, why should this (Satcharita) be written? And where is its necessity?

The answer is plain and simple. The life of Sai Baba is as wide and deep as the infinite ocean; and all can dive deep into the same and take out precious gems (of knowledge and Bhakti), and distribute them to the aspiring public. The stories, parables, and teachings of Sai Baba are very wonderful. They will give peace and happiness to the people, who are afflicted with sorrows and heavily loaded with miseries of this worldly existence, and also bestow knowledge and wisdom, both in the worldly and in spiritual domains.

If these teachings of Sai Baba, which are as interesting and instructive as the Vedic lore, are listened to and meditated upon, the devotees will get, what they long for, viz., Union with Brahman, mastery in eight-fold Yoga, Bliss of meditation etc...So I thought that I should call these stories together that would be my best Upasana. This collection would be most delightful to those simple souls, whose eyes were not blessed with Sai Baba's darshan. So, I set about collecting Sai Baba's teachings and expressions - the outcome of His boundless and natural self-realization. It was Sai Baba, who inspired me in this matter; in fact, I surrendered my ego at His feet, and thought that my path was clear; and that He would make me quite happy here, and in the next world.

I could not myself ask Sai Baba to give me permission for this work; so I requested Mr. Madhavrao Deshpande alias Shama, Baba's most intimate devotee, to speak to Him for me. He pleaded for my cause and said to Sai Baba, "This Annasaheb wishes to write Your biography, don't say that You are a poor begging Fakir, and there is no necessity to write it, but if You agree and help him, he will write or rather, Your feet (grace) will accomplish the work. Without Your consent and blessing, nothing can be done successfully."

When Sai Baba heard this request, He was moved and blessed me by giving me His Udi (sacred ashes) and placing His boon-bestowing hand on my head said :- "Let him make a collection of stories and experiences, keep notes and memos; I will help him. He is only an outward instrument. I should write Myself, My autobiography and satisfy the wishes of My devotees. He should get rid of his ego, place (or surrender) it at My feet. He who acts like this in life, him I help the most. What of My life stories? I serve him in his house in all possible ways. When his ego is completely annihilated and there is left no trace of it, I, Myself shall enter into him and shall Myself write My own life. Hearing my stories and teachings will create faith in devotees' hearts and they will easily get self - realization and Bliss; let there be no insistence on establishing one's own view, no attempt to refute other's opinions, no discussions of pros and cons of any subject."

The word 'discussion' put me in mind of my promise to

explain the story of my getting the title of Hemadpant and now I begin to relate the same. I was on close friendly terms with Kakasaheb Dixit and Nanasaheb Chandorkar. They pressed me to go to Shirdi and have Baba's darshan, and I promised them to do so. But something in the interval turned up, which prevented me from going to Shirdi. The son of a friend of mine at Lonavala fell ill. My friend tried all possible means, physical and spiritual, but the fever would not abate. At length he got his Guru to sit by the bedside of his son, but this too was of no avail. Hearing this, I thought 'what was the utility of the Guru, if he could not save my friend's son? If the Guru can't do anything for us, why should I go to Shirdi at all?' Thinking in this way, I postponed my Shirdi-trip; but the inevitable must happen and it happened in my case as follows:

Mr. Nanasaheb Chandorkar, who was a Prant Officer, was going on tour to Bassein. From Thana he came to Dadar and was waiting for a train bound for Bassein. In the meanwhile, a Bandra Local turned up. He sat in it and came to Bandra; and sent for me and took me to task for putting off my Shirdi trip. Nana's argument for my Shirdi trip was convincing and delightful, and so I decided to start for Shirdi, the same night. I packed up my luggage and started for Shirdi. I planned to go to Dadar and there to catch the train for Manmad, and so I booked myself for Dadar and sat in the train.

While the train was to start, a Mohammedan came hastily to my compartment and seeing all my paraphernalia, asked me where I was bound to. I told him my plan. He then suggested that I should straight go to Boribunder, and not get down at Dadar, for the Manmad Mail did not get down at Dadar at all. If this little miracle or Leela had not happened, I would not have reached Shirdi next day as settled, and many doubts would have assailed me. But that was not to be. As fortune favored me, I reached Shirdi the next day before 9 or 10am, Mr. Bhausaheb (Kaka) Dixit was waiting for me there. This was in 1910, when there was only one place, Sathe's Wada for lodging pilgrim devotees. After alighting from the Tonga, I was anxious to have darshan. Then the great devotee, Tatyasaheb Noolkar returned from the Masjid and said that Sai Baba was at the corner of the Wada, and that I should first get the preliminary darshan and then, after bath, see Him at leisure. Hearing this I ran and prostrated before Baba and then my joy knew no bounds. I found more than what Nana Chandorkar had told me. All my senses were satisfied and I forgot thirst and hunger.

The moment I touched Sai Baba's feet, I began a new lease of life. I felt myself much obliged to those who spurred and helped me to get the darshan; and I considered them as my real relatives, and I cannot repay their debt. I only remember them and prostrate (mentally) before them. The peculiarity of Sai Baba's darshan, as I found it, is that by His darshan our thoughts are changed, the force of previous actions is abated and gradually non-attachment of dis-passion towards worldly objects grows up. It is by the merit of actions in many past births that such darshan is got, and if only you see Sai Baba, really all the world becomes or assumes the form of Sai Baba.

Hot Discussion

On the first day of my arrival in Shirdi, there was a discussion between me and Balasaheb Bhate regarding the necessity of a Guru. I contended, "Why should we lose our freedom and submit to others? When we have to do our duty, why a Guru is necessary? One must try his best and save himself. What can the Guru do to a man who does nothing but sleeps indolently?" Thus I pleaded freewill, while Mr. Bhate took up the other side, viz.., Destiny, and said, "Whatever is bound to happen must happen; even great men have failed, man proposes one way, but God disposes the other (contrary) way. Brush aside your cleverness; pride or egoism won't help you." This discussion, with all its pros and cons went on for an hour or so, and as usual no decision was arrived at. We had to stop the discussion ultimately as we were exhausted. The net result of this was that I lost my peace of mind and found that unless there is strong body-consciousness and egoism, there would be no discussion; in other words, it is egoism which breeds discussion.

Then when we went to the Masjid with others, Baba asked Kakasaheb Dixit the following:

"What was going on in the (Sathe's) Wada? What was the

discussion about?" and staring at me, Baba further added, "What did this Hemadpant say?"

Hearing these words, I was much surprised. The Masjid was at a considerable distance from Sathe's Wada where I was staying and where the discussion was going on. How could Baba know our discussion unless He be omniscient and Inner Ruler of us all?

Significant and Prophetic Title

I began to think why Sai Baba should call me by the name Hemadpant. This word is a corrupt form of Hemadripant. This Hemadripant was a well-known Minister of the kings Mahadev and Ramadev of Devgiri of the Yadav dynasty. He was very learned, good-natured and the author of good works, such as Chaturvarga Chintamani (dealing with spiritual subjects) and Rajprashasti. He invented and started new methods of accounts and was the originator of the Modi (Marathi Shorthand) script. But I was quite the opposite, an ignoramus, and of dull, mediocre intellect. So I could not understand why the name or title was conferred upon me, but thinking seriously upon it, I thought that the title was a dart to destroy my ego, so that, I should always remain meek and humble. It was also a compliment paid to me for the cleverness in the discussion.

Looking to the future history, we think that Baba's word (calling Mr. Dabholkar by the name Hemadpant) was significant and prophetic, as we find that he looked after the management of Sai Sansthan very intelligently, kept nicely all the accounts and was also the author of such a good work "Sai Satcharita", which deals with such important and spiritual subjects as Jnana, Bhakti and dis-passion, self-surrender and self-realization.

About the Necessity of a Guru

Hemadpant has left no note, no memo about what Baba said regarding this subject, but Kakasaheb Dixit has published his notes regarding this matter. Next day after Hemadpant's meeting with Sai Baba; Kakasaheb went to Baba and asked whether he should leave Shirdi. Baba Said, "Yes". Then someone asked - "Baba, where to go?" Baba said, "High up." Then the man said,

"How is the way?" Baba said, "There are many ways leading there; there is one way also from here (Shirdi). The way is difficult. There are tigers and wolves in the jungles on the way." I (Kakasaheb) asked - "But Baba, what if we take a guide with us?" Baba answered, - "Then there is no difficulty. The guide will take you straight to your destination, avoiding wolves, tigers and ditches etc... On the way, if there be no guide, there is the danger of your being lost in the jungles or falling into ditches."

Mr. Dabholkar was present on this occasion and he thought that this was the answer Baba gave to the question whether Guru was a necessity (Vide Sai Leela Vol. I, No.5, Page 47); and he thereupon took the hint that no discussion of the problem, whether man is free or bound, is of any use in spiritual matters, but that on the contrary real Paramartha is possible only as the result of the teachings of the Guru, as is illustrated in this chapter of the original work in the instances of great Avatars like Rama and Krishna, who had to submit themselves to their Gurus, Vasishtha and Sandipani respectively, for getting self-realization and that the only virtues necessary for such progress are faith and patience.

Bow to Shri Sai - Peace be to all

Chapter III

Sai Baba's Sanction and Promise - Assignment of Work to
Devotees - Baba's Stories as Beacon - Light - His Motherly Love
Rohilla's Story - His sweet and Nectar-like Words

Sai Baba's Sanction and Promise

As described in the previous chapter, Sai Baba gave His
complete assent to the writing of the Sat-Charita and said, "I fully
agree with you regarding the writing of Sat Charita. You do your
duty, don't be afraid in the least, steady your mind and have faith
in My words. If my Leelas are written, the Avidya (prescience)
will vanish and if they are attentively, and devoutly listened to,
the consciousness of the worldly existence will abate, and strong
waves of devotion, and love will rise up and if one dives deep into
My Leelas, he would get precious jewels of knowledge."

Hearing this, author was much pleased, and he at once became
fearless and confident, and thought that work was bound to be a
success. Then turning to Shama (Madhavrao Deshpande)
Sai Baba said:

"If a man utters My name with love, I shall fulfill all his
wishes, increase his devotion. And if he sings earnestly My life
and My deeds, him I shall beset in front and back and on all sides.
Those devotees, who are attached to Me, heart and soul, will
naturally feel happiness, when they hear these stories. Believe Me
that if anybody sings My Leelas, I will give him infinite joy and
everlasting contentment. It is My special characteristic to free any
person, who surrenders completely to Me, and who does worship
Me faithfully, and who remembers Me, and meditates on Me
constantly. How can they be conscious of worldly objects and
sensations, who utter My name, who worship Me, who think of
My stories and My life and who thus always remember Me? I
shall draw out My devotees from the jaws of Death. If My stories
are listened to, all the diseases will be got rid of. So, hear My
stories with respect; and think and meditate on them, assimilate
them. This is the way of happiness and contentment. The pride
and egoism of My devotees will vanish, the mind of the hearers

12

will be set at rest; and if it has wholehearted and complete faith, it will be one with Supreme Consciousness. The simple remembrance of My name as 'Sai, Sai' will do away with sins of speech and hearing".

Different Works Assigned to Devotees

The Lord entrusts different works to different devotees. Some are given the work of building temples and maths, or ghats (flight of steps) on rivers; some are made to sing the glories of God; some are sent on pilgrimages; but to me was allotted the work of writing the Sat Charita.

Being a jack of all trades but master of none, I was quite unqualified for this job. Then why should I undertake such a difficult job? Who can describe the true life of Sai Baba? Sai Baba's grace alone can enable one to accomplish this difficult work. So, when I took up the pen in my hand, Sai Baba took away my egoism and wrote Himself His stories. The credit of relating these stories, therefore, goes to Him and not to me.

Though Brahmin by birth, I lacked the two eyes. (i.e. the sight or vision) of Shruti and Smriti and therefore was not at all capable of writing the Sat-Charita, but the grace of the Lord makes a dumb man talk, enables a lame man to cross a mountain. He alone knows the knack of getting things done as He likes. Neither the flute, nor the harmonium knows how the sounds are produced. This is the concern of the Player. The oozing of Chandrakant jewel and the surging of the sea are not due to the jewel and the sea but to the rise of the moon.

Baba's Stories as Beacon - Light

Lighthouses are constructed at various places in the sea, to enable the boatmen to avoid rocks and dangers, and make them sail safely. Sai Baba's stories serve a similar purpose in the ocean of worldly existence. They surpass nectar in sweetness, and make our worldly path smooth and easy to traverse. Blessed are the stories of the saints. When they enter our hearts through the ears, then our egoism and the sense of duality vanishes; and when they are stored in the heart, doubts fly out to all sides, pride of the body will fall, and wisdom will be stored in abundance. The description of Baba's pure fame, and the hearing of the same, with love, will destroy the sins of the devotee and, therefore, this is the simple Sadhana for attaining salvation.

The Sadhana for Krita or Sat Yuga was Shama Dama (tranquility of mind and body via control), for Treta Yuga, sacrifice, for Dwapara Yuga it was worship, and for Kali Yuga (our present age), it is the singing of the name and glory of the Lord. This last Sadhana is open to all the people of the four varnas (castes, Brahmins, etc...).

The other Sadhanas, viz. Yoga, Yagya (sacrifice), Dhyana (meditation) and Dharana (concentration) are very difficult to practice, but singing and hearing the stories and the glory of the Lord (Sai Baba) is very easy. We have only to turn our attention towards them. The listening and singing of the stories will remove the attachment to the senses and their objects, and will make the devotees dispassionate, and will ultimately lead them to self-realization. With this end in view, Sai Baba made me or helped me to write His stories, Sat-Charitamrita.

Devotees may now easily read and hear these stories of Sai Baba and while doing so, meditate on Him, His form and thus attain devotion to Guru and God (Sai Baba), get detachment and self-realization. In the preparation and writing of this work, Sat-Charitamrita, it is Sai Baba's grace which has accomplished everything, making use of me as a mere instrument.

Motherly Love of Sai Baba

Everybody knows how a cow loves her infant calf. Her udder is always full and when the calf wants milk and dashes at the udder, out comes the milk in an unceasing flow. Similarly a human mother knows the wants of her child and feeds it, at her breast in time. In case of dressing and adorning the child, the mother takes particular care to see that this is well done. The child knows or cares nothing about this, but the mother's joy knows no bounds, when she sees her child beautifully dressed and adorned. The love of mother is peculiar, extraordinary and disinterested, and has no parallel. Sadgurus feel this motherly love towards their disciples. Sai Baba had this same love towards me, and I give an instance of it below:

In 1916, I retired from Government Service. The pension that was settled in my case was not sufficient to maintain my family decently. On Guru Purnima (15th of Ashadha) day of that year, I went to Shirdi with other devotees. There, Mr. Anna Chinchanikar, of his own accord, prayed to Baba for me as follows: - "Please look kindly on him, the pension he gets is quite insufficient, his family is growing. Give him some other appointment, remove his anxiety and make him happy." Baba replied- "He will get some other job, but now he should serve Me and be happy. His dishes will be ever full and never empty. He should turn all his attention towards Me and avoid the company of atheists, irreligious and wicked people. He should be meek and humble towards all and worship Me heart and soul. If he does this, he will get eternal happiness".

The question Who is this HE, Whose worship is advocated, is already answered in a note on "Who is Sai Baba" in the prologue, at the beginning of this work.

Rohilla's Story

The story of the Rohilla illustrates Sai Baba's all-embracing love. One Rohilla, tall and well-built, strong as a bull, came to Shirdi, wearing a long Kafni (robe) and was enamored of Sai who stayed there. Day and night he used to recite in a loud and harsh tone Kalma (verses from Holy Koran) and shout "ALLAH HO AKBAR" (God is Great).

Most people of Shirdi were working in their fields by day and when they returned to their homes at night, they were welcomed with the Rohilla's harsh cries and shouts. They could get no sleep and felt much trouble and inconvenience. They suffered in silence this nuisance for some days, and when they could stand it no longer, they approached Baba, and requested Him to check the Rohilla and stop the nuisance. Baba did not attend to their complaint. On the contrary, Baba took the villagers to task, and asked them to mind their own business, and not the Rohilla. He said to them that the Rohilla had a very bad wife, a Zantippi, who tried to come in and trouble the Rohilla and Himself; but hearing

15

the Rohilla's prayers, she dared not to enter and they were at peace and happy. In fact, the Rohilla had no wife and by his wife Baba meant DURBUDDHI, i.e. bad thoughts. As Baba liked prayers and cries to God better than anything else, He took the side of the Rohilla, and asked the villagers to wait and suffer the nuisance, which would abate in due course.

Baba's Sweet and Nectar-like Words

One day at noon after the Arati, devotees were returning to their lodgings, when Baba gave the following beautiful advice:

"Be wherever you like, do whatever you choose, remember this well that all what you do is known to Me. I am the Inner Ruler of all and seated in their hearts. I envelope all the creatures, the movable and immovable world. I am the Controller - the wire-puller of the show of this Universe. I am the mother - origin of all beings - the Harmony of three Gunas, the propeller of all senses, the Creator, Preserver and Destroyer. Nothing will harm him, who turns his attention towards Me, but Maya will lash or whip him who forgets Me. All the insects, ants, the visible, movable and immovable world, is My Body or Form".

Hearing these beautiful and precious words, I at once decided in my mind to serve no man henceforward, but my Guru only; but the reply of Baba to Anna Chinchanikar's query (which was really mine) that I would get some job, began to revolve in my mind, and I began to think whether it would come to happen. As future events showed, Baba's words came true and I got a Government job, but that was of short duration. Then I became free and solely devoted myself to the service of my Guru- Sai Baba.

Before concluding this Chapter, I request the readers to leave out the various hindrances viz. indolence, sleep, wandering of mind, attachments to senses, etc... and turn their whole and undivided attention to these stories of Sai Baba. Let their love be natural, let them know the secret of devotion; let them not exhaust themselves by other Sadhanas, let them stick to this one simple remedy, i.e. listening to Sai Baba's stories. This will destroy their ignorance and will secure for them salvation. A miser may stay at various places; but he always thinks of his buried treasure. So let Sai Baba be enthroned in the hearts of all.

In the next chapter, I shall speak of Sai Baba's appearance in Shirdi.

Bow to Shri Sai - Peace be to all

Chapter IV

SAI BABA'S FIRST ADVENT (Appearance) IN SHIRDI

Mission of the Saints - Shirdi a Holy Tirth - Personality of
Sai Baba - Dictum of Goulibuva - Appearance of Vithal
Kshirsagar's Story - Das Ganu's Bath in Prayag - Immaculate
Conception of Sai Baba and His First Advent in Shirdi
Three Wadas

In the last chapter, I described the circumstances which led me
to write Sai-SatCharita. Let me now describe the first advent
of Sai Baba in Shirdi.

Mission of the Saints

Lord Krishna says in Bhagavad Gita (Chapter IV, 7-8) that
"Whenever there is a decay of Dharma (righteousness) and an
ascendancy of unrighteousness, I manifest Myself; and for the
protection of the virtuous, the destruction of the vicious and for
the establishment of righteousness, I manifest Myself in age after
age".

This is the mission of Lord, and the Sages and Saints, Who are
His representatives and Who appear here at proper times, help in
their own way to fulfill that mission. For instance, when the twice
born, i.e. the Brahmins, the Kshatriyas and the Vaishyas neglect
their duties and when the Sudras try to usurp the rights of the
higher classes, when spiritual preceptors are not respected but
humiliated, when nobody cares for religious instructions, when
everybody thinks himself very learned, when people begin to
partake of forbidden foods and intoxicating drinks, when under
the cloak of religion, people indulge in malpractices, when people
belonging to different sects fight amongst themselves, when
Brahmins fail to do Sandhya adoration, and the orthodox their
religious practices, when Yogis neglect their meditation, when
people begin to think that wealth, progeny, wife are their sole
concern, and thus turn away from the true path of salvation, then
do Saints appear and try to set matters right by their words and

action. They serve us as beacon-lights, and show us the right path, and the right way for us to follow. In this way, many saints, viz. Nivritti, Jnanadev, Muktabai, Namdev, Gora, Gonayi, Ekanath, Tukaram, Narahari, Narsi Bhai, Sajan Kasai, Sawata, Ramdas, and various others did appear at various times to show the right path to the people, and so presently came Shri Sai Baba of Shirdi.

Shirdi - A Holy Tirth

The banks of the Godavari river, in the Ahmednagar District, are very fortunate for they gave birth and refuge to many a Saint, prominent amongst them being Jnaneshwar. Shirdi also falls in the Kopargaon Taluka of the Ahmednagar District. After crossing the Godavari river at Kopargaon, one gets the way to Shirdi. When you go three Koss (9 miles), you come to Nimgaon, from whence, Shirdi is visible. Shirdi is as famous and well-known as other holy places like Gangapur, Narsinhwadi, and Audumbar on the banks of Krishna river. As the devotee Damaji flourished in and blessed Mangalvedha (near Pandharpur) as Samarth Ramdas at Sajjangad, as Shri Narasimha Saraswati at Saraswatiwadi, so Sainath flourished at Shirdi and blessed it.

Personality of Sai Baba

It is on account of Sai Baba that Shirdi grew into importance. Let us see what sort of a personage Sai Baba was. He conquered this Samara (worldly existence), which is very difficult and hard to cross. Peace or mental calm was His ornament, and He was the repository of wisdom. He was the home of Vaishnava devotees, most liberal (like Karna) amongst liberals, the quint-essence of all essences. He had no love for perishable things, and was always engrossed in self-realization, which was His sole concern. He felt no pleasure in the things of this world or of the world beyond. His Antarang (heart) was as clear as a mirror, and His speech always rained nectar. The rich or poor people were the same to Him. He did not know or care for honor or dishonor. He was the Lord of all beings. He spoke freely and mixed with all people, saw the acting and dances of Nautchgirls and heard Gajjal songs. Still, He swerved not an inch from Samadhi (mental equilibrium). The

19

name of Allah was always on His lips. While the world awoke, He slept; and while the world slept, He was vigilant. His abdomen (Inside) was as calm as the deep sea. His Ashram could not be determined, nor His actions could be definitely determined, and though He sat (lived) in one place, He knew all the transactions of the world. His Darbar was imposing. He told daily hundreds of stories; still He swerved not an inch from His vow of silence.

He always leaned against the wall in the Masjid or walked morning, noon and evening towards Lendi (Nala) and Chavadi; still He at all times abided in the Self. Though a Siddha, He acted like a Sadhaka. He was meek, humble and ego-less, and pleased all. Such was Sai Baba, and as the soil of Shirdi was trodden by Sai Baba's Feet, it attained extraordinary importance.

As Jnaneshwar elevated Alandi, Ekanath did to Paithan, so Sai Baba raised Shirdi. Blessed are the grass leaves and stones of Shirdi, for they could easily kiss the Holy Feet of Sai Baba, and take their dust on their head. Shirdi became to us, devotees, another Pandharpur, Jagannath, Dwarka, Banaras (Kashi) and Rameshwar, Badrikedar, Nasik, Tryambakeshwar, Ujjain, and Maha Kaleshwar or Mahabaleshwar Gokarn. Contact of Sai Baba in Shirdi was like our Veda and Tantra; it quieted our Samsara (world consciousness) and rendered self-realization easy. The darshan of Sri Sai was our Yoga-Sadhana, and talk with Him removed our sins. Shampooing His Legs was our bath in Triveni Prayag, and drinking the holy water of His Feet destroyed our desires. To us, His commands were Vedas, and accepting (eating) His Udi (sacred ashes) and Prasad was all purifying. He was our Shri Krishna and Shri Rama who gave us solace and He was our Para Brahma (Absolute Reality). He was Himself beyond the Pair of dwandwas (opposite), never dejected Nor elated. He was always engrossed in His Self as 'Existence, Knowledge and Bliss.' Shirdi was His center; but His field of action extended far wide, to Punjab, Calcutta, North India, Gujarat, Dacca (Now in Bangladesh) and Konkan. Thus the fame of Sai Baba spread, far, and wide, and people from all parts came to take His darshan and be blessed. By mere darshan, minds of people, whether, pure or impure, would become at once quiet. They got here the same sort of unparalleled joy that devotees get at Pandharpur by seeing

Vithal Rakhumai. This is not an exaggeration. Consider what a devotee says in this respect:

Dictum of Goulibuva

An old devotee by name Goulibuva, aged about 95 years, was a Varkari of Pandhari. He stayed eight months at Pandharpur and four months - Ashadha to Kartik (July - November) on the banks of the Ganges. He had an ass with him for carrying his luggage, and a disciple, as his companion. Every year he made his Vari or trip to Pandharpur and came to Shirdi to see Sai Baba, Whom he loved most. He used to stare at Baba and say, "This is Pandharinath Vithal incarnate, the merciful Lord of the poor and helpless." This Goulibuva was an old devotee of Vithoba, and had made many a trip to Pandhari; and he testified that Sai Baba was real Pandharinath.

Vithal Himself Appeared

Sai Baba was very fond of remembering and singing God's name. He always uttered Allah Malik (God is Lord) and in His presence made others sing God's name continuously, day and night, for 7 days. This is called Namasaptaha. Once He asked Das Ganu Maharaj to do the Namasaptaha. He replied that he would do it, provided he was assured that Vithal would appear at the end of the 7th day. Then Baba, placing His hand on his breast assured him that certainly Vithal would appear, but that the devotee must be 'earnest and devout'. The Dankapuri (Takore) of Takurnath, the Pandhari of Vithal, the Dwarka of Ranchhod (Krishna) is here (Shirdi). One need not go far out to see Dwarka. Will Vithal come here from some outside place? He is here. Only when the devotee is bursting with love and devotion, Vithal will manifest Himself here (Shirdi).

After the Saptaha was over, Vithal did manifest Himself in the following manner. Kakasaheb Dixit was, as usual, sitting in meditation after the bath, and he saw Vithal in a vision. When he went at noon for Baba's darshan, Baba asked him point-blank - "Did Vithal Patil come? Did you see Him? He is a very truant fellow, catch Him firmly, otherwise, he will escape, if you be a little inattentive." This happened in the morning and at noon there was another Vithal darshan. One hawker from outside, came there for selling twenty-five or thirty pictures of Vithoba. This picture exactly tallied with the figure that appeared in Kakasaheb's vision. On seeing this and remembering Baba's words, Kakasaheb Dixit was much surprised and delighted. He bought one picture of Vithoba, and placed it in his shrine for worship.

Bhagwantrao Kshirsagar's Story

How fond was Baba for Vithal worship was illustrated in Bhagwantrao Kshirsagar's story. The father of Bhagwantrao was a devotee of Vithoba, and used to make Varis (annual trips) to Pandharpur. He also had an image of Vithoba at home, which he worshipped. After his death, the son stopped everything - the Vari, the worship and shraddha ceremony etc... When Bhagwantrao came to Shirdi, Baba on remembering his father, at once said - "His father was my friend, so I dragged him (the son) here. He never offered naivaidya (offering of food) and so he starved Vithal and Me. So I brought him here. I shall remonstrate him now and set him to worship."

Das Ganu's Bath in Prayag

The Hindus think that a bath in the holy Tirth of Prayag, where the Ganga and Yamuna rivers meet, is very meritorious and thousands of pilgrims go there, at periodical times, to have the sacred bath there. Once, Das Ganu thought that he should go to Prayag for a bath, and came to Baba to get His permission for doing so. Baba replied to him - "It is not necessary to go so long. Our Prayag is here, believe me." Then wonder of wonders! When Das Ganu placed his head on Baba's Feet, out came or flowed streams, of Ganga - Yamuna water, from both the toes of Baba. Seeing this miracle, Das Ganu was overwhelmed with feelings of love and adoration and was full of tears. Inwardly, he felt inspired, and his speech burst forth into a song in praise of Baba and His Leelas.

Immaculate Conception of Sai Baba and His First Advent in Shirdi

Nobody knew the parents, birth or birth-place of Sai Baba. Many inquiries were made, many questions were put to Baba and others regarding these items, but no satisfactory answer or information has yet been obtained. Practically we know nothing about these matters. Namdev and Kabir were not born like ordinary mortals. They were found as infants in mother-of-pearls, Namdev being found on the bank Bhimrathi river by Gonayee, and Kabir on the bank Bhagirathi river by Tamal.

Similar was the case with Sai Baba. He first manifested Himself as a young lad of sixteen under a Neem tree in Shirdi, for the sake of Bhaktas. Even then He seemed to be full with the knowledge of Brahman. He had no desire for worldly objects even in dream. He kicked out Maya; and Mukti (deliverance) was serving at His feet. One old woman of Shirdi, the mother of Nana Chopdar, described Him thus. This young lad, fair, smart and very handsome, was first seen under the Neem tree, seated in an Asan. The people of the village were wonder-struck to see such a young lad practising hard penance, not minding heat and cold. By day he associated with none, by night he was afraid of nobody. People were wondering and asking, whence this young chap had turned up. His form and features were so beautiful that a mere look endeared Him to all. He went to nobody's door, always sat near the Neem tree. Outwardly he looked very young; but by His action he was really a Great Soul. He was the embodiment of dis-passion and was an enigma to all.

One day it so happened, that God Khandoba possessed the body of some devotee and people began to ask Him, "Deva (God), you please enquire what blessed father's son is this lad and whence did He come". God Khandoba asked them to bring a pick-axe and dig in a particular place. When it was dug, bricks were found underneath a flat stone. When the stone was removed, a corridor led to a cellar where cow-mouth-shaped structures, wooden boards, necklaces were seen. Khandoba said - "This lad practiced penance here for 12 years." Then the people began to question the lad about this. He put them off the scent by telling them that it was His Guru's place, His holy Watan and requested them to guard it well. The people then closed the corridor as before. As Ashwattha and Audumbar trees are held sacred, Baba regarded this Neem tree equally sacred and loved it most. Mhalasapati and other Shirdi devotees regard this site as the resting place (Samadhi-Sthana) of Baba's Guru and prostrate before it.

Three Wadas

(1) The site with the Neem tree and surrounding space was bought by Mr. Hari Vinayak Sathe, and on this site a big building styled Sathe's Wada was erected. This Wada was the sole resting place for pilgrims, who flocked there. A Par (platform) was built round the neem tree and lofts with steps were constructed. Under the steps, there is a niche facing South and devotees sit on the Par (platform) facing north. It is believed, that he who burns incense there, on Thursday and Friday evenings will, by God's grace, be happy. This Wada was old and dilapidated and wanted repairs. The necessary repairs, additions and alterations have been made now by the Sansthan.

(2) Then after some years another Wada, Dixit's Wada was constructed. Kakasaheb Dixit, Solicitor of Bombay, had gone to England. He had injured his leg by an accident there. The injury could not be got rid of by any means. Nanasaheb Chandorkar advised him to try Sai Baba. So he saw Sai Baba in 1909, and requested Him to cure rather the lameness of his mind than that of his leg. He was so much pleased with the darshan of Sai Baba that he decided to reside in Shirdi.

So he built a Wada for himself and other devotees. The foundation of this building was laid on tenth December 1910. On this day, two other important events took place.

(1) Mr. Dadasaheb Khaparde was given permission to return home, and

(2) the night Arati in Chavadi was commenced. The Wada was complete and was inhabited on the Rama-Navami day in 1911, with due rites and formalities.

(3) Then another Wada or palatial mansion was put up by the famous millionaire, Mr. Booty, of Nagpur. Lots of money was

spent on this building, but all the amount was well utilized, as Sai Baba's body is resting in this Wada, which is now called the Samadhi Mandir. The site of this Mandir had formerly a garden, which was watered and looked after by Baba. Three Wadas thus sprang up, where there was none formerly. Of these, Sathe's Wada was most useful to all, in the early days.

The story of the garden, attended to by Sai Baba with the help of Vaman Tatya, the temporary absence of Sai Baba from Shirdi, and His coming again to Shirdi with the marriage-party of Chand Patil, the company of Devidas, Jankidas and Gangagir, Baba's wrestling match with Mohdin Tamboli, residence in Masjid, love of Mr. Dengale and other devotees; and other incidents will be described in the next Chapter.

Bow to Shri Sai - Peace be to all

Chapter V

Baba's Return with Chand Patil's Marriage-party
Addressed as "Sai" - Contact with Other Saints
His Dress and Daily Routine - The Story of the Padukas
Wrestling Bout with Mohdin and Change in Life
Turning Water into Oil - The Pseudo-Guru Javhar Ali

Return with Chand Patil's Marriage - Party

As hinted in the last Chapter, I shall now describe first how Sai Baba returned to Shirdi after His disappearance.

There lived in the Aurangabad District (Nizam State), in a village called Dhoop, a well-to-do Mohammedan gentleman by name Chand Patil. While he was making a trip to Aurangabad, he lost his mare. For two long months, he made a diligent search but could get no trace of the lost mare. After being disappointed, he returned from Aurangabad with the saddle on his back. After travelling four Koss and a half, he came, on the way, to a mango tree under the foot of which sat a RATNA (queer fellow). He had a cap on His head, wore Kafni (long robe) and had a "Satka" (short stick) under His arm-pit and He was preparing to smoke a Chillum (pipe).

On seeing Chand Patil pass by the way, He called out to him and asked him to have a smoke and to rest a little. The Fakir asked him about the saddle. Chand Patil replied that it was of his mare which was lost. The queer fellow or Fakir asked him to make a search in the Nala close by. He went and the wonder of wonders! he found out the mare. He thought that this Fakir was not an ordinary man, but an Avalia (a great saint). He returned to the Fakir with the mare. The Chillum was ready to be smoked, but two things were wanting; (1) fire to light the pipe, and (2) water to wet the chhapi (piece of cloth through which smoke is drawn up). The Fakir took His prong and thrust it forcibly into the ground and out came a live burning coal, which He put on the pipe. Then He dashed the Satka on the ground, from whence water began to ooze. The chhapi was wetted with that water, was

26

then wrung out and wrapped round the pipe. Thus everything being complete, the Fakir smoked the Chillum and then gave it also to Chand Patil.

On seeing all this, Chand Patil was wonder-struck. He requested the Fakir to come to his home and accept his hospitality. Next day He went to the Patil's house and stayed there for some time. The Patil was a village officer of Dhoop. His wife's brother's son was to be married and the bride was from Shirdi. So Patil made preparations to start for Shirdi for the marriage. The Fakir also accompanied the marriage-party. The marriage went off without any hitch, the party returned to Dhoop, except the Fakir alone stayed in Shirdi, and remained there forever.

How the Fakir Got the Name Sai

When the marriage-party came to Shirdi, it alighted at the foot of a Banyan tree in Bhagata Mhalsapati's field near Khandoba's temple. The carts were loosened in the open court-yard of Khandoba's temple. The carts were loosened in the open court-yard of Khandoba's temple, and the members of the party descended one by one, and the Fakir also got down. Bhagat Mhalsapati saw the young Fakir getting down and accosted Him "YA SAI" (Welcome Sai). Others also addressed Him as Sai and thence-forth he became known as Sai Baba.

Contact with Other Saints

Sai Baba began to stay in a deserted Masjid. One Saint named Devidas was living in Shirdi many years before Baba came there. Baba liked his company. He stayed with him in the Maruti temple, in the Chavadi, and sometime lived alone. Then came another Saint by name Jankidas. Baba spent most of His time in talking with him, or Jankidas went to Baba's residence. So also one Vaishya (house-holder Saint), from Puntambe by name Gangagir always frequented Shirdi. When he first saw Sai Baba, carrying pitchers of water in both hands, for watering the garden, he was amazed and said openly, "Blessed is Shirdi, that it got this precious Jewel. This man is carrying water to-day; but He is not an ordinary fellow. As this land (Shirdi) was lucky and

27

meritorious, it secured this Jewel." So also one famous Saint by name Anandnath of Yewala Math, a disciple of Akkalkot Maharaj came to Shirdi with some Shirdi people. When he saw Sai Baba, he said openly, "This is a precious Diamond in reality. Though he looks like an ordinary man, he is not a 'gar' (ordinary stone) but a Diamond. You will realize this in the near future." Saying this he returned to Yewala. This was said while Sai Baba was a youngster.

Baba's Dress and Daily Routine

In his young days, Sai Baba grew hair on His head; never had His head shaved. He dressed like an athlete. When He went to Rahata (3 miles from Shirdi), He brought with Him small plants of Marigold, Jai and Jui, and after cleaning, he planted and watered them. A devotee by name Vaman Tatya supplied Him daily with two earthen pitchers. With these Baba Himself used to water the plants. He drew water from the well and carried the pitchers on His shoulders. In the evening the pitchers were kept at the foot of the Neem tree. As soon as they were placed there, they were broken, as they were made of raw earth and not baked. Next day, Tatya supplied two fresh pitchers. This course went on for three years; and with Sai Baba's toil and labor, there grew a flower-garden. On this site, at present, stands the big mansion - the Samadhi Mandir of Baba, which is now frequented and used by so many devotees.

The Story of Padukas (foot-prints) under the Neem Tree

A devotee of Akkalkot Maharaj by name Bhai Krishnaji Alibagkar worshipped the photo of Akkalkot Maharaj. He once thought of going to Akkalkot (Sholapur District), taking the darshan of the Padukas (foot-prints) of the Maharaj and offering his sincere worship there; but before he could go there, he got a vision in his dream. Akkalkot Maharaj appeared in the vision and said to him - "Now Shirdi is my resting place, go there and offer your Worship." So Bhai changed his plan and came to Shirdi, worshipped Baba, stayed there for six months and was happy. As a reminiscence of this vision etc..., he prepared the Padukas and installed them on an auspicious day of Shravan, Shaka 1834 (1912 A.D.) under the Neem tree with due ceremonies and formalities, conducted by Dada Kelkar and Upasani. One Dixit Brahmin was appointed for worship, and the management was entrusted to devotee Sagun.

Complete Version of this Story

Mr. B.V. Deo, Retired Mamalatdar of Thana, and a great devotee of Sai Baba, made enquired about this matter with Sagun Meru Naik and Govind Kamlakar Dixit and has published a full version of the Padukas in Sai Leela Vol.... 11, No. 1, page 25. It runs as follows:

In 1834 Shaka (1912 A.D.) one Doctor Ramarao Kothare of Bombay came to Shirdi for Baba's darshan. His compounder; and his friend, Bhai Krishnaji Alibagkar, accompanied him. The compounder and Bhai became intimate with Sagun Meru Naik and G.K. Dixit. While discussing things, these persons thought that there must be some memorial of the fact of Sai Baba's first coming to Shirdi and sitting under the holy Neem tree. They thought of installing Baba's Padukas there and were going to make them of some rough stones. Then Bhai's friend, the compounder, suggested that if this matter be made known to his master, Dr. Ramarao Kothare, who would prepare nice Padukas for this purpose. All liked the proposal and Dr. Kothare was informed of it. He came to Shirdi and drew a plan of the Padukas. He went to Upasani Maharaj in Khandoba's temple, and showed him his plan. The latter made many improvements, drew lotuses, flowers, conch, disc, man etc., and suggested that the following SHLOKA (verse) regarding Neem tree's greatness and Baba's Yogi powers be inscribed. The verse was as follows:

"Sada Nimbarvrikshasya mooladhiwasat, Sudhasravinam tik-tamapi-apriyam tam, Tarum Kalpavrikshadhikam sadhayantam Namameeshwaram Sadgurum Sai Natham".

Upasani's suggestions were accepted and carried out. The Padukas were made in Bombay and sent to Shirdi with the compounder. Baba said that they should be installed on the Purnima

(15th) of Shravan. On that day at 11 a.m., G.K. Dixit brought them on his head from Khandoba's temple to the Dwarkamai (Masjid) in procession. Baba touched the Padukas, saying that these are the feet of the Lord and asked the people to install them, under foot of the Neem tree.

A day before, one Parsi devotee of Bombay named Pastha Shet sent Rs.25 by money order. Baba gave this sum for the installation of the Padhukas. The total expense of installation came up to Rs.100 out of which Rs.75 were collected by subscriptions. For the first 5 years, G.K. Dixit worshipped the Padukas daily and then this was done by Laxman Kacheshwar Jakhadi. In the first five years, Dr. Kothare sent Rs.2 per month for lighting and he also sent the railing round the Padukas. The expense of bringing the railing from the station to Shirdi (Rs.7-8-0) (presently Rs.7.50p) and roofing was paid by Sagun Meru Naik. Now, Jakhadi (Nana Pujari) does the worship and Sagun Meru Naik offers the naivaidya and lights the evening lamps.

Bhai Krishnaji was originally a devotee of Akkalkot Maharaj. He had come to Shirdi at the installation of the Padukas, in Shaka 1834 on his way to Akkalkot. He wanted to go to Akkalkot after taking the darshan of Baba. He asked Baba's permission for this. Baba said - "Oh, what is there in Akkalkot? Why do you go there? The incumbent Maharaj of that place is here, Myself." Hearing this Bhai did not go to Akkalkot. He came to Shirdi off and on, after the installation of the Padukas.

Mr. B.V. Deo concluded that Hemadpant did not know these details. Had he known them, he would not have failed to depict them in his Satcharita.

Wresting Bout with Mohdin Tamboli and Change in Life

To return to other stories of Baba: There was a wrestler in Shirdi, by name Mohdin Tamboli. Baba and he did not agree on some items, and both had a fight. In this Baba was defeated. Thenceforth, Baba changed His dress and mode of living. He donned Kafni, wore a Langot (waist band) and covered His head with a piece of cloth. He took a piece of sack-cloth for His seat, sack-cloth for His bed and was content with wearing torn and worn out rags. He always said that "Poverty is better than Kingship, far better than Lordship. The Lord is always brother (befriender) of the poor." Gangagir was also very fond of wrestling. While he was once wrestling, a similar feeling of dis-passion came over him, and at the proper time he heard the voice of an adept, saying that he should wear out his body, playing with God. So he too gave up Samsara and turned towards God-realization. He established a math (spiritual residence) on the banks of the river near Puntambe, and lived there with disciples.

Sai Baba did not mix and speak with the people. He only gave answers when he was questioned. By day he always sat under the Neem tree, sometimes under the shade of a branch of a Babul tree near the stream at the outskirts of the village. In the afternoon, He used to walk at random and go at times to Nimgaon. There He frequented the house of Balasaheb Dengale. Baba loved Mr. Balasaheb. His younger brother, named Nanasaheb, had no son, though he married a second wife. Balasaheb sent Nanasaheb for taking darshan of Sai Baba, and after some time with His grace, Nanasaheb got a son. From that time onwards, people began to come in numbers to see Sai Baba, and His fame began to spread and reached Ahmednagar; from thence Nanasaheb Chandorkar and Keshav Chidamber, and many others began to come to Shirdi. Baba was surrounded by His devotees during day; and slept at night in an old and dilapidated Masjid. Baba's paraphernalia at this time consisted of a Chillum, tobacco, a "Tumrel" (tin pot), long flowing Kafni, a piece of cloth round His head, and a Satka (short stick), which He always kept with Him. The piece of white cloth on the head was twisted like matted hair, and flowed down from the left ear on the back. This was not washed for weeks. He wore no shoes, no sandals. A piece of sack-cloth was His seat for most of the day. He wore a coupin (waist-cloth-band) and for warding off cold he always sat in front of a Dhuni (sacred fire) facing south with His left hand resting on the wooden railing.

In that Dhuni, He offered as oblation; egoism, desires and all thoughts and always uttered Allah Malik (God is the sole owner). The Masjid in which He sat was only of two room dimensions, where all devotees came and saw Him. After 1912, there was a change. The old Masjid was repaired and a pavement was con-

31

structed. Before Baba came to live in this Masjid, He lived for a long time in a place Takia, where with ghungur (small bells) on His legs, Baba danced beautifully, sang with tender love.

Turning Water into Oil

Sai Baba was very fond of lights. He used to borrow oil from shop-keepers, and keep lamps burning the whole night in the Masjid and temple. This went on for some time. The Banias, who supplied oil gratis, once met together and decided not to give Him oil. When, as usual, Baba went to ask for oil, they all gave Him a distinct, "No". Unperturbed, Baba returned to the Masjid and kept the dry wicks in the lamps. The banias were watching Him with curiosity. Baba took the Tumrel (tin pot) which contained very little (a few drops) of oil, put water into it and drank it and forced it fall in the container. After consecrating the tin-pot in this way, He again took water in the tin-pot and filled all the lamps with it and lighted them. To the surprise and dismay of the watching Banias, the lamps began to burn and kept burning the whole night. The Banias repented and apologized. Baba forgave them and asked them to be more truthful in future.

The Pseudo-Guru Javhar Ali

Five years after the wrestling bout mentioned above, one Fakir from Ahmednagar by name Javhar Ali, came to Rahata (a village two miles south of Shirdi) with his disciples and stayed in Bakhal (spacious room) near Virabhadra temple. The Fakir was learned, could repeat the whole Koran and had a sweet tongue. Many religious and devout people of the village came to him and began to respect him. With the help of the people, he started to build an Idgah (a wall before which Mohammedans pray on Idgah day), near the Virabhadra temple.

There was some quarrel about this affair, on account of which, Javhar Ali had to leave Rahata. Then he came to Shirdi and lived in the Masjid with Baba. People were captured by his sweet talk, and he began to call Baba his disciple. Baba did not object and consented to be his Chela. Then both Guru and Chela decided to return to Rahata and live there. The Guru (Teacher) never knew his disciple's worth, but the disciple knew the defects of the Guru, still he never disrespected him, observing carefully his duties. He even served the Master in various ways. They used to come to Shirdi off and on, but their main stay was in Rahata. The loving devotees of Baba in Shirdi did not like, that Baba should stay away from them in Rahata. So they went in a deputation to bring Baba back to Shirdi. When they met Baba near the Idgah and told the purpose for which they came, Baba said to them that the Fakir was an ill-tempered fellow, he would not leave him and that they should better return to Shirdi without him, before the Fakir returned. While they were thus talking, the Fakir turned up and was very angry with them for trying to take away his disciple. There was some discussion and altercation and it was finally decided that both the Guru and Chela should return to Shirdi. And so they returned and lived in Shirdi. But after a few days the Guru was tested by Devidas and he was found wanting.

Twelve years before Baba arrived in Shirdi with the marriage-party, this Devidas aged about 10 or 11 came to Shirdi and lived in the Maruti temple. Devidas had fine features and brilliant eyes, and he was dis-passion incarnate and a Jnani. Many persons, namely Tatya Kote, Kashinath and others regarded him as their Guru. They brought Javhar Ali in his presence, and in the discussion that followed, Javhar was worsted and fled from Shirdi. He went and stayed in Bijapur and returned after many years to Shirdi, and prostrated himself before Sai Baba. The delusion that he was Guru and Sai Baba his Chela was cleared away, and as he repented, Sai Baba treated him with respect. In this case Sai Baba showed by actual conduct how one should get rid of egoism and do the duties of a disciple to attain the highest end, viz., self-realization. This story is told here according to the version given by Mhalsapati (a great devotee of Baba).

In the next Chapter will be described Rama-Navami Festival, the Masjid, its former condition and later improvement etc...

Bow to Shri Sai - Peace be to all

Chapter VI

RAMA-NAVAMI FESTIVAL AND MASJID REPAIRS

Efficacy of the Touch of Guru's Hand
Rama-Navami Festival - Its Origin, Transformation etc...
Repairs to the Masjid

Before describing Rama-Navami Festival and Masjid Repairs, the author makes some preliminary remarks about Sadguru as follows:

Efficacy of the Touch of Guru's Hand

Where Real or Sadguru is the helmsman, he is sure to carry us safely and easily beyond the worldly ocean. The word Sadguru brings to mind Sai Baba. He appears to me, as if standing before me, and applying Udi (scared ashes) to my fore-head and placing his hand of blessing on my head. Then joy fills my heart and love overflows through my eyes. Wonderful is the power of the touch of Guru's hand. The subtle-body (consisting of thoughts and desires), which cannot be burnt by the world dissolving fire, is destroyed by the mere touch of the Guru's hand, and the sins of many past births are cleaned and washed away. Even the speech of those, whose heads feel annoyed when they hear religious and Godly talks, attains calmness. The seeing of Sai Baba's handsome form, chokes our throat with joy, makes the eyes overflowing with tears, and overwhelms the heart with emotions. It awakens in us 'I am He (Brahman)' consciousness, manifests the joy of self-realization, and dissolving the distinction of I and Thou, then and there, makes us one with the Supreme (One Reality).

When I begin to read scriptures, at every step I am reminded of my Sadguru, and Sai Baba, assumes the form of Rama or Krishna and makes me listen to his Life. For instance when I sit to listen to Bhagwat, Sai becomes Krishna from top to toe, and I think he sings the Bhagwat or Uddhava Gita (song of teachings by Lord Shri Krishna to His disciple, Uddhava) for the welfare of the devotees. When I begin to chitchat, I am at once put in mind of Sai's stories for enabling me to give suitable illustrations. When I myself start to write anything, I cannot compose a few words or sentences, but when He of his own accord makes me write, I go on writing and writing and there is no end to it. When the disciple's egoism props up, He presses it down with His hand and giving him His own power, makes him gain His object, and thus satisfies and blesses him.

If anyone prostrates before Sai and surrenders heart and soul to Him, then unsolicited, all the chief objects of life viz. Dharma (Righteousness), Artha (Wealth), Kama (Desire) and Moksha (Deliverance), are easily and unsolicitedly attained. The Four paths, of Karma, Jnana, Yoga and Bhakti lead us separately to God. Of these, the path of Bhakti is thorny and full of pits and ditches, and thus difficult to traverse, but if you, relying on your Sadguru, avoid the pits and thorns and walk straight, it will take you to the destination (God). So says definitely, Sai Baba.

After philosophizing about the Self-Existent Brahman, His Power (Maya) to create this world and the world created, and stating that all these three are ultimately one and the same, the author quotes Sai Baba's words guaranteeing the welfare of the Bhaktas:

"There will never be any dearth or scarcity, regarding food and clothes, in any devotees' homes. It is my special characteristic, that I always look to, and provide, for the welfare of those devotees, who worship Me whole-heartedly with their minds ever fixed on Me. Lord Krishna, has also said the same in the Gita. Therefore, strive not much for food and clothes. If you want anything, beg of the Lord, leave worldly honors, try to get Lord's grace and blessings, and be honored in His Court. Do not be deluded by worldly honor. The form of the Deity should be firmly fixed in the mind. Let all the senses and mind be ever devoted to the worship of the Lord, let there be no attraction for any other thing; fix the mind in remembering Me always, so that it will not wander elsewhere, towards body, wealth and home. Then it will be calm, peaceful and care-free. This is the sign of the mind, being well engaged in good company. If the mind is vagrant, it cannot be called well-merged."

After quoting these words, the author goes on to relate the

story of Rama Navami festival in Shirdi. As Rama-Navami is the greatest festival celebrated at Shirdi, another fuller account, as published in Sai Leela Magazine of 1925, pg. 197, is also referred to and a summary of the festival, as related in both these accounts is attempted here.

Origin

One, Mr. Gopalrao Gund, was a Circle Inspector at Kopergaon. He was a great devotee of Baba. He had three wives, but had no issue. With Sai Baba's blessings, a son was born to him. In the joy that he felt regarding the event, an idea of celebrating a fair or 'Urus' occurred to him in the year 1897, and he placed it for consideration before other Shirdi devotees, viz. Tatya Patil, Dada Kote Patil and Madhavrao Deshpande (Shama). They all approved of the idea, and got Sai Baba's permission and blessings. Then an application for getting the Collector's sanction for celebrating the Urus was made, but as the village Kulkarni reported against holding the fair, the sanction was refused. But as Sai Baba had blessed it, they tried again, and ultimately succeeded in getting the Collector's sanction. The day for the Urus was fixed on the Rama-Navami day, after having consultation with Sai Baba. It seems, He had some end in view, in this, viz., the Unification of the two fairs of festivals, the Urus and the Rama-Navami and the unification of the two communities - the Hindus and the Mohammedans. As future events showed, this end or object was achieved.

Though the permission was obtained, but other difficulties cropped up. Shirdi was a village, and there was scarcity of water. There were two wells in the village, the one in use, dried up soon, and the water from the second was brackish. This brackish water was turned into sweet one by Sai Baba, by throwing flowers into it. The water of this well was insufficient, so Tatya Patil had to arrange to get water, from a well by fixing Moats (leather sacks) thereon, at a considerable distance. Then temporary shops had to be constructed, and wrestling bouts arranged. Gopalrao Gund had a friend, by name Damu Anna Kasar, of Ahmednagar. He also was similarly unhappy in the matter of progeny, though he married two wives. He too was blessed by Sai Baba with sons, and Mr. Gund prevailed upon his friend to prepare and supply one simple flag for the procession of the fair; he also succeeded in inducing Mr. Nanasaheb Nimonkar to supply another embroidered flag. Both these flags were taken in procession through the village, and finally fixed at the two ends or corners of the Masjid, which is called by Sai Baba as Dwarkamai. This is being done even now.

The 'Sandal' Procession

There was another procession which was started in this fair. This idea of 'Sandal' procession originated with one Mr. Amir Shakkar Dalal, a Mohammedan Bhakta from Korhla. This procession is held in honor of great Muslim Saints. Sandal i.e. Chandan paste and scrappings are put in the THALI (flat dishes), and these are carried with incense burning before them in procession to the accompaniment of band and music through the village and then after returning to the Masjid, the contents of the dishes are thrown on the 'Nimbar' (niche) and walls of the Masjid with hands. This work was managed by Mr. Amir Shakkar for the first three years, and then afterwards by his wife. So on one day, the two processions, the 'Flags' by the Hindus and that of 'Sandal' by the Muslims, went on side by side, and are still going on without any hitch.

Arrangement

This day was very dear and sacred to the devotees of Sai Baba. Most of them turned out on the occasion, and took a leading part in the management of the fair. Tatya Kote Patil looked to all outward affairs, while the internal management was entirely left to one Radha Krishna Mai, a female devotee of Baba. Her residence was full of guests on the occasion, and she had to look to their needs, and also to arrange for all the paraphernalia of the fair. Another work, which she willingly did, was to wash out and clean and white-wash the entire Masjid, its walls and floor, which were blackened and were full of soot on account of the ever-burning Dhuni (sacred fire) of Sai Baba. This work, she did during the night, when Sai Baba went to sleep every alternate day in the Chavadi. She had to take out all the things, including even the Dhuni, and after thorough cleaning and whitewashing replace them, as they were before. Feeding the poor which was so dear to Sai Baba, was also a great item in this fair. For this purpose, cooking on a grand scale and preparing various sweet dishes, was done in Radha-Krishna Mai's lodging, and various rich and wealthy devotees took a leading part in this affair.

Transformation of Urus into Rama-Navami Festival

Things were going on in this way and the Festival was gradually increasing in importance till 1912, when a change took place; That year one devotee, Mr. Krishnarao Jageshwar Bhisma (the author of the pamphlet 'Sai Sagunopasana'), came for the fair with Dadasaheb Khaparde of Amraoti, and was staying on the previous day in the Dixit Wada. While he was lying on the verandah, and while Mr. Laxmanrao alias Kaka Mahajani, was going down with Puja materials to the Masjid, a new thought arose in his mind and he accosted the latter thus - There is some providential arrangement in the fact that the Urus (or fair) is celebrated in Shirdi on the Rama-Navami day; this day is very dear to all the Hindus; then why not begin the Rama-Navami Festival - the celebration of the birth of Shri Rama here on this day?

Kaka Mahajani liked the idea, and it was arranged to get Baba's permission in this matter. The main difficulty was how to secure a Haridas, who would perform 'Kirtan' and sing the glories of the Lord on the occasion. But Bhishma solved the difficulty, by saying that his 'Rama Akhyan' (composition on Rama's birth) was ready, and he would do the 'Kirtan' himself, while Kaka Mahajani should play on the harmonium.

It was also arranged to get the 'Sunthavada' (ginger-powder mixed with sugar) as Prasad prepared by Radha-Krishna Mai. So they immediately went to the Masjid to get Baba's permission. Baba, who knew all things and what was passing there, asked Mahajani, as to what was going on in the Wada. Being rather perturbed, Mahajani could not catch the purport of the question and remained silent. Then Baba asked Bhishma, what he had to say. He explained the idea of celebrating Rama-Navami festival, and asked for Baba's permission and Baba gladly gave it. All rejoiced and made preparations for the Jayanti-festival.

Next day, the Masjid was decorated with buntings etc.., a cradle was supplied by Radha-Krishna Mai and placed in front of Baba's seat and the proceedings started. Bhishma stood up for Kirtan and Mahajani played on the harmonium. Sai Baba sent a man to call Mahajani. He was hesitating to go, doubting whether Baba would allow the festival to go on; but when he went to Baba, the latter asked him as to what was going on and why the cradle was placed there. He answered that the Rama-Navami festival had commenced, and the cradle was put on for that purpose. Then Baba took a garland from the 'Nimbar' (niche), and placed it round his neck and sent another garland for Bhishma. Then commenced the Kirtan. When it came to a close, pound sounds of "Victory to Rama" went up; and Gulal (red-powder) was thrown up all-round, amidst band and music. Everybody was overjoyed, when suddenly roaring was heard. The red-powder thrown promiscuously all round, went up, somehow entered Baba's eyes. Baba got wild and began to scold and abuse loudly. People got frightened by this scene and took to their heels.

Those intimate devotees, who knew Baba well, took these scoldings and outpourings of Baba, as blessings in disguise. They thought that when Rama was born, it was proper for Baba to get wild and enraged to kill Ravana; and his demons, in the form of egoism and wicked thoughts etc... Besides they knew that whenever a new thing was undertaken at Shirdi, it was usual with Baba to get wild and angry, and so they kept quiet. Radha-Krishna Mai was rather afraid; and thought that Baba might break her cradle, and she asked Mahajani to get the cradle back. When he went to loosen and unfasten the cradle, Baba went to him, and asked him not to remove it. Then after some time, Baba became calm, and that day's program, including Mahapuja and Arati was finished.

Later on, Mr. Mahajani asked Baba, for permission to remove the cradle, Baba refused the same saying, that the festival was not yet finished. Next day, another 'Kirtan' and Gopal-Kala ceremony (an earthen pot containing parched rice mixed with curds is hung, only to be broken after the 'Kirtan', and the contents distributed to all, as was done by Lord Krishna amongst His cowherd (friends), were performed, and then Baba allowed the cradle to be removed. While the Rama-Navami festival was thus going on, the procession, of the two flags by day and that of the 'Sandal' by night, went off with the usual pomp and show. From this time onwards, the 'Urus of Baba' was transformed into the Rama-Navami festival.

From next year (1913), the items in the program of Rama-Navami began to increase. Radha-Krishna Mai started a 'Nama-Saptah' (singing the glory of God's name continuously day and night for seven days), from 1st of Chaitra, For this, all devotees took part by turns, and she also joined it, sometimes early in the morning. As Rama-Navami Festival is celebrated in many places all over the country, the difficulty of getting a Haridas was felt again. But 5 or 6 days before the festival, Mahajani met accidentally Balabuva Mali, who was known as modern Tukaram, and got him to do the 'Kirtan' that year. The next year (1914), another Balabuva Satarkar of Brihadsiddha Kavate, District Satara, could not act as a Haridas in his own town, as plague was prevailing in his town, and so he came to Shirdi; With Baba's permission, which was secured through Kakasaheb Dixit, he did the Kirtan; and was sufficiently recompensed for his labor. The difficulty of getting a new Haridas every year was finally solved from 1914 by Sai Baba, as He entrusted this function to Das Ganu Maharaj permanently, and since that time, he has been successfully and creditably conducting that function up till now.

Since 1912, this festival began to grow gradually year by year. From the 8th to 12th of Chaitra, Shirdi looked like a bee-hive of men. Shops began to increase. Celebrated wrestlers took part in wrestling bouts. Feeding of the poor was done on a grander scale. Hard work and sincere efforts of Radha-Krishna Mai turned Shirdi into a Sansthan (State). Paraphernalia increased. A beautiful horse, a palanquin, chariot and many silver things, pots, buckets, pictures, mirrors etc... were presented. Elephants were also sent for the procession. Though all this paraphernalia increased enormously, Sai Baba ignored all these things, and maintained His simplicity as before. It is to be noted that both the Hindus and Mohammedans have been working in unison in both the processions, and during the entire festival, there has been no hitch or quarrel between them at all so far. In the early days about five to seven thousand people used to collect, but that figure went up to 75,000 in some years; still there was no outbreak of any epidemic or any riots worth the name during so many past years.

Repairs to the Masjid

Another important idea occurred to Gopal Gund. Just as he started the Urus or fair, he thought that he should put the Masjid in order. So in order to carry out the repairs, he collected stones and got them dressed. But this work was not assigned to him. This was reserved for Nanasaheb Chandorkar and the pavement-work for Kakasaheb Dixit. First, Baba was unwilling to allow them to have these works done, but with the intervention of Mhalsapati, a local devotee of Baba, His permission was secured.

When the pavement was completed in one night in the Masjid, Baba took a small Gadi for His seat, discarding the usual piece of sack - cloth used till then. In 1911, the Sabha-Mandap (courtyard) was also put in order with great labor and effort. The open space in front of the Masjid was very small and inconvenient. Kakasaheb Dixit wanted to extend it and put on it roofing. At great expense, he acquired iron columns, and pillars and trusses and started the work.

At night, all the devotees worked hard and fixed the posts; but Baba, when he returned from Chavadi next morning, uprooted them all and threw them out. Once it so happened that Baba got very excited, caught a pole with one hand, and began to shake and uproot it, and with the other hand caught the neck of Tatya Patil. He took by force Tatya's Pheta, struck a match, set it on fire and threw it in a pit. At that time, Baba's eyes flashed like burning embers. None dared to look at Him. All got terribly frightened. Baba took out a rupee from his pocket and threw it there, as if it were an offering on an auspicious occasion. Tatya also was much frightened. None knew what was going to happen to Tatya, and none dared to interfere.

Bhagoji Shinde, the leper devotee of Baba, made a little boldly advance, but he was pushed out by Baba. Madhavrao was also similarly treated, he being pelted with brick pieces. So all those, who went to intercede, were similarly dealt with. But after some time, Baba's anger cooled down. He sent for a shopkeeper, got from him an embroidered Pheta and Himself tied it on Tatya's head, as if he was being given a special honor. All the people were wonder-struck to see this strange behavior of Baba. They were at a loss to know, what enraged Baba so suddenly and what led Him to assault Tatya Patil, and why His anger cooled down, the next moment. Baba was sometimes very calm and quiet and talked sweet things with love, but soon after, with or without any pretext, got enraged. Many such incidents may be related; but I do not know which to choose and which to omit. I, therefore, refer them as they occur to me.

In the next Chapter the question whether Baba was a Hindu or a Mohammedan will be taken up; and His Yogic practices and powers, and other matters will be dealt with.

Bow to Shri Sai Baba - Peace be to all

Chapter VII

Wonderful Incarnation - Behavior of Sai Baba - His Yoga
Practices - His All-pervasiveness
Leper Devotee's service - Master Khaparde's Plague-case
Going to Pandharpur

Wonderful Incarnation

Sai Baba knew all Yogic Practices. He was well-versed in the six processes including Dhauti (Stomach-cleaning by a moistened piece of linen 3" in breadth and 22 1/2" in length), Khandayoga, i.e., separating His limbs and joining them again, and Samadhi, etc... If you think that He was a Hindu, He looked like a Yavan. If you think Him to be a Yavan, He looked like a pious Hindu. No one definitely knew whether He was a Hindu or a Mohammedan. He celebrated the Hindu festival of Rama Navami with all due formalities, and at the same time permitted the 'Sandal' procession of the Mohammedans. He encouraged wrestling bouts in this festival, and gave good prizes to winners. When the Gokul Ashtami came, He got the 'Gopal-Kala' ceremony duly performed and on Eid festivals, He allowed Mohammedans to say their prayers (Namaj) in His Masjid.

Once in the Muhurram festival, some Muslims proposed to construct a Taziya in the Masjid, keep it there for some days and afterwards take it in procession through the village. Sai Baba allowed the keeping of the Taziya for four days, and on the fifth day removed it out of the Masjid without the least compunction. If we say that He was a Mohammedan, His ears were pierced (i.e. had holes according to Hindu fashion). If you think that He was a Hindu, He advocated the practice of circumcision (though according to Mr. Nanasaheb Chandorkar, who observed Him closely, He was not Himself circumcised. Vide article in Sai Leela on "Baba Hindu Ki Yavan" by B.V. Deo, page 562).

If you call Him Hindu, He always lived in the Masjid; if Mohammedan, He had always the Dhuni - sacred fire there, and the following things which are contrary to Mohammedan religion, i.e., grinding on the hand-mill, blowing of the conch and bells, oblation in the fire, Bhajan, giving of food, and worship of Baba's Feet by means of ARGHYA (water) were always allowed there. If you think that He was a Mohammedan, the best of Brahmins and Agnihotris, leaving aside their orthodox ways, fell prostrate at His Feet.

Those who went to make enquiries about his nationality were dumb-founded and were captured by his darshan. So none could definitely decide whether Sai Baba was Hindu or Mohammedan*. (see below this paragraph) This is no wonder; for he who completely surrenders himself to the Lord, by getting rid of his egoism; and body - consciousness thus becomes one with Him, and has nothing to do with any questions of caste or nationality. Such a one as Sai Baba was, saw no difference between caste and caste and even beings and beings. He took meat and fish with Fakirs, but did not grumble when dogs touched the dishes with their mouths.

[* Note--(1) Mhalsapati, an intimate Shirdi devotee of Baba, who always slept with Him in the Masjid and Chavadi, said that Sai Baba told him that He was a Brahmin of Pathari and was handed over to a Fakir in his infancy, and when He told this, some men from Pathari had come, and Baba was enquiring about some men from that place. Vide Sai Leela 1924, Page 179. (2) Mrs. Kashibai Kanitkar, the famous learned woman of Poona says in the experience No.8, published on Page 79, Sai Leela Vol. 11,1934, - "On hearing of Baba's miracles, we were discussing according to our theosophical convention and fashion whether Sai Baba belonged to Black or White Lodge. When once I went to Shirdi, I was thinking seriously about this in my mind. As soon as I approached the steps of the Masjid, Baba came to the front and pointing to His chest and staring at me spoke rather vehemently -"This is a Brahmin, pure Brahmin. He has nothing to do with black things. No Mussulmen can dare to step in here. He dare not." Again pointing to his chest - "This Brahmin can bring lakhs of men on the white path and take them to their destination. This is a Brahmin's Masjid and I won't allow any black Mohammedan to cast his shadow here."]

Such a unique and wonderful incarnation was Sai Baba. On account of the merits in my past birth, I had the good fortune to sit at His Feet and enjoy His blessed company. The joy and delight I derived there from was incomparable. In fact Sai Baba was pure Ananda and Consciousness. I cannot sufficiently describe Him, His greatness and uniqueness. He who took delight at His Feet, was established in His own self. Many Sanyasis, Sadhakas and all sorts of men aspiring for salvation came to Sai Baba. He always walked, talked and laughed with them and always uttered with His tongue 'Allah Malik' (God is the sole owner). He never liked discussion or arguments. He was always calm and controlled, though irritable at times, always preached full Vedanta and nobody knew till the last Who was Baba. Princes and poor people were treated alike by Him. He knew the inmost secrets of all, and when He gave expression to them, all were surprised. He was the repository of all knowledge, still He feigned ignorance. He also disliked honor. Such were the characteristics of Sai Baba. Though, He had a human body, His deeds testified to HIS Godhood. All people considered Him as the Lord God in Shirdi.

Behavior of Sai Baba

Fool that I am, I cannot describe Baba's miracles. He got almost all the temples in Shirdi repaired. Through Tatya Patil, the temples of Shani, Ganapati, Shankar-Parvati, Village Deity, and Maruti were put in order. His charity was also remarkable. The money He used to collect as Dakshina was freely distributed, Rs.20 to some, Rs.15 or 50, to others every day. The recipients thought that this was 'pure' charity money, and Baba wished that it should be usefully employed.

People were immensely benefited by having a darshan of Baba. Some became hale and hearty; wicked people were turned into good ones. Kushtha (Leprosy) was cured in some cases, many got their desires fulfilled, without any drops or medicine being put in the eyes, some blind men got back their sight and some lame ones got their legs. Nobody could see the end of His extraordinary greatness. His fame spread far and wide, and pilgrims from all sides flocked to Shirdi. Baba sat always near the Dhuni and eased Himself there and always sat in meditation; sometimes with and on other times without a bath.

He used to tie a white turban on his head; and wear a clean Dhotar round his waist, and a shirt on his body. This was his dress in the beginning. He started practising medicine in the village, examined patients and gave medicines. He was always successful, and He became famous as a Hakim (Doctor). A curious case may be narrated here. One devotee got his eye balls quite red and swollen. No Doctor was available in Shirdi. The other devotees took him to Baba. Other Doctors would use ointments, Anjans, cow's milk and camphorated drugs etc.., in such cases. Baba's remedy was quite unique. He pounded some 'BEEBA' (Some Carpus Ana Cardium i.e. marking nuts) and made two balls of them, thrust them on in each eye of the patient and wrapped a cloth-bandage round them (eyes). Next day, the bandage was removed and water was poured over them in a stream. The inflammation subsided and the pupils became white and clear. Though the eyes are very delicate, the BEEBA caused no smarting; but removed the disease of the eyes. Many such cases were cured and this is only an instance in point.

Baba's Yoga Practices

Baba knew all the processes and practices of Yoga. Two of them will be described here:

(1)   DHAUTI or CLEANING PROCESS: Baba went to the well near a Banyan tree at a considerable distance from the Masjid every third day and washed his mouth and had a bath. On one occasion, He was seen to vomit out his intestines, clean them inside and outside and place them on a Jamb tree for drying. There are persons in Shirdi, who have actually seen this, and who have testified to this fact. Ordinary Dhauti is done by a moistened piece of linen, 3 inches broad 22 1/2ft. long. This piece is gulped down the throat and allowed to remain in the stomach for about half an hour for being reacted there and then taken out. But Baba's Dhauti was quite unique and extraordinary.

(2)   KHANDA YOGA: In this practice, Baba extracted the
various limbs from His body, and left them separately at
different places in the Masjid. Once, a gentleman went to the
Masjid, and saw the limbs of Baba lying separately at separate
places. He was much terrified; and he first thought of running
to the village officers, and informing them of Baba being
hacked to pieces and murdered. He thought that he would be
held responsible, as he was the first informant, and knew
something of the affair. So he kept silent. But next day when
he went to the masjid, he was very much surprised to see
Baba, hale and hearty and sound, as before. He thought that
what he had seen the previous day was only a dream.

Baba practiced Yoga since His infancy and nobody knew or
guessed the proficiency He attained. He charged no fees for His
cures; became renowned and famous by virtue of His merits, gave
health to many a poor and suffering person. This famous Doctor
of doctors cared not for His interests, but always worked for the
good and welfare of others, Himself suffering unbearable and
terrible pain many a time in the process. One such instance, I give
below, which will show the all-pervasive and most merciful
character of Sai Baba.

Baba's All-pervasiveness and Mercy

In the year 1910, Baba was sitting near the Dhuni on Divali
holiday and warming Himself. He was pushing fire-wood into the
Dhuni, which was brightly burning. A little later, instead of
pushing logs of woods, Baba pushed His arm into the Dhuni; the
arm was scorched and burnt immediately. This was noticed by the
servant Madhava, and also by Madhavrao Deshpande (Shama).
They at once ran to Baba and Madhavarao clasped Baba by His
waist from behind and dragged Him forcible backward and asked,
"Deva, for what have You done this?" Then Baba came to His
senses and replied, "The wife of a blacksmith at some distant
place was working the bellows of a furnace; her husband called
her. Forgetting that her child was on her waist, she ran hastily and
the child slipped into the furnace. I immediately thrust My hand

into the furnace and saved the child. I do not mind My arm being burnt, but I am glad that the life of the child is saved."

Leper Devotee's Service

On hearing the news of Baba's hand being burnt from Shama (Madhavrao Deshpande), Mr. Nanasaheb Chandorkar, accompanied by the famous Doctor Parmanand of Bombay with his medical outfit consisting of ointments, lint and bandage etc... rushed to Shirdi, and requested Baba to allow Dr. Parmanand to examine the arm, and dress the wound caused by the burn. This was refused. Ever since the burn, the arm was dressed by the leper devotee, Bhagoji Shinde. His treatment consisted in massaging the burnt part with ghee and then placing a leaf over it and bandaging it tightly with Pattis (bandages). Mr. Nanasaheb Chandorkar solicited Baba many a time to unfasten the Pattis and get the wound examined and dressed and treated by Dr. Parmanand, with the object that it may be speedily healed. Dr. Parmanand himself made similar requests, but Baba postponed saying that Allah was His Doctor; and did not allow His arm to be examined. Dr. Paramanand's medicines were not exposed to their air of Shirdi, as they remained intact, but he had the good fortune of getting a darshan of Baba. Bhagoji was allowed to treat the hand daily. After some days, the arm healed and all were happy. Still, we do not know whether any trace of pain was left or not. Every morning, Bhagoji went through his program of loosening the Pattis, massaging he arm with ghee and tightly bandaging it again. This went on till Sai Baba's Samadhi (death). Sai Baba, a perfect Siddha, as He was, did not really want this treatment, but out of love to His devotee, He allowed the 'Upasana' - service of Bhagoji to go on un-interrupted all along.

When Baba started for Lendi, Bhagoji held an umbrella over Him and accompanied Him. Every morning, when Baba sat near the post close to the Dhuni, Bhagoji was present and started his service. Bhagoji was a sinner in his past birth. He was suffering from leprosy, his fingers had shrunk, and his body was full of pus and smelling badly. Though outwardly he seemed so unfortunate, he was really very lucky and happy, for he was the premier servant of Baba, and got the benefit of His company.

Master Khaparde's Plague-Case

I shall now relate another instance of Baba's wonderful Leela. Mrs. Khaparde, the wife of Mr. Dadasaheb Khaparde of Amraoti, was staying at Shirdi with her young son for some days. One day the son got high fever, which further developed into Bubonic plague. The mother was frightened and felt most uneasy. She thought of leaving the place for Amraoti, and went near Baba in the evening, when He was coming near the Wada (now Samadhi Mandir) in His evening rounds, for asking His permission. She informed Him in a trembling tone that her dear young son was down with plague. Baba spoke kindly and softly to her, saying that the sky is beset with clouds; but they will melt and pass off and everything will be smooth and clear. So saying, He lifted up His Kafni up to the waist and showed to all present, four fully developed buboes, as big as eggs, and added, "See, how I have to suffer for My devotees; their difficulties are Mine." Seeing this unique and extraordinary deed (Leela), the people were convinced as to how the Saints suffer pains for their devotees. The mind of the saints is softer than wax, it is soft, in and out, as butter. They love their devotees without any idea of gain, and regard them as their true relatives.

Going to Pandharpur and Staying There

I shall now close this Chapter after relating a story illustrating how Sai Baba loved His devotees and anticipated their wishes and movements. Mr. Nanasaheb Chandorkar, who was a great devotee of Baba, was Mamlatdar at Nandurbar in Khandesh. He got an order of transfer to Pandharpur. His devotion to Sai Baba bore fruit, as he got an order to go and stay at Pandharpur which is regarded as the 'BHUVAIKUNTHA' - Heaven on earth. Nanasaheb had to take immediate charge, so he left, immediately, for the place, without even writing or informing anybody at Shirdi. He wanted to give a surprise visit to Shirdi - his Pandharpur, see and salute his Vithoba (Baba), and then proceed. Nobody dreamt of Nanasaheb's departure for Shirdi, but Sai Baba knew all about this, as His eyes were everywhere (omniscient). As soon as

Nanasaheb approached Neemgaon, a few miles from Shirdi, there was stir in the Masjid at Shirdi. Baba was sitting and talking with Mhalsapati, Appa Shinde and Kashiram, when He at once said, "Let us all four do some Bhajan, the doors of Pandhari are open, let us merrily sing." Then they began to sing in chorus, the burden of the song being "I have to go to Pandharpur and I have to stay on there, for it is the house of my Lord."

Baba sang and the devotees followed Him. In a short time Nanasaheb came there with his family, prostrated before Baba and requested Him to accompany them to Pandharpur and stay with them there. This solicitation was not necessary, as the devotees told Nanasaheb that Baba was already in the mood of going to Pandharpur and staying there. Hearing this Nanasaheb was moved and fell at Baba's Feet. Then getting Baba's permission, Udi (sacred ashes) and Blessings, Nanasaheb left for Pandharpur.

There is no end to Baba's stories, but let me now make a halt here, reserving for the next Chapter other topics, such as importance of human life, Baba's living on alms, Bayajabai's service and other stories.

Bow to Shri Sai -- Peace be to all

Chapter VIII

Importance of Human Birth - Sai Baba Begging Food
Bayajabai's Service - Sai Baba's Dormitory
His Affection for Khushalchand

As hinted in the last Chapter, Hemadpant now explains at length, in his preliminary remarks, on the importance of human birth; and then proceeds to relate how Sai Baba begged His food, how Bayajabai served Him, how He slept in the Masjid with Tatya Kote Patil and Mhalsapati and how He loved Khushalchand of Rahata.

Importance of a Human Birth

In this wonderful universe, God has created billions (84 lacs according to Hindusastra calculation) of creatures or beings (including Gods, demigods, insects, beasts and men) inhabiting heaven, hell, earth, ocean, sky and other intermediate regions. Of these, those creatures or souls, whose merits preponderate, go to heaven and live there till they enjoy the fruits of their actions, and when this is done, they are cast down while those souls, whose sins or demerits preponderate, go down to hell, and suffer the consequences of their misdeeds for so long a time as they deserve. When their merits and demerits balance each other, they are born on earth as human beings, and are given a chance to work out their salvation. Ultimately when their merits and demerits both drop down (are got rid of) completely, they get their deliverance and become free. To put the matter in a nutshell, souls get their births or transmigrations according to their deeds and intelligence (development of their minds).

Special Value of the Human Body

As we all know, four things are common to all the creatures, viz. food, sleep, fear and sexual union. In the case of man, he is endowed with a special faculty, viz. knowledge, with the help of which he can attain God-vision, which is impossible in any other

51

birth. It is for this reasons that Gods envy man's fortune and aspire to be born as men on earth, so as to get their final deliverance.

Some say, that there is nothing worse than the human body, which is full of filth, mucus, phlegm and dirt, and which is subject to decay, disease and death. This is no doubt true to a certain extent; but in spite of these drawbacks and defects, the special value of the human body is - that man has got the capacity to acquire knowledge: it is only due to the human knowledge that one can think of the perishable and transitory nature of the body itself, and of the world and get a disgust for the sense-enjoyments and can discriminate between the unreal and the real, and thus attain God-vision. So, if we reject or neglect the body because it is filthy, we lose the chance of God-vision, and if we fondle it, and run after sense - enjoyments, because it is precious, we go to hell. The proper course, therefore, for us to pursue is the following; that the body should neither be neglected nor fondled, but should be properly cared for, just as a traveler on horse-back takes care of his pony on the way till he reaches his destination and returns home. Thus the body should ever be used or engaged to attain God-vision or self-realization, which is the supreme end of life.

It is said that though God created various sorts of creatures he was not satisfied, for none of them was able to know and appreciate His work. So he had to create a special being - Man, and endow him with a special faculty, viz. Knowledge and when He saw that man was able to appreciate His Leela - marvelous work and intelligence. He was highly pleased and satisfied. (Vide, Bhagawat 11-9-28). So really it is good luck to get a human body, better luck to get birth in a Brahmin family, and best one, to get an opportunity of having recourse to Sai Baba's Feet and surrendering to Him.

Man's Endeavour

Realizing how precious the human life is, and knowing that Death is certain and may snatch us at any time, we should be ever alert to achieve the object of our life, we should not make the least delay but make every possible haste to gain our object, just as a widower is most anxious to get himself married to a new bride, or just as a king leaves no stone unturned to seek his lost son. So with all earnestness and speed, we should strive to attain our end, i.e., self-realization. Casting aside sloth and laziness, warding off drowsiness, we should day and night meditate on the Self. If we fail to do this, we reduce ourselves to the level of beasts.

How to Proceed?

The most effective and speedy way to gain our object is to approach a worthy Saint or Sage - Sadguru, who has Himself attained God-vision. What cannot be achieved by hearing religious lectures and study of religious works is easily obtained in the company of such worthy souls. Just as the sun alone gives light, which all the stars put together cannot do, so the Sadguru alone imparts spiritual wisdom which all the sacred books and sermons cannot infuse. His movements and simple talks give us 'silent' advice. The virtues of forgiveness, calmness, disinterested-ness, charity, benevolence, control of mind and body, egolessness etc... are observed by the disciples as they are being practiced in such pure and holy company. This enlightens their minds and lifts them up spiritually. Sai Baba was such a Sage or Sadguru. Though He acted as a Fakir (mendicant), He was always engrossed in the Self. He always loved all beings in whom He saw God or Divinity. By pleasures He was not elated. He was not depressed by misfortunes. A king and a pauper were the same to Him. He, whose glance would turn a beggar into a king, used to beg His food from door to door in Shirdi, and let us now see how He did it.

Baba Begging Food

Blessed are the people of Shirdi, in front of whose houses, Baba stood as a beggar and called out, "Oh Lassie, give Me a piece of bread" and spread out His hand to receive the same. In one hand He carried a Tumrel (tin pot) and in the other a zoli or choupadari, i.e., a rectangular piece of cloth. He daily visited certain houses and went from door to door. Liquid or semi-liquid things such as soup, vegetables, milk or butter-milk were received in the tin pot, while cooked rice, bread, and such solid things were taken in the zoli. Baba's tongue knew no taste, as He had acquired control over it. So how could He care for the taste of the different things collected together? whatever things He got in His zoli and in the tin pot were mixed together and partaken by Baba to His heart's content. Whether particular things were tasty or otherwise was never noticed by Baba as if His tongue was devoid of the sense of taste altogether.

Baba begged till noon, but His begging was very irregular. Some days He went a few rounds, on other days up to twelve noon. The food thus collected was thrown in a kundi, i.e. earthen pot. Dogs, cats and crows freely ate from it and Baba never drove them away. The woman who swept the floor of the Masjid took some ten or twelve pieces of bread to her house, and nobody prevented her from doing so. How could, He, who even in dreams never warded off cats and dogs by harsh words and signs, refuse food to poor helpless people? Blessed indeed is the life of such a noble person! People in Shirdi took Him in the beginning for a mad Fakir. He was known in the village by this name. How could one, who lived on alms by begging a few crumbs of bread, be revered and respected? But this Fakir was very liberal of heart and hand, disinterested and charitable. Tough He looked fickle and restless from outside. He was firm and steady inside. His way was inscrutable. Still even in that small village, there were a few kind and blessed people who recognized and regarded Him as a Great Soul. One such instance is given below.

Bayajabai's Brilliant Service

Tatya Kote's mother, Bayajabai, used to go to the woods every noon with a basket on her head containing bread and vegetables. She roamed in the jungles koos (about 3 miles) after koss, trampling over bushes and shrubs in search of the mad Fakir, and after hunting Him out, fell at His feet. The Fakir sat calm and motionless in meditation, while she placed a leaf before Him, spread the food, bread, vegetables etc... thereon and fed Him forcibly. Wonderful was her faith and service. Every day she roamed at noon in the jungles and forced Baba to partake of lunch. Her service, Upasana or Penance, by whatever name we call it, was never forgotten by Baba till his Maha Samadhi. Remembering fully what service she rendered, Baba benefited her son magnificently. Both the son and the mother had great faith in the Fakir, Who was their God. Baba often said to them that "Fakir (Mendicancy) was the real Lordship as it was everlasting, and the so called Lordship (riches) was transient". After some years, Baba left off going into the woods, began to live in the village and take His food in the Masjid. From that time Bayajabai's troubles of roaming in the jungles ended.

Dormitory of Trio

Even blessed are the Saints in whose heart Lord Vasquez dwells, and fortunate, indeed, are the devotees who get the benefit of the company of such Saints. Two such fortunate fellows, Tatya Kote Patil and Bhagat Mhalsapati, equally shared the company of Sai Baba. Baba also loved them both equally. These three persons slept in the Masjid with their heads towards the east, west and north and with their feet touching one another at the center. Stretching their beds, they lay on them, chitchatting and gossiping about many things, till late at midnight. If any one of them showed any signs of sleep, others would wake him up. For instance, if Tatya began to snore, Baba at once got up and shook him from side to side and pressed his head. If it was Mhalsapati, He hugged him close, stroked his legs and kneaded his back. In this way for full fourteen years, Tatya leaving his parents at home slept in the Masjid on account of his love for Baba. How happy and never to be forgotten were those days!

How to measure that love and how to value the grace of Baba? After the passing away of his father, Tatya took charge of the household affairs and began to sleep at home.

Khushalehand of Rahata

Baba loved Ganpat Kote Patil of Shirdi. He equally loved Chandrabhanshet Marwadi of Rahata. After the demise of the Shet, Baba loved his nephew Khushalchand equally or even perhaps more, and watched his welfare, day and night. Sometimes in a bullock cart, at other times in a tanga with intimate friends,

Baba went to Rahata.

People of that village came out, with band and music, and received Baba at the Ves or gate of the village and prostrated before Him. Then He was taken into the village with great pomp and ceremony. Khushalchand took Baba to his house, seated Him on a comfortable seat and gave Him a good lunch. Then they talked freely and merrily for some time, after which Baba returned to Shirdi, giving delight and blessing to all.

Shirdi is midway between and equidistant from Rahata on one side (south) and Nimgaon on the other (north). Baba never went beyond these places during His life time. He never saw any railway train nor travelled by it. Still, He knew exactly the timing of arrival and departure of all trains. Devotees who acted according to Baba's instructions (re : their departure)which were given by him at the time of taking His leave fared well, while those who disregarded them suffered many a mishap and accident. More about this and other matters will be told in the next Chapter.

Bow to Shri Sai-- Peace to be all

NOTE: An incident, given in the footnote at the end of this Chapter, showing Baba's love for Khusalchand how He asked one afternoon Kakasaheb Dixit to go to Rahata and fetch Khushalchand to Him, and at the same time appeared before Khushalchand in his noon-nap dream asking him to come to Shirdi, is not given here as it is described in the body of the book (Sai-Charita) later on (Chapter 30).

Chapter IX

Effect of compliance and Non-compliance with Baba's Orders at
the Time of Taking Leave
Mendicancy and Its Necessity
Devotees' (Tarkhad family's) Experiences
Baba fed sumptuously - How?

At the end of the last chapter, it was barely stated that the
Bhaktas, who obeyed Baba's orders at the time of taking
leave, fared well and those, who disobeyed them, suffered
many a mishap. This statement will be amplified and
illustrated, with a few striking instances; and by other matters
dealt with in this Chapter.

Characteristic of Shirdi - Pilgrimage

One special peculiarity of Shirdi-pilgrimage was this, that
none could leave Shirdi, without Baba's permission; and if he did,
he invited untold sufferings, but if anyone was asked to quit
Shirdi, he could stay there no longer. Baba gave certain suggestions or hints, when Bhaktas went to bid good-bye and take leave.
These suggestions had to be followed. If they were not followed
or were departed from, accidents were sure to befall them, who
acted contrary to Baba's directions. We give below a few instances.

Tatya Kote Patil

Tatya Kote was once going in a tanga to Kopargaon bazaar.
He came in haste to the Masjid, saluted Baba, and said that he
would go to Kopargtaon bazaar. Baba said, "Don't make haste,
stop a little, let go the bazaar, don't go out of the village". On
seeing has anxiety to go, Baba asked him to take Shama
(Madhavrao Deshpande) at least with him. Not minding this
direction, Tatya Kote immediately drove his tanga. Of the two
horses one, which cost Rs.300 was very active and restless. After
passing Sawul well, it began to run rashly, got a sprain in its waist

and fell down. Tatya was not much hurt, but was reminded of Mother Sai's direction. On another occasion while proceeding to Kolhar village, he disregarded Baba's direction, and drove in a tanga, which met with a similar accident.

European Gentleman

One European gentleman of Bombay once came to Shirdi, with an introductory note from Nanasaheb Chandorkar, and with some object in view. He was comfortably accommodated in a tent. He wanted to kneel before Baba and kiss His hand.

He tried thrice to step into the Masjid, but Baba prevented him from doing so. He was asked to sit in the open court-yard below and take Baba's darshan from there. Not pleased with this reception he got, he wanted to leave Shirdi at once and came to bid goodbye. Baba asked him to go the next day and not to hurry. People also requested him to abide by Baba's direction.

Not listening to all this, he left Shirdi in a tanga. The horses ran at first all right, but when Sawul well was passed, a bicycle came in front, seeing which the horses were frightened and ran fast. The tanga was turned topsy-turvy and the gentleman fell down and was dragged some distance. He was immediately re-leased; but had to go and lie in Kopargaon hospital for the treatment of the injuries. Because of such experiences all people learnt the lesson that those who disobeyed Baba's instruction met with accidents in one way or the other and those who obeyed them were safe and happy.

The Necessity of Mendicancy

Now to return to the question of mendicancy. A question may arise in the minds of some that if Baba was such a great personage - God in fact, why should He have recourse to the begging bowl, all His lifetime? This question may be considered and replied from two standpoints.

(1) Who are the fit persons, who have a right to live by the begging bowl? Our Shastras say that those persons, who, getting rid of, or becoming free from the three main Desires, (1) for progeny, (2) for wealth, (3) for fame, except Sannyas, are the fit

persons to live by begging alms. They cannot make cooking arrangements and dine at home. The duty of feeding them rests on the shoulders of house-holders. Sai Baba was neither a house-holder nor Vanaprastha. He was a celibate sannyasi, i.e., brahmachari from boyhood. His firm conviction was that the universe was His home; He was the Lord Devastate - the Supporter of the universe and the Imperishable Brahman. So He had the full right to have recourse to the begging-bowl.

(2) Now from the standpoint of (1) Pancha-soona - the five sins and their atonement. In order to prepare food-stuffs and meals, the householders have to go through five actions or processes, the five sins, (1) Kandani- Pounding, (2) Peshani- Grinding, (3) Udakumbhi- Washing pots, (4) Marjani- Sweeping and cleaning, (5) Chulli- Lighting of the hearth. These processes involve destruction of a lot of small insects and creatures, and thus the householders incur a lot of sin. In order to atone for this sin, the Shastras prescribe five kinds of sacrifices, (1) Brahma-Yajna, or Veda-Dhyayan- offerings to Brahman or the study of the Vedas. (2) Pitra-Yajna- offerings to the ancestors, (3)Deva-Yajna-offerings to the Gods, (4) Bhoota-Yajna- offerings to the beings, (5) Manushya-Atithi-Yajna- offerings to men or uninvited guests.

If these sacrifices, enjoined by the Shastras are duly performed, the purification of the mind is effected and this helps the house-holder to get knowledge and self-realization. Baba, in going from house to house, reminded the inmates of their sacred duty, and fortunate were the people, who got the lesson at their homes from Baba.

Devotee's Experiences

Now to return to the other more interesting subject. Lord Krishna has said in the Bhagavad Gita (9-26) "Whosoever devoutly offers to me a leaf, a flower, or a fruit or water, of that pure-hearted man, I accept that pious offering." In the case of Sai Baba, if a devotee really longed to offer anything to Sai Baba, and if he afterwards forgot to offer the same, Baba reminded him, or his friend about the offering, and made him present it to Him, and then accepted it and blessed the devotee. A few instances are given below.

Tarkhad Family (father and son)

Mr. Ramachandra Atmaran alias Babasaheb Tarkhad, former-ly a Prarthana-Samajist, was a staunch devotee of Sai Baba. His wife and son loved Baba equally or perhaps more. It was once proposed that Master Tarkhad should go with his mother to Shirdi and spend his May vacation there, but the son was unwilling to go, as he thought that in case he left his home at Bandra, the worship of Sai Baba in the house would not be properly attended to, as his father being a Prarthana Samajist, would not care to worship Sai Baba's enlarged portrait. However, on his father's giving an assurance of oath, that he would perform the worship exactly as the son was doing, the mother and the son left for Shirdi on one Friday night.

Next day (Saturday) Mr. Tarkhad got up early, took his bath and before proceeding with the Puja, prostrated himself before the Shrine and said - "Baba, I am going to perform the Puja exactly as my son has been doing, but please let it not be a formal drill." After he performed the Puja, he offered a few pieces of lump sugar as naivedya (offering), which were distributed at the time of the lunch.

That evening and on Sunday, everything went on well. The following Monday was a working day and it also passed well. Mr. Tarkhad, who had never performed Puja like this in all his life, felt great confidence within himself, that everything was passing on quite satisfactorily according to the promise given to his son. On Tuesday, he performed the morning Puja as usual and left for his work. Coming home at noon, he found that there was no Prasad (sugar) to partake of, when the meal was served. He asked the servant - cook, who told him that there was no offering made that morning, and that he had completely forgotten then to per-form that part of the Puja (offering naivedya). After hearing that he left his seat and prostrated himself before the Shrine, expressed his regret, at the same time chiding Baba for the want of guidance in making the whole affair a matter of mere drill. Then he wrote a letter to his son stating the facts and requested him to lay it before Baba's feet and ask His pardon for his neglect. This happened in Bandra at Tuesday noon.

At about the same time, when the noon Arati was just about to commence in Shirdi, Baba said to Mrs. Tarkhad, "Mother, I had been to your house in Bandra, with a view to having something to eat. I found the door locked. I somehow got an entrance inside and found to My regret, that Bhau (Mr. Tarkhad) had left nothing for Me to eat. so I have returned from there without eating anything."

The lady could not understand anything; but the son, who was close by, understood that there was something wrong with the Puja in Bandra and he, therefore, requested Baba to permit him to go home. Baba refused the permission, but allowed him to perform Puja there. Then, the son wrote a letter to his father, stating all that took place at Shirdi and implored his father not to neglect the Puja at home. Both these letters crossed each other and were   delivered to the respective parties the next day. Is this not astonishing?

Mrs. Tarkhad

Let us now take up the case of Mrs. Tarkhad herself. She offered three things, (1) Bharit (roasted brinjal eggplant mixed curds and spice). (2) Kacharya (circular pieces of brinjal fried in ghee), (3) Peda (sweet-ball). Let us see how Baba accepted them.

Once Mr. Raghuvir Bhaskar Purandare of Bandra, a great devotee of Baba started for Shirdi with his family. Mrs. Tarkhad went to Mrs. Purandare, and gave her two brinjals and requested her to prepare Bharit of one brinjal and Kacharya of the other, when she went to Shirdi and serve Baba with them. After reaching Shirdi, Mrs. Purandare went with her dish of Bharit to the Masjid when Baba was just about to start his meals. Baba found the Bharit very tasty. So He distributed it to all and said that He wanted Kacharyas now. A word was sent to Radha Krishna-Mai, that Baba wanted Kacharyas. She was in a fix, as that was no season of brinjals. How to get brinjals was the question? When an enquiry was made as to who brought the Bharit, it was found that Mrs. Purandare was also entrusted with the duty of serving Kacharyas. Everybody then came to know the significance of Baba's enquiry regarding Kacharyas, and was wonder-struck at Baba's all-pervasive knowledge.

In December 1915, one Govind Balaram Mankar wanted to go to Shirdi to perform the obsequies of his father. Before he left, he came to see Mr. Tarkhad. Then Mrs. Tarkhad wanted to send something with him to Baba. She searched the whole house but found nothing, except a Peda, which had already been offered as naivedya. Mr. Mankar was in mourning. Still out of great devotion to Baba, she sent the Peda with him, hoping that Baba would accept and eat it. Govind went to Shirdi and saw Baba, but forgot to take the Peda with him. Baba simply waited. When again he went to Baba in the afternoon, he went empty-handed without the Peda. Baba could wait no longer and, therefore, asked him straight, "What did you bring for me?" "Nothing" was the reply. Baba asked him again. The same reply came forth again. Then Baba asked him the leading question, "Did not the mother (Mrs. Tarkhad) give some sweetmeat to you for Me at the time of your starting?" The boy then remembered the whole thing. He felt abashed, asked Baba's pardon, ran to his lodging, brought the Peda and gave it to Baba. As soon as Baba got it in His hand. He put it into His mouth and gulped it down. Thus the devotion of Mrs. Tarkhad was recognized and accepted. "As men believe in Me, so do I accept them" (Gita, 4-11) was proved in this case.

Baba Fed Sumptuously, -- How?

Once, Mrs. Tarkhad was staying in a certain house in Shirdi. At noon, meals were ready and dishes were being served, when a hungry dog turned up there and began to cry, Mrs. Tarkhad got up at once and threw a piece of bread, which the dog gulped with great relish. In the afternoon, when she went to the Masjid and sat at some distance, Sai Baba said to her, "Mother, you have fed Me sumptuously up to my throat; My afflicted pranas (life-forces) have been satisfied. always act like this, and this will stand you in good stead. Sitting in this Masjid I shall never, never speak untruth. Take pity on Me like this. First give bread to the hungry, and then eat yourself. Note this well." She could not at first understand the meaning of what Baba said. So she replied -- "Baba, how could I feed You? I am myself dependent on others and take my food from them on payment." Then Baba replied -- "Eating that lovely bread I am heartily contended and I am still belching. The dog which you saw before meals and to which you gave the piece of bread is, one with Me, so also other creatures (cats, pigs, flies, cows etc...) are one with Me. I am roaming in their forms.

He, who sees Me in all these creatures, is My beloved. So abandon the sense of duality and distinction, and serve Me, as you did today." Drinking these nectar-like words, she was moved, her eyes were filled with tears, her throat was choked and her joy knew no bounds.

Moral

"See God in all beings" is the moral of this chapter. The Upanishads, the Greta and the Bhagwat, all exhort us to perceive God or Divinity in all the creatures. By the instance given at the end of this Chapter and others too numerous to mention. Sai Baba has practically demonstrated to us how to put the Upanishadic teachings into practice. In this way Sai Baba stands as the best Exponent or Teacher of the Upanishadic doctrines.

Bow to Shri Sai - Peace be to all

Chapter X

Sai Baba's Mode of Life - His Sleeping Board
His Stay in Shirdi - His Teachings
His Humility - The Easiest Path

Remember Him (Sai Baba) always with love, for He was engrossed in doing good to all, and always abided in His Self. To remember Him only is to solve the riddle of life and death. This is the best and easiest of Sadhanas, as it involves no expenditure. A little exertion here brings great rewards. So as long as our senses are sound, we should, minute my minute, practice this Sadhana. All other Gods are illusory; Guru is the only God. If we believe in Sadguru's holy feet, he can change our fortune for the better. If we serve Him nicely, we get rid of our Samara. We need not study any philosophy like the Nyaya and the Mimansa. If we make Him our Helmsman, we can easily cross over the sea of all our pains and sorrows. As we trust the helmsman in crossing rivers and seas, so we have to trust our Sadguru in getting over the ocean of worldly existence. The Sadguru looks to the intense feeling and devotion of his devotees, endows them with knowledge and eternal bliss.

In the last chapter, Baba's mendicancy, and devotees' experiences and other subjects are dealt with. Let the readers now hear, where and how Baba lived, how He slept, and how He taught etc...

Baba's Wonderful Bedstead

Let us first see where and how Baba slept, Mr. Nanasaheb Dengale brought, for Sai Baba, a wooden plank, amount 4 cubits in length and only a span in breath, for sleeping upon. Instead of keeping the plank on the floor and then sleeping on it, Baba tied it like a swing to the rafters of the Masjid with old shreds or rags and commenced to sleep upon it. The rags were so thin and worn out that it was a problem how they could bear or support even weight of the plank itself, let alone the weight of Baba. But somehow or other, it was Baba's sheer Leela that the worn out rags did sustain the plank, with the weight of Baba on it. On the four corners of this plank, Baba lighted panatis (earthen lamps), one at each corner, and kept them burning the whole night. It was a sight for the Gods to see Baba sitting or sleeping on this plank! It was a wonder to all, how Baba got up and down the plank. Out of curiosity, many careful observers kept watching the process of mounting and dismounting, but none succeeded. As crowds began to swell so to detect this wonderful feat, Baba one day broke the plank into pieces and threw it away. Baba had all the eight Siddhis (powers) at His command. He never practiced nor craved for them. They came to Him naturally, as a result of His perfection.

Sagun Manifestation of Brahman

Though Sai Baba looked like a man, three cubits and a half in length, still He dwelt in the hearts of all. Inwardly, he was unattached and indifferent, but outwardly, He longed for public welfare. Inwardly most disinterested, He looked outwardly full of desires, for the sake of His devotees. Inwardly an abode of peace, he looked outwardly restless. Inwardly He had the state of Brahman; outwardly He acted like a devil. Inwardly He had the state of Brahman; outwardly he acted like a devil.

Inwardly He loved Adwaita (union or monism); outwardly He got entangled with the world. Sometimes He looked on all with affection, and at times He threw stones at them; sometimes He scolded them, while at times He embraced them and was calm, composed, tolerant and well-balanced. He always abided and was engrossed in the Self and was well-disposed towards His Bhaktas. He always sat on one Asan and never travelled. His 'band' was a small stick, which He always carried in His hand. He was calm, being thought-free. He never cared for wealth and fame and lived on begging. Such a life He led. He always uttered 'Allah Malik' (God the real owner).

Entire and unbroken was His love for the Bhaktas. He was the mine or store-house for self-knowledge and full of Divine Bliss. Such was the Divine Form of Sai Baba, boundless, endless and undifferentiated. One principle which envelopes the whole universe, (from a stone pillar to Brahma) incarnated in Sai Baba. The really meritorious and fortunate people got this treasure-trove in their hands, while those people who not knowing the real worth of Sai Baba took or take Him to be a man, a mere human being, were and are indeed miserable.

His Stay in Shirdi and Probable Birth-date

None knew or knows the parents and exact birth-date of Sai Baba; but it can be approximately determined by His stay in Shirdi. Baba first came to Shirdi, when he was a young lad of sixteen and stayed there for three years. Then all of a sudden He disappeared for some time. After some time, He reappeared in the Nizam state near Aurangabad, and again came to Shirdi with the marriage-party of Chand Patil, when He was twenty years old. Since then, He stayed in Shirdi continuously for a period of sixty years, after which Baba took His Mahasamadhi in the year 1918. From this we can say that the year of Baba's birth is approximately 1838.

Baba's Mission and Advice

Saint Ramadas (1608-1681) flourished in the 17th century, and fulfilled to a great extent his mission of protecting cows and Brahmins against the Yavanas (Mohammedans), but within two centuries after him, the split between the two communities -- Hindus and Mohammedans widened again, and Sai Baba came to bridge the gulf. His constant advice to all was to this effect. "Rama (the God of the Hindus) and Rahim (the God of the Mohammedans) were one and the same; there was not the slightest difference between them; then why should their devotees and quarrel among themselves? You ignorant folk, children, join hands and bring both the communities together, act sanely and thus you will gain your object of national unity. It is not good to dispute and argue. So don't argue, don't emulate others. Always consider your interest and welfare. The Lord will protect you. Yoga, sacrifice, penance, and knowledge are the means to attain God. If you do not succeed in this by any means, vain is your birth. If any one does any evil unto you, to do not retaliate. If you can do anything, do some good unto other." This in short was Sai Baba's advice to all; and this will stand in good stead both in material and spiritual matters.

Sai Baba as Sadguru

There are Gurus and Gurus. There are many so-called Gurus, who go about from house to house with cymbals and veena in their hands, and make a show of their spirituality. They blow mantras into the ears of their disciples and extract money from them. They profess to teach piety and religion to their disciples, but are themselves impious and irreligious. Sai Baba never thought of making the least show of His worth (piety). Body-consciousness, He had none, but He had great love for the disciples. There are two kinds of Gurus (1) 'Niyat' (appointed or fixed) and (2) 'Aniyat' unappointed or general). The latter by their advice develop the good qualities in us, purify our hearts and set us on the path of salvation; but contact with the former, dispels our quality (sense of difference); and establishes us in Unity by making us realize "Thou art that".

There are various Gurus imparting to us various kinds of worldly knowledge, but he, who fixes us in our Nature (Self) and carries us beyond the ocean of worldly existence, is the Sadguru. Sai Baba was such a Sadguru. His greatness is indescribable. If anybody went to take His darshan, he, without being asked, would give every detail of his past, present and future life. He saw Divinity in all beings. Friends and foes were alike to Him. Disinterested and equal-balanced, He obliged the evil-doers. He was the same in prosperity and adversity. No doubt, ever touched Him. Though He possessed the human body, He was not in the least attached to His body or house. Though He looked embodied, He was really disembodied, i.e., free in this every life.

Blessed are the people of Shirdi, who worshipped Sai as their God. While eating, drinking, working in their backyards and fields and doing various household works, they always remembered Sai and sang His glory. They knew no other God except Sai. What to speak of the love, the sweetness of the love, of the women of Shirdi! They were quite ignorant, but their pure love inspired them to compose poems or songs in their simple rural language. Letters or learning they had none, still one can discern real poetry in their simple songs. It is not intelligence, but love, that inspires real poetry as such. Real poetry is the manifestation of true love; and this can be seen and appreciated by intelligent listeners. Collection of these folk songs is desirable and Baba willing, some fortunate devotee may undertake the task of collecting and publishing these folk-songs, either in the Sai Leela magazine or separately in a book-form.

Baba's Humility

Lord or Bhagwan is said to have six qualities, viz. (1) Fame, (2) Wealth, (3) Non-attachment, (4) Knowledge, (5) Grandeur, and (6) Generosity. Baba had all these in Him. He incarnated in flesh for the sake of the Bhaktas. Wonderful was His grace and kindness! He drew the devotees to Him, or how else one could have known Him! For the sake of His Bhaktas Baba spoke such words, as the Goddess of Speech dare not utter. Here is a specimen. Baba spoke very humbly as follows: - "Slave of slaves I am your debtor, I am satisfied at your darshan. It is a great favor that I saw your feet. I am an insect in your excreta. I consider Myself blessed thereby". What humility is this? If anybody would think that by publishing this, any disrespect is shown to Sai, we beg His pardon and to atone for this we sing and chant Baba's name.

Though Baba seemed outwardly to enjoy sense-objects, he had not the least flavor in them, or even the consciousness of enjoying them. Though He ate, he had no taste and though He saw, He never felt any interest in what He saw. Regarding passion, He was as perfect a celibate as Hanuman. He was not attached to anything. He was pure consciousness, the resting place of desire, anger, and other feelings. In short, He was disinterested, free and perfect. A striking instance may be citied in illustration of this statement.

Nanavalli

There was in Shirdi, a very quaint and strange fellow, by name Nanavalli. He looked to Baba's work and affairs. He once approached Baba who was seated on His Gadi (seat) and asked Him to get up, as he wanted to occupy the same. Baba at once got up and left the seat, which he occupied. After sitting there awhile Nanavalli got up, and asked Baba to take His seat. Then Baba sat on the seat and Nanavalli fell at His feet, and then went away. Baba did not show the slightest displeasure in being dictated to and ousted.

This Nanavalli loved Baba so much that he breathed his last, on the thirteenth day of Baba's taking Maha Samadhi.

The Easiest Path

Hearing the stories of the Saints and Being in their Company:

Though Sai Baba acted outwardly like an ordinary man, His actions showed extraordinary intelligence and skill. Whatever He did, was done for the good of His devotees. He never prescribed any asana, regulation of breathing or any rites to His Bhaktas, nor did He blow any mantra into their ears. He told them to leave off all cleverness and always remember "Sai" "Sai". "If you did that" He said, "all your shackles would be removed and you would be free".

Sitting between five fires, sacrifices, chanting, eight-fold Yoga are possible for the Brahmins only. They are of no use to the other classes. The function of the mind is to think, it cannot remain for a minute without thinking. If you give it a Sense-object, it will think about it. If you give it to a Guru, it will think about Guru. You have heard most attentively the greatness, grandeur of Sai. This is the natural remembrance, worship and Kirtan of Sai. Hearing the stories of the Saints is not so difficult, as the other Sadhanas mentioned above. They (stories) remove all fear of this Samara (worldly existence), and take you on to the spiritual path. So listen to these stories, meditate on them, and assimilate them. If this is done, not only the Brahmins, but women and lower castes will get pure and holy.

You may do or attend to your worldly duties, but give your mind to Sai and His stories, and then, He is sure to bless you. This is the easiest path, but why do not all take to it? The reason is that without God's grace, we do not get the desire to listen to the stories of Saints. With God's grace everything is smooth and easy. Hearing the stories of the Saints is, in a way, keeping their company. The importance of the company of Saints is very great. It removes our body-consciousness and egoism, destroys completely the chain of our birth and death, cuts asunder all the knots of the heart, and takes us to God, Who is pure Consciousness. It certainly increases our non-attachment to sense-objects, and makes us quite indifferent to pleasures and pains, and leads us on the spiritual path.

If you have no other Sadhana, such as uttering God's name, worship or devotion etc..., but if you take refuge in them (Saints) whole-heartedly, they will carry you off safety across the ocean of worldly existence. It is for this reason that the Saint manifest themselves in this world. even sacred rivers such as the Ganges, Godavari, Krishna and Kaveri etc.., which wash away the sins of the world, desire that the Saints should come to them, for a bath and purify them. Such is the grandeur of the Saints. It is on account of the store of merit in past births that we have attained the feet of Sai Baba.

We conclude this chapter with meditation on Sai's Form. He, the beautiful and handsome Sai, standing on the edge of the Masjid and distributing Udi to each and every Bhakta, with a view to his welfare. He who thinks the world as naught and Who is ever engrossed in Supreme Bliss -- before Him -- we humbly prostrate ourselves.

Bow to Shri Sai -- Peace be to all

Chapter XI

Sai, as Sagun Brahman -- Dr. Pandit's Worship
Haji Sidik Falke
Control over the Elements

Let us now, in this Chapter, describe the manifested (Sagun)
Brahman Sai. How He was worshipped and how He controlled
the elements.

Sai as Sagun Brahman

There are two aspects of God or Brahman: (1) the Unmanifested (Nirgun) and (2) the Manifested (Sagun). The Nirgun is
formless, while the Sagun is with form, though both denote the
same Brahman. Some prefer to worship the former, some the
latter.

As stated in the Gita (chapter XII) the worship of the latter is
easy and preferable. As man has got a form (body, senses, etc...),
it is natural and easy for him to worship the God with form. Our
love and devotion do not develop unless we worship Sagun
Brahman for a certain period of time, and as we advance; it leads
us to the worship (meditation) of Nirgun Brahman. So let us start
with Sagun worship. Image, altar, fire, light, sun, water, Brahman
are the seven objects of worship, but Sadguru is better than all
these. Let us, on this occasion, bring to our mind the form of Sai,
Who was non-attachment Incarnate, and Who was a resting-place
for His whole-hearted devotees.

Our faith in His words is the seat of Asan; and our Sankalpa
(determination to start and finish the Puja) is the abandonment of
all our desires. Some say that Sai was a Bhagwad-bhakta (devotee
of the Lord), others say He was a Maha-Bhagwat (a great
devotee), but to us He is God Incarnate. He was extremely for-
giving, never irritable, straight, soft, tolerant and content beyond
comparison. Though He looked embodied (as having the form),
He was really dis-embodied, emotionless, unattached and internally free. The Ganges on its way to the sea, cools and refreshes

71

the creatures affected with heat, gives life to the crops and trees, and quenches the thirst of many. Similarly Saints (Souls) like Sai, while they live their own life, give solace and comfort to all. Lord Krishna has said that 'the Saint is My soul, My living image, I am He or He is My pure form (Being).' This in-describable Shakti or Power of God, known as Pure Existence, Knowledge and Bliss, incarnated in the form of Sai in Shirdi. The Shruti (Taitiriya Upanishad) describes Brahman as Bliss. This we read or hear daily in the books, but the devout people experienced this Brahman or Bliss in Shirdi. Baba, the support of all, required no prop or support (Asan) from anybody. He always used a piece of sack-cloth for His seat, which was covered with a small beautiful bed by His bhaktas and has a bolster placed by them, as a rest to His back.

Baba respected the feelings of His devotees and allowed them to worship Him as they liked. Some waved Chamara or fans before Him, some played on musical instruments, some washed His hands and Feet, some others applied scent and chandan, some gave betel nut with leaves and other things, and some others offered naivedya. Though He looked like living in Shirdi, He was present everywhere. This all-pervasiveness of His way daily experienced by His devotees. Our humble prostration to this all-pervasive Sadguru.

Dr. Pandit's Worship

One Dr. Pandit, a friend of Tatyasaheb Noolkar, once came to Shirdi for Baba's darshan. After saluting Baba, he stayed in the Masjid for some time. Baba asked him to go to Dadabhat Kelkar. He went to Dadabhat, by whom he was well received. Then Dababhat left his house for Puja and Dr. Pandit accompanied him. Dadabhat worshipped Baba. Nobody until then dared to apply sandal paste to Baba's forehead. Only Mhalsapati used to apply it to His throat. But this simple-hearted devout, Dr. Pandit, took Dabadhat's dish containing Puja-materials and taking sandal-paste out of it, drew a Tripundra, i.e. there horizontal lines on Baba's forehead.

To the surprise of all, Baba kept silent without uttering a single word. Then Dababhat that evening asked Baba, "How is it, that though You object to the sandal-paste being applied by others to Your forehead, but You allowed Dr. Pandit to do so now?" Baba replied that Dr. Pandit believed Him to be the same as his Guru, Raghunath Maharaja of Dhopeshwar, known as Kaka Puranik, and he applied the paste to His forehead, as he was doing to his Guru. Hence He could not object. On enquiry, Dr. Pandit told Dadabhat that he took Baba as his Guru Kaka Puranik, and hence he marked the Tripundra on Baba's forehead, as he did on his Guru's head.

Though Baba allowed the devotees to worship Him as they pleased, still sometimes, He acted in a strange way. Sometimes, He threw away the Puja-dish and was wrath Incarnate, then who could approach Him? Sometimes, He scolded the devotees, at times, He looked softer than wax, a statue of peace and forgiveness. Though He seemed to shake with anger and His red eyes rolled round and round, still, He was internally a stream of affection and motherly love. Immediately, He called out His devotees and said, that He ever angry with His devotees; that if mothers kicked their children and if the sea turned back the rivers, He would neglect the devotees' welfare: that He, the slave of His devotees, always stood by them, and responded to them, whenever they called upon Him, and that He always longed for their love.

Haji Sidik Falke

There was no knowing, when Baba would accept a devotee. That depended on His sweet will. Sidik Falke's story is to the point. One Mohammedan gentleman by name Sidik Falke of Kalyan, after making a pilgrimage to Mecca and Medina, came to Shirdi. He lived in a Chavadi, facing north, and sat in the open court-yard of the Masjid. For nine months, Baba ignored him, and did not allow him to step into the Masjid. Falke felt much disconsolate, and did not know what to do.

Somebody advised him not to be disappointed; but to try to approach Baba through Shama (Madhavarao Deshpande), a close and intimate devotee of Baba. He told him that as they approach the God Shiva through his servant and devotee, Nandi, so Baba should be approached through Shama. Falke liked the idea and implored Shama to intercede for him. Shama agreed and on a convenient occasion spoke to Baba about him thus:- "Baba, why don't You allow the old Haji to step into the Masjid, while so many persons freely come and go, after taking Your darshan; why not bless him once?" Baba replied "Shama, you are too young to understand things. If the Fakir (Allah) does not allow, what can I do? Without His grace, who will climb into the masjid?

Well, go to him and ask him whether he will come to the narrow footpath near the Barvi well." Shama went and returned with an affirmative answer. Again Baba said to Shama, "Ask him whether he is willing to pay me the sum of Rs. 40,000 in four installments." Shama went and returned with the answer that he was willing to pay even 40 lacs. Again Baba said to Shama- "We are going to butcher a goat in the Masjid, so ask him, whether he would like to have mutton, haunch or testicles of the goat." Shama returned with the answer that the Haji would be happy to receive a small crumb from Baba's kolamba (clay pot). Hearing this Baba got excited and with His hands threw away the earthen jars and kolamba and straight away advanced to the Haji and lifting His Kafni up with His hands said - "Why do you brag and fancy yourself great and pose yourself as an old Haji? Do you read   Koran like this? You are proud of your pilgrimage to Mecca, but you do not know Me." Being thus scolded, the Haji was confounded. Baba then went back to the Masjid, purchased a few baskets of mangoes and sent them to the Haji. Then again Baba went to the Haji and taking out Rs.55 from His pocket, gave them to the Haji. From that time, Baba loved the Haji, invited him for meals and the Haji, thereafter, came into the Masjid whenever he liked. Baba gave him at times some rupees, and thus the Haji was enlisted in Baba's Darbar.

Baba's Control over the Elements

We shall close this Chapter after describing two incidents showing Baba's control over the elements.

(1) Once at evening time, there was a terrible storm at Shirdi. The sky was overcast with thick black clouds. The winds began to blow forcibly; the clouds roared and the lighting began to flash, and the rains began to descend in torrents. In a short time, the

whole place was flooded with water, All the creatures, birds, beasts and men got terribly frightened; and they all flocked to the Masjid for shelter. There are many local deities in Shirdi, but none of them came to their help. So they all prayed to Baba - their God, Who was fond of their devotion, to intercede and quell the storm. Baba was much moved. He came out and standing at the edge of the Masjid, addressed the storm in a loud and thunderous voice - "Stop, stop your fury and the calm." In a few minutes the rains subsided, the winds ceased to blow, and the storm came to a stop. Then the moon rose in the sky, and the people then went back home well-pleased,

(2) On another occasion at noon the fire in the Dhuni began to burn brightly, its flames were seen to be reaching the rafters above. The people who were sitting in the Masjid did not know what to do. They dared not to ask Baba to pour water or do anything to quench the flames. But Baba soon came to realize, what was happening. He took up His Satka (short stick) and dashed it against a pillar in front, saying - "Get down, Be calm." At each stroke of the Satka, the flames began to lower and slow down; and in a few minutes the Dhuni became calm and normal.

This is our Sai, an Incarnation of God. He will bless any man who will prostrate and surrender himself to Him. He, who will read the stories of this Chapter daily with faith and devotion, will soon be free from all calamities; not only this, but always attached and devoted to Sai, he will get very soon God-vision: all his desires will be fulfilled and being ultimately desire-less, he will attain the Supreme. Amen!

Bow to Shri Sai -- Peace be to all

Chapter XII

Sai Leelas - Experience of (1) Kaka Mahajani
(2) Dhumal Pleader (3) Mrs. Nimonkar
(4) Moolay Shastri (5) A Doctor

Now let us see in this Chapter how devotees were received
and treated by Baba.

Saints' Mission

We have seen before, that the purpose or object of Divine
Incarnation is to protect the good and destroy the wicked. But the
mission of the Saints is quite different. To them the good and the
wicked are the same. First they feel for the evil-doers and set
them on the right path. They are like the Agasti to destroy the
Bhava-sagar (the ocean of worldly existence) or like the Sun to
the darkness of ignorance. The Lord (God) dwells in the Saints. In
fact they are not different from Him. Our Sai is One of these, Who
incarnated for the welfare of the devotees, Supreme in knowledge
and surrounded with divine lustre, He loved all beings equally. He
was unattached. Foes and friends, kings and paupers, were the
same to Him. Hear His powers. For the sake of devotees, He spent
His stock of merits and was ever alert to help them. But the
devotees could never approach Him, unless He meant to receive
them. If their turn did not come, Baba did not remember them,
and His Leelas could not reach their ears.

Then, how could they think of seeing Him? Some men desired
to see Sai Baba but they did not get any opportunity of taking His
darshan, till His Mahasamadhi. There are many such persons,
whose desire for Baba's darshan was not thus satisfied. If these
persons, believing in Him, listen to His Leelas, their quest for
milk (darshan) will be, to a great extent, satisfied by the butter-
milk (Leelas). If some persons went there by sheer luck and took
Baba's darshan, were they able to stay there longer? No. Nobody
could go there of his own accord, and nobody could stay there
long even if he so wished. They could stay there, so long as Baba
permitted them to stay, and had to leave the place when asked to

do so by Baba; so everything depended of Baba's will.

Kala Mahajani

Once, Kaka Mahajani went to Shirdi from Bombay. He wanted to stay there for one week, and enjoy the Gokul-Ashtami festival. As soon as he took Baba's darshan, Baba asked him - "When are you returning home?" He was rather surprised at this question, but he had to give an answer. He said that he would go home when Baba ordered him to do so. Then Baba said - "Go tomorrow". Baba's word was law and had to be obeyed. Kaka Mahajani, therefore, left Shirdi, immediately. When he went to his office in Bombay, he found that his employer was anxiously waiting for him. His munim, i.e., the manager, suddenly fell ill; hence Kaka's presence was absolutely necessary. He had sent a letter to Kaka at Shirdi, which was redirected to him at Bombay.

Bhausaheb Dhumal

Now listen to an opposite story. Once Bhausaheb Dhumal, a pleader (lawyer), was going to Niphad for a case. On the way he came to Shirdi, took Baba's darshan and wanted to proceed to Niphad immediately. But, Baba did not permit him to do so. He made him stay at Shirdi, for a week or more. In the meanwhile, the magistrate at Niphad suffered intensely from pain in his abdomen, and the case was adjourned. Mr. Dhumal was then allowed to go and attend to his case. It went on for some months and was tried by four magistrates. Ultimately Mr. Dhumal won the case, and his client was acquitted.

Mrs. Nimonkar

Mr. Nanasaheb Nimonkar, Watandar of Nomon & Honorary Magistrate, was staying at Shirdi with his wife. Mr. and Mrs. Nimonkar were spending most of their time in the Masjid with Baba and serving Him. It so happened, that their son fell ill at Belapur and the mother decided, with Baba's consent, to go to Belapur, and see her son and other relatives; and stay there for a few days, but Mr. Nanasaheb asked her to return the next day. The lady was in a fix and did not know what to do; but her God Sai came to her aid. While leaving Shirdi she went to Baba, who was standing in front of Sathe's wada with Mr. Nanasaheb and others, and prostrated at His Feet and asked His permission to go. Baba said to her, "Go, go quickly, be calm and unperturbed. Stay comfortably at Belapur for four days. See all your relatives and then return to Shirdi." How opportune were Baba's words! Mr. Nanasaheb's proposal was overruled by Baba's decree.

Moolay Shastri of Nasik

An orthodox Agnihotri Brahmin of Nasik, by name Moolay Shastri, who had studied the six Shastras and was well-versed in astrology and palmistry, once, came to Shirdi to see Mr. Bapusaheb Booty, the famous millionaire of Nagpur. After seeing him, he and others went to see Baba in the Masjid. Baba bought various fruits and other things from vendors with His own money, and distributed them to the persons present in the Masjid. Baba used to press the mango on all sides so skillfully that when any person received it from Baba and sucked it, he got all the pulp at once in his mouth and could throw away the stone and the skin forthwith. Plantains were peeled off by Baba and the kernel was distributed to the devotees, while the skins were retained by Baba for Himself. Moolay Shastri, as a palmist, wanted to examine Baba's hand or palm and requested Him to extend the same. Baba ignored his request and gave four plantains to him.

Then, they all returned to the Wada and Moolay Shastri bathed, wore sacred clothes, and started his routine duties, viz. Agnihotra etc... Then Baba as usual started for Lendi and said - "Take some Geru (i.e. a red miry substance, to dye clothes in saffron-color), we shall today don saffron-colored cloth. None understood what Baba meant. Then after some time when Baba returned, and preparations for the noon-Arati were being made. Bapusaheb Jog asked Moolay Shastri, whether he would accompany him for the Arati. He replied that he would see Baba in the afternoon. Very soon Baba sat on his seat, was worshipped by the devotees and Arati commenced.

Then Baba said - "Get some Dakshina from the new (Nasik) Brahmin." Booty himself went to get the Dakshina; and when he gave Baba's message to Moolay Shastri, he was sorely perplexed.

He thought in his mind thus: "I am a pure Agnihotri Brahmin, why should I pay Dakshina? Baba may be a great Saint. I am not His dependent." But as a great Saint like Sai Baba was asking for Dakshina through a millionaire like Booty, he could not refuse. So leaving his routine unfinished, he forthwith started with Booty to the Masjid. Thinking himself holy and sacred, and the Masjid otherwise, he remained at a distance, and joining his hands threw flowers at Baba. Then lo! all of a sudden, he saw no Baba on the seat, but saw his late Guru Gholap Swami there. He was wonder-struck. Could this be a dream? No, it was not, as he was wide awake; but though awake, how could his late Guru Gholap be there? He was speechless for some time. He pinched himself and thought again, but could not reconcile the fact of his late Guru Gholap being in the Masjid. Ultimately, leaving all doubt, he went up, fell at his Guru's feet and then getting up stood there with folded hands. Other people sang Baba's Arati, while Moolay Shastri chanted his Guru's name. Then casting off all pride of caste and ideas about sacredness, he fell flat at his Guru's feet and closed his eyes.

When he got up and opened his eyes, he saw Baba asking for Dakshina. Seeing Baba's blissful form, and His inconceivable power, Moolay Shastri forgot himself. He was extremely pleased; his eyes were full of tears of joy. He again saluted Baba and gave the Dakshina. He said that his doubt was removed and that he saw his own Guru. On seeing his wonderful Leela of Baba all the people, including Moolay Shastri, were much moved, and they realized the meaning of Baba's words, "Bring Geru, we shall don saffron-colored garment." Such is the wonderful Leela of Baba.

A Doctor

Once a Mamlatdar came to Shirdi with a doctor friend of his. The Doctor said that his Deity was Rama and that he would not bow before a Mohammedan, and so, he was unwilling to go to Shirdi. The Mamlatdar replied that nobody would press him to make a bow, nor would ask him to do so. So he should come and give the pleasure of his company. Accordingly, they came to Shirdi, and went to the Masjid for Baba's darshan. All were wonder-struck to see the Doctor going ahead and saluting Baba.

They asked him how he forgot his resolve and bowed before a Mussulmen. Then the Doctor replied that he saw his beloved Deity, Rama, on the seat and he, therefore prostrated himself before Him. Then as he was saying this, he saw Sai Baba there again. Being dismayed, he said, "Is this a dream? How could He be a Mohammedan? He is a great Yogasampanna (full of Yoga) Avatar."

Next day, he made a vow and began to fast. He absented himself from the Masjid, resolving not to go there, until Baba blessed him. Three days passed and on the fourth day, a close friend of his from Khandesh, turned up, and with him, he went to the Masjid for Baba's darshan. After the salutation, Baba asked him, whether anybody had gone to call him, so that he had come. Hearing this vital question, the doctor was moved. The same night he was blessed by Baba, and he experienced the Bliss supreme, in his sleep. Then he left for his town, where the experienced the same state of a fortnight. Thus his devotion to Sai Baba increased manifold.

The moral of all the stories mentioned above, specially, that of Moolay Shastri, is this that we should have firm faith in our Guru and nowhere else.

More Leelas of Sai Baba will be described in the next Chapter.

Bow to Shri Sai -- Peace be to all

Chapter XIII

More Sai Leelas - Diseases Cured (1) Bhimaji Patil (2) Bala
Shimpi (3) Bapusaheb Booty
(4) Alandi Swami (5) Kaka Mahajani (6) Dastopant of Harda

The Inscrutable Power of Maya

Baba's words were always short, pithy, deep, full of meaning,
efficient and well-balanced. He was ever content and never cared
for anything. He said, "Though I have become a Fakir, have no
house or wife, and though leaving off all cares, I have stayed at
one place, the inevitable Maya teases Me often. Though I forgot
Myself I cannot forget Her. She always envelops Me. This Maya
(illusive power) of the Lord (Shri Hari) teases God Brahma and
others; then what to speak of a poor Fakir like Me? Those who
take refuge in the Lord will be freed from Her clutches with his
grace".

In such terms Baba spoke about the power of Maya. Lord Shri
Krishna has said to Uddhava in the Bhagwat that the Saints are
His living forms; and see what Baba had said for the welfare of
His devotees: "Those who are fortunate and whose demerits have
vanished; take to My worship. If you always say 'Sai, Sai' I shall
take you over the seven seas; believe in these words, and you will
be certainly benefited. I do not need any paraphernalia of worship
- either eight-fold or sixteen-fold. I rest there where there is full
devotion". Now read what Sai, the friend of those, who surrendered themselves to Him, did for their welfare.

Bhimaji Patil

One Bhimaji Patil of Narayanagaon, Taluka Junnar, Poona,
suffered in the year 1909, from a severe and chronic chest-disease
which ultimately developed into Tuberculosis. He tried all sorts of
pathos (remedies), but to no effect. Losing all hopes, he ultimately prayed to God - "Oh Lord Narayana, help me now".

It is a well-known fact that, when our circumstances are well
off, we do not remember God, but when calamities and adversi-
ties overtake us, we are reminded of Him, So Bhimaji now turned

to God. It occurred to him that he should consult Mr. Nanasaheb Chandorkar, a great devotee of Baba, in this respect. So he wrote to him a letter, giving all details of his malady, and asking for his opinion. In reply, Mr. Nanasaheb wrote to him that there was only one remedy left, and that was to have recourse to Baba's Feet. Relying on Mr. Nanasaheb's advice, he made preparations for going to Shirdi.

He was brought to Shirdi and taken to the Masjid, and placed before Baba. Mr. Nanasaheb and Shama (Madhavrao Deshpande) were then present. Baba pointed out that the disease was due to the previous evil karma, and was not at first disposed to interfere. But the patient cried out in despair that he was helpless, and sought refuge in Him, as He was his last hope, and prayed for mercy. Then Baba's heart melted and He said, "Stay, cast off your anxiety, your sufferings have come to an end. However, oppressed and troubled one may be as soon as he steps into the Masjid, he is on the pathway to happiness. The Fakir here is very kind and He will cure the disease, and protect all with love and kindness."

The patient vomited blood every five minutes, but there was no vomiting in the presence of Baba. From the time, Baba uttered the words of hope and mercy; the malady took a favorable turn. Baba asked him to stay in Bhimabai's house, which was not a convenient and healthy place, but Baba's order had to be obeyed. While he was staying there, Baba cured him by two dreams. In the first dream, he saw himself as a boy suffering the severe pain of a flogging, which he received for not reciting his 'Swami-poetry' lesson before his class master. In the second dream, someone caused him intense pain, and torture, by rolling a stone up and down over his chest. With the pain thus suffered in dream, his cure was complete, and he went home.

He then often came to Shirdi, gratefully remembering what Baba did for him, and prostrated before Him. Baba also did not expect anything from devotees, but grateful remembrance, unchanging faith and devotion. People in the Maharashtra, always celebrate Satya-Narayana Puja in their homes every fortnight or month. But it was this Bhimaji Patil, who started a new Sai Satya-Vrata Puja, instead of Satya-Narayana-Vrata Puja, in his house, when he returned to his village.

Bala Ganpat Shimpi

Another devotee of Baba by name Bala Ganapat Shimpi, suffered much from a malignant type of Malaria. he tried all sorts of medicines and decoctions, but in vain. The fever did not abate a jot and so he ran to Shirdi and fell on Baba's Feet. Baba gave him a strange recipe, in this case as follows: - "Give a black dog some morsels of rice mixed with curds in front of the Laxmi temple". Bala Shimpi did not know, how to execute this recipe; but no sooner he went home, then he found rice and curds. After mixing them together, he brought the mixture near the Laxmi temple, when he found a black dog waving its tail. He placed the curds and rice before the dog. The dog ate it and, strange to say, Bala got rid of his Malaria.

Bapusaheb Booty

Shriman Bapusaheb Booty suffered, once from dysentery and vomiting. His cupboard was full of patent drugs and medicines, but none of them had any effect. Bapusaheb got very weak, on account of purgings and vomiting and, therefore, was not able to go to the Masjid for Baba's darshan. Baba then sent for him and made him sit before Him and said, "Now take care, you should not purge any more" and waving His index-finger "The vomiting must also stop". Now look at the force of Baba's words. Both the maladies took to their heels (disappeared) and Booty felt well.

On another occasion he had an attack of Cholera, and suffered from severe thirst. Dr. Pillai tried all sorts of remedies but could give him no relief. Then he went to Baba and consulted Him as what to drink that would allay his thirst and cure the disease. Baba prescribed an infusion of almonds, walnuts, pistachio (a kind of dry fruit), boiled in sugared milk. This would be considered, as a fatal aggravation of the disease by any other doctor or physician, but in implicit obedience to Baba's order, the infusion was administered and strange to say, the disease was cured.

Alandi Swami

A Swami from Alandi, wishing to take Baba's darshan, came

to Shirdi. He suffered from a severe pain in his ear, which prevented him from getting the sleep. He was operated for this, but it served no purpose. The pain was severe and he did not know what to do. While he was returning, he came to take Baba's leave, when Shama (Madhavrao Deshpande) requested Baba to do something for the pain in the Swami's ear. Baba comforted him saying, "Allah Accha Karega (God will do good)." The Swami then returned to Poona, and after a week sent a letter to Shirdi, stating that the pain in his ear had subsided though the swelling was there, and in order to get the swelling removed, he went to Bombay for operation, but the surgeon on examining the ear said that no operation was then necessary. Such was the wonderful effect of Baba's words.

Kaka Mahajani

Another devotee named Kaka Mahajani suffered once from diarrhea. In order that there should be no break in his services to Baba, Kaka kept a tambya (pot) with water in some corner of the Masjid and whenever there was a call, he would go out. As Sai Baba knew everything, Kaka did not inform Him of his disease, thinking that Baba would of His own cure it soon. The work of constructing the pavement in front of the Masjid was permitted by Baba, but when the actual work was begun, Baba got wild and shouted out loudly. Everybody ran away, and as Kaka was also doing the same, Baba caught hold of him and made him sit there. In the confusion that followed, somebody left a small bag of peanuts. Baba took a handful of groundnut, rubbed them in His hands, blew away the skins, and gave the clean nuts to Kaka and made him eat them. Scolding and cleaning the nuts, and making Kaka eat them, went on simultaneously. Baba Himself ate some of them. Then, when the bag was finished, Baba asked him to fetch water as He felt thirsty. Kaka brought a pitcher full of water. Then Baba drank some water and made Kaka also drink it. Baba then said, "Now your diarrhea has stopped, and you may attend to the work of the pavement." In the meanwhile other persons, who had run away, returned and started the work; and Kaka, whose motions had stopped, also joined them. Are groundnut medicine for diarrhea? According to current medical opinion, groundnut would aggravate the disease, and not cure it. The true medicine, in this as in other cases, was Baba's word.

Dattopant of Harda

A gentleman from Harda by name Dattopant suffered from stomach-ache for fourteen years. None of the remedies gave him any relief. Then hearing of Baba's fame, that He cures diseases by sight he ran to Shirdi, and fell at Baba's Feet. Baba looked at him kindly and gave him blessings. When Baba placed His hand on his head, and when he got Baba's Udi with blessing, he felt relieved and there was no further trouble about the malady.

Towards the end of this Chapter three cases are cited in footnotes:

1. Madhavrao Deshpande suffered from Piles. Baba gave him decoction of Sonamukhi (senna pods). This relieved him. Then after two years the trouble again recurred and Mahdavrao took the same decoction without consulting Baba. The result was that the disease aggravated but later on it was cured by Baba's grace.

2. Kaka Mahajani's elder brother, Gangadharpant, suffered for many years from stomach pain. Hearing Baba's fame he came to Shirdi and requested Baba to cure him. Baba touched his belly and said, "God will cure". From that time there was no stomach pain and he was completely cured.

3. Nanasaheb Chandorkar also once suffered from intense stomach-pain; he was restless the whole day and night. Doctors administered syringes which produced no effect. Then he approached Baba, who told him to eat Burfi (a kind of sweet) mixed with ghee. This recipe gave him complete relief.

All these stories go to show, that the real medicine that cured the various diseases permanently was Baba's word, and grace, and not any medicines or drugs.

Bow to Shri Sai - Peace be to all

Chapter XIV

Ruttonji Wadia of Nanded - Saint Moulisaheb - Dakshina
Mimansa

In the last Chapter, we described how Baba's word and grace
cured many incurable diseases. Now, we shall describe, how
Baba blessed Mr. Ruttonji Wadia with an issue.

The life of this Saint is naturally sweet in and out. His various
doings, eating, walking and His natural sayings are also sweet.
His life is Bliss incarnate. Sai gave it out as a means of His
devotee's remembrance to Him. He gave them various stories of
duty and action, which ultimately led them to true religion. His
object may be that people should live happily in this world, but
they should be ever cautious and gain the object of their life, viz.
self-realization. We get human body as a result of merits in past
births and it is worth-while that with its aid, we should attain
devotion and liberation in this life. So we should never be lazy,
but always be on the alert to gain our end and aim of life.

If you daily hear the Leelas (stories) of Sai, you will always
see Him. Day and night you will remember Him in your mind,
When you assimilate Sai in this way, your mind will lose its
fickleness and if you go on in this manner, it will finally be
merged in pure Consciousness.

Ruttonji of Nanded

Now let us come to the main story of this Chapter. In
Nanded, in the Nizam state, there lived a Parsi mill-contractor and
trader, by name Ruttonji Shapurji Wadia. He had amassed a large
amount of money and had acquired fields and lands. He had got
cattle, horses and conveyances and was very prosperous. To all
outward appearances he looked very happy and contented, but
inwardly he was not so.

Providential dispensation is such, that no one in this world is
completely happy and rich; Ruttonji was no exception to this. He

was liberal and charitable, gave food and clothing to the poor and helped all in various ways. The people took him to be a good and happy man, but Ruttonji thought himself miserable as he had no issue, male or female, for a long time. As Kirtan (singing glories of the Lord) without love or devotion, music of singing without rhythmical accompaniments, Brahmin without the sacred thread, proficiency in all arts without common-sense, pilgrimage without repentance and ornamentation without a necklace, are ugly and useless, so is the house of a man or house-holder without a male issue. Ruttonji always brooded on this matter and said in his mind, "Would God be ever pleased to grant me a son?" He thus looked morose, had no relish for his food. Day and night, he was enveloped with anxiety whether he would ever be blessed with a son. He had a great regard for Dasganu Mahajat. He saw him and opened his heart before him. Dasganu advised him to go to Shirdi, take Baba's darshan, fall at His Feet and seek His blessing and pray for issue. Ruttonji liked the idea, and decided to go to Shirdi. After some days he went to Shirdi, took Baba's darshan and fell at His Feet. Then opening a basket, he took out a beautiful garland of flowers and placed it around Baba's neck and offered Him a basket of fruits. With great respect he then sat near Baba, and prayed to Him saying- "Many persons who find themselves in difficult situations come to You, and You relieve them immediately. Hearing this, I have sought anxiously Your Feet; please, therefore, do not disappoint me." Sai Baba then asked him for Dakshina of Rs. five which Ruttonji intended to give, but added that He has already received Rs. 3-14-0 from him, and that he should pay the balance only. Hearing this, Ruttonji was rather puzzled. he could not make out what Baba meant. That was the first time, he thought, that he went to Shirdi and how was it that Baba said that He had formerly got Rs. 3-14-0 from him? He could not solve the riddle. But he sat at Baba's Feet and gave the balance of the Dakshina asked for, explained to Baba fully, as to why he came and sought His help, and prayed that Baba should bless him with a son. Baba was moved and told him not to be worried, and that that time his bad days had ended. He then gave him Udi, placed His hand on his head and blessed him saying that Allah would satisfy his heart's desire.

Then after taking Baba's leave, Ruttonji returned to Nanded and told Dasganu everything that took place at Shirdi, He said that everything went on well there, that he got Baba's darshan and blessing with Prasad, but there was one thing which he could not understand. Baba said to him that he had got Rs. 3-14-0 before. Please explain as to what Baba meant by this remark. He said to Dasganu, "I never went to Shirdi before, and how cold I give Him the sum to which Baba referred?" To Dasganu also, it was a puzzle, and he pondered much over it for a long time. Sometime afterwards it struck him that Ruttonji had received some days ago a Mohammedan Saint, by name Moulisaheb, in his house and had spent some money for his reception. This Moulisaheb was coolie-saint well-known to the people of Nanded. When Ruttonji decided to go the Shirdi, this Molisaheb accidentally came to Ruttonji's house. Ruttonji knew him and loved him. So he gave a small party in his honor. Dasganu got from Ruttonji the yadi or memo of expenses of this reception, and everybody was wonder-struck to see, that the expenses amounted to exactly Rs. 3-14-0, nothing more, nothing less. They all came to know, that Baba was omniscient, that though He lived in Shirdi, He knew what happened outside far away from Shirdi. In fact He knew the past, present and future, and could identify Himself heart and soul with anybody. In this particular instance how could He know the reception given to Moulisaheb, and the amount spent therefore, unless He could identify Himself with him, and be One with him?

Ruttonji was satisfied with this explanation and his faith in Baba was confirmed and increased. In due time afterwards, he was blessed with a son and his joy knew no bounds. It is said that he had in all a dozen (12) issues out of which only four survived.

In a foot-note towards the end of this Chapter, it is stated that Baba told Rao Bahadur Hari Vinayak Sathe, after the death of his first wife, to remarry and that he would get a son. R.B. Sathe married second time. The first two issues by this wife were daughters and he, therefore, felt very despondent. But the third issue was a son. Baba's word did turn out true and he was satisfied.

Dakshina - Mimansa

Now we shall close this Chapter with a few remarks about Dakshina. It is a well-known fact that Baba always asked for Dakshina from people who went to see Him. Somebody may ask a question, "If Baba was a Fakir and perfectly non-attached, why should he ask for Dakshina and care for money?" We shall consider this question broadly now.

First for a long time, Baba did not accept anything. He stored burnt matches and filled His pocket with them. He never asked anything from anybody--whether he be a devotee or otherwise. If anybody placed before Him a pice or two, He purchased oil or charas (cannabis). He was fond of charas (Baba smoked a blend of tobacco & charas, which is a high resin handmade type of cannabis and is smoked by rolling into a ball), for He always smoked a bidi or Chillum (an earthen pipe). Then some persons thought that they could not see the Saints empty-handed, and they, therefore, placed some copper coins before Baba. If a pice was placed before Him, He used to pocket it; if it was a two pice coin, it was returned immediately. Then after Baba's fame had spread far and wide, people began to flock in numbers; and Baba began to ask Dakshina from them. It is said in the Shruti (Veda) that Puja of the Gods is not complete, unless a golden coin was offered. If a coin was necessary in the Puja of the Gods, why should it be not so in the Puja of the Saints also? Ultimately, the Shastras expounded upon it, that when one goes to see God, King, Saint or Guru, he should not go empty-handed. He should offer something, preferably coin or money. In this connection we may notice the precepts recommended by the Upanishads. The Brihadaranyak Upanishad says that the Lord Prajapati advised the Gods, men and demons by one letter "Da". The Gods understood by this letter that they should practice (1) "Dama" i.e. self-control; the men thought or understood that they should practice (2) "Dana" i.e. charity; the demons understood that they should practice (3) "Daya" i.e. compassion. To men Charity or giving was recommended.

The teacher in the Taittiriya Upanishad exhorts his pupils to practice charity and other virtues. Regarding charity he says, "Give with faith, give with magnanimity, i.e. liberally, give with modesty, with awe and with sympathy. In order to teach the devotees the lesson of charity and to remove their attachment to money and thus to purify their minds, Baba extracted Dakshina from them; but there was this peculiarity, as Baba said, that He had to give back hundred times more of what He received.

There are many instances, in which this has happened. To quote an instance, Mr. Ganpatrao Bodas, the famous actor, says in his Marathi autobiography, that on Baba's pressing him often and often for Dakshina, he emptied his money-bag before Him. The result of this was, as Mr. Bodas says, that in later life he never lacked money, as it came to him abundantly.

There were also secondary meanings of Dakshina, in many cases, in which Baba did not want any pecuniary amount. To quote two instances - (1) Baba asked Rs.15 as Dakshina from Prof. G. G. Narke, who replied that he did not have even a pie. Then Baba said, "I know you have no money; but you are reading Yoga-Vashistha. Give Me Dakshina from that." Giving Dakshina in this case meant - 'deriving lessons from the book and lodging them in the heart where Baba resides'. (2) In the second case Baba asked a certain lady (Mrs. R. A. Tarkhad) to give Rs.6 as Dakshina. The lady felt pained, as she had nothing to give. Then her husband explained to her that Baba wanted six inner enemies (lust, anger, avarice etc...) to be surrendered to Him. Baba agreed with this explanation.

It is to be noted, that though Baba collected a lot of money by Dakshina, He would distribute the whole amount the same day, and the next morning He would become a poor Fakir as usual. When Baba took His Mahasamadhi, after receiving thousands and thousands of Rupees as Dakshina for about ten years, He had only a few Rupees in His possession.

In short, Baba's main object in taking Dakshina, from His devotees was to teach them the lessons of Renunciation and Purification.

Postscript

Mr. B. V. Deo of Thana, retired Mamlatdar, and a great devotee of Baba, has written an article on this subject (Dakshina) in "Shri Sai Leela" magazine, Vol.VII, P.6-26, in which he says amongst other things, as follows:

"Baba did not ask Dakshina from all. If some gave Dakshina without being asked, He sometimes accepted it; and at other times He refused it. He asked it from certain devotees only. He never demanded it, from those devotees, who thought in their minds that Baba should ask them for it, and then they should pay it. If anybody offered it against His wish, He never touched it, and if he kept it there, He asked him to take it away. He asked for small or big amounts from devotees, according to their wish, devotion and convenience. He asked it, even from women and children. He never asked all the rich for it, or from all the poor."

"Baba never got angry with those from whom He asked Dakshina, and who did not give it. If any Dakshina was sent, through some friend, who forgot to hand over the same to Baba, He reminded him somehow of it and made him pay it. On some occasions, Baba used to return some sum from the amount tendered as Dakshina, and ask the donor to guard it or keep it in his shrine for worship. This procedure benefited the donor or devotee immensely. If anybody offered more than he originally intended to give, He returned the extra amount. Sometimes, He asked more Dakshina from some, than what they originally intended to give and, if they had no money, asked them to get or borrow from others. From some, He demanded Dakshina three or four times a day."

"Out of the amount collected as Dakshina, Baba spent very little for His own sake, viz., for buying Chillum (clay pipe) and fuel for His Dhuni (sacred fire), and all the rest, He distributed as charity in varying proportions to various persons. All the paraphernalia of the Shirdi Sansthan was brought, by various rich devotees at the instance and suggestion of Radha-Krishna-Mai. Baba always used to get wild and scolded those, who brought costly and rich articles. He said to Mr. Nanasaheb Chandorkar, that all His property consisted of one coupin (codpiece), one stray piece of cloth, one Kafni and a tumbrel (tin pot), and that all the people troubled Him by bringing all these unnecessary, useless and costly articles."

Woman and wealth are the two main obstacles in the way of our Pramartha (spiritual life); and Baba and provided in Shirdi

two institutions, viz., Dakshina and Radha- Krishna-Mai. Whenever they came to Him, He demanded Dakshina from them, and
asked them to go to the 'SCHOOL' (Radha-Krishna-Mai's house).
If they stood these two tests well, i.e. if they showed that they
were free from attachment for woman and wealth, their progress
in spirituality was rapid and assured by Baba's grace and
blessings.

Mr. Deo has also quoted passages from the Gita and Upanishads; and shown that charity given in a holy place and to a
holy personage conduces to the donors' welfare to a great
degree. What is more holy than Shirdi and its Presiding Deity -
- Sai Baba?

Bow to Shri Sai - Peace be to all

Chapter XV

Naradiya Kirtan - Paddhati - Mr. Cholkar's Sugarless Tea
Two Lizards

The readers may remember that mention was made in the 6th Chapter regarding the Rama-Navami Festival in Shirdi; how the festival originated and how in the early years there was a great difficulty in getting a good Hardidas for performing Kirtan on that occasion, and how Baba permanently entrusted this function (Kirtan) to Dasganu permanently. Now in this Chapter we shall describe the manner in which Dasganu was performing the Kirtan.

Naradiya Kirtan-Paddhati

Generally our Haridasas, while performing the Kirtan, wear a gala and full dress. They put on a head-dress, either a pheta or a turban, a long flowing coat with a shirt inside, an uparane (short dhotar) on the shoulders and the usual long dhotar from the waist below. Dressed in this fashion for some Kirtan in the Shirdi village, Dasganu once went to bow to Baba. Baba asked him - "Well, bridegroom! where are you going dressed so beautifully like this?" 'For performing a Kirtan' was the reply. Then Baba said - "Why do you want all this paraphernalia, coat, uparani (shawl) and pheta (turban) etc., doff all that before Me, why wear them on the body?" Dasganu immediately took them off and placed them at the Baba's Feet. From that time Dasganu never wore these things while performing the Kirtan. He was always bare from waist upwards, a pair of 'chiplis' was in his hand and a garland round his neck. This is not in consonance with the practice generally followed by all the Hardidasa, but this is the best and the purest method. The sage Narada, from whom the Kirtan-Paddhati originated, wore nothing on his trunk and head. He carried a 'veena' in his hand, and wandered from place to place everywhere singing the glory of the Lord.

Mr. Cholkar's Sugarless Tea

Initially, Baba was known in Poona and Ahmednagar Districts, but Nanasaheb Chandorkar, by his personal talks and by Dasganu, by his splendid Kirtans, spread the fame of Baba in the Konkan (Bombay Presidency). In fact, it was Dasganu - May God bless him - who by his beautiful and inimitable Kirtans, made Baba available to so many people there. The audience, who come to hear the Kirtans have different tastes, some like the erudition of the Haridas; some his gestures, some his singing, some his wit and humor, some his preliminary dissertation on Vedanta, and some others, his main stories and so on; but among them, there are very few, who by hearing the Kirtan get faith and devotion or love for God or saints. The effect of hearing Dasganu's kirtan on the minds of audience was however electric, as it were.

We give an instance here Dasganu was once performing his Kirtan and singing the glory of Sai Baba, in the Koupineshwar temple in Thana. One Mr. Cholkar, a poor man serving as a candidate in the Civil Courts in Thana, was amongst the audience. He heard Dasganu's Kirtan most attentively and was much moved. He there and then mentally bowed and vowed to Baba saying - "Baba, I am a poor man, unable to support my family. If by your grace, I pass the departmental examination, and get a permanent post, I shall go to Shirdi, fall at Your Feet and distribute sugar-candy in Your name." As good luck would have it, Mr. Cholkar did pass the examination and did get the permanent post and now it remained for him to fulfill his vow, the sooner the better. Mr. Cholkar was a poor man with a large family to support; and he could not afford to pay for the expenses of a Shirdi trip.

As is well said, one can easily cross over Nahne ghat in Thana District or even the Sahyadri Range; but it is very difficult for a poor man to cross Umbareghat, i.e., the threshold of his house. As Mr. Cholkar was anxious to fulfill his vow as early as possible, he resolved to economize, cut down his expenses, and save money. He determined not to use sugar in his diet; and began to take his tea without it. After he was able to save some money in this way, he came to Shirdi, took Baba's darshan, fell at His Feet, offered a coconut, distributed it with a clean conscience along with sugar-candy as per his vow and said to Baba that he was much pleased with His darshan and that his desires were fulfilled that day. Mr. Cholkar was in the Masjid with his host Bapusaheb Jog.

When the host and the guest both got up and were about to leave the Masjid, Baba spoke to Jog as follows:- "Give him (your guest) cups of tea, fully saturated with sugar." Hearing these significant words, Mr. Cholkar was much moved, he was wonder-struck, his eyes were be-dewed with tears, and he fell at Baba's Feet again. Mr. Jog was also curious about this direction, regarding the tea cups to be given to his guest. Baba wanted by His words to create faith and devotion in Cholkar's mind. He hinted as it were, that He got the sugar-candy as per his vow and that He knew full well his secret determination not to use sugar in his diet. Baba meant to say, "If you spread your palms with devotion before Me, I am immediately with you, day and night. Though, I am here bodily, still I know what you do; beyond the seven seas. Go wherever you will, over the wide world, I am with you. My abode is in your heart and I am within you. Always worship Me, Who is seated in your heart, as well as, in the hearts of all beings, Blessed and fortunate, indeed, is he who knows Me thus."

What a beautiful and important lesson was thus imparted by Baba to Mr. Cholkar!

Two Lizards

Now we close this Chapter, with a story of two little lizards. Once Baba was sitting in the Masjid, a devotee sat in front of Him, when a lizard tick-ticked. Out of curiosity, the devotee asked Baba whether this tick-ticking of the lizard signified anything; was it a good sign or a bad omen? Baba said that the lizard was overjoyed as her sister from Aurangabad was coming to see her. The devotee sat silent, not making out the meaning of Baba's words. Just then a gentleman from Aurangabad came on horse-back to see Baba. He wanted to proceed further, but his horse would not go, as it was hungry and wanted grams. He took out a bag from his shoulders to bring grams and dashed it on the ground to remove dirt. A lizard came out there, and in the presence of all climbed up the wall. Baba asked the questioner devotee to mark her well. She at once went strutting to her sister. Both sisters met each other after a long time, kissed and embraced each other, whirled round and danced with love! Where is Shirdi and where is Aurangabad? How should the man on horse-back come there from Aurangabad with the lizard? And how should Baba make the prophesy of the meeting of the two sisters? All this is really very wonderful and proves the omniscience -- the all-knowing nature of Baba.

Post Script
He who respectfully reads this Chapter or studies it daily, will get all his miseries removed by the grace of the Sadguru Sai Baba, Hence:

Bow to Shri Sai - Peace be to all

Chapters XVI & XVII

These two Chapters relate the story of a rich gentleman,
who wanted Brahma-Jnana quickly from Sai Baba

Preliminary

The last Chapter described how Mr. Cholkar's vow of small
offering was completed and accepted. In that story, Sai Baba
showed that He would accept with appreciation any small thing
offered with love and devotion, but if the same thing was offered
with pride and haughtiness, He would reject it. Being Himself full
of SatChitAnanda (Existence, Knowledge and Bliss), He did not
care much for more outward formalities, but if an offering was
made in meek and humble spirit, the same was welcome and He
accepted it with pleasure and avidity. In fact there is no person
more liberal and benevolent than a Sadguru like Sai Baba. He
cannot be compared to the Chintamani jewel (the Philosopher's
stone which satisfies desires), the Kalpataru (the Celestial Tree
which fulfills our desires) or the the Kamadhenu (the Celestial
Cow which yields what we desire), for they give us only what we
desire; but the Sadguru gives us the most precious thing that is
inconceivable and inscrutable (The Reality). Now let us hear how
Sai Baba disposed of a rich man, who came to Him and implored
Him to give him Brahma-Jnana.

These was a rich gentleman (unfortunately his name and
whereabouts are not mentioned) who was very prosperous in his
life. He had amassed a large quantity of wealth, houses, field and
lands, and had many servants and dependents. When Baba's fame
reached his ears, he said to a friend of his, that he was not in want
of anything, and so he would go to Shirdi and ask Baba to give
him Brahma-Jnana which, if he got, would certainly make him
happier. His friend dissuaded him, saying, "it is not easy to know
Brahman, and especially so for an avaricious man like you, who is
always engrossed in wealth, wife and children. Who will, in your
quest of Brahma-Jnana, satisfy you that won't give away even a
pice in charity?"

Not minding his friend's advice, the fellow engaged a return-

journey tanga (horse drawn carriage) and came to Shirdi. He went
to the Masjid, saw Sai Baba, fell at His Feet and said, "Baba,
hearing that You show the Brahman to all who come over here
without any delay, I have come here all the way from my distant
place. I am much fatigued by the journey and if I get the Brahman
from You, my troubles will be well-paid and rewarded." Baba
then replied, "Oh, My dear friend, do not be anxious, I shall
immediately show you the Brahman; all My dealings are in cash
and never on credit. So many people come to Me, and ask for
wealth, health, power, honor, position, cure of diseases and other
temporal matters. Rare is the person, who comes here to Me and
asks for Brahma-Jnana. There is no dearth of persons asking for
worldly things, but as persons interested in spiritual matters are
very rare, I think it a lucky and auspicious moment, when persons
like you come and press Me for Brahma-Jnana. So I show to you
with pleasure, the Brahman with all its accompaniments and
complications."

Saying this, Baba started to show him the Brahman. He made
him sit there and engaged him in some other talk or affair and
thus made him forget his question for the time being. Then He
called a boy and told him to go to one Nandu Marwari, and get
from him a hand-loan of Rs. five. The boy left and returned
immediately, saying that Nandu was absent and his house was
locked. Then Baba asked him to go to Bala grocer and get from
him, the said loan. This time also, the boy was unsuccessful. This
experiment was repeated again twice or thrice, with the same result.

Sai Baba was, as we know, the living and moving Brahman
Incarnate. Then, someone may ask - "Why did He want the paltry
sum of five rupees, and why did He try hard to get it on loan?
Really He did not want that sum at all. He must have fully known
that Nandu and Bala were absent, and he seems to have adopted
this procedure as a test for the seeker of Brahman. That gentleman
had a roll or bundle of currency notes in his pocket, and if he was
really earnest, he would not have sat quiet and be a mere onlooker, when Baba was frantically trying to get a paltry sum of Rs.
five. He knew that Baba would keep His word and repay the debt,
and that the sum wanted was insignificant. Still he could not make

up his mind and advance the sum.

Such a man wanted from Baba the greatest thing in the world, viz., the Brahma-Jnana! Any other man, who really loved Baba, would have at once given Rs. five, instead of being a mere onlooker. It was otherwise with this man. He advanced no money nor did he sit silent, but began to be impatient, as he was in a haste to return and implored Baba saying- "Oh Baba, please show me the Brahman soon." Baba replied - "Oh my dear friend, did you not understand all the procedure that I went through, sitting in this place, for enabling you to see the Brahman? It is, in short this. For seeing Brahman one has to give five things, i.e. surrender five things viz. (1) Five Pranas (vital forces), (2) Five senses (five of action and five of perception), (3) mind, (4) intellect and (5) ego. This path of Brahma-Jnana of self-realization is 'as hard as to tread on the edge of a razor'.

Sai Baba then gave rather a long discourse on the subject, the purport of which is given below:

Qualifications for Brahma-Jnana or Self-Realization

All persons do not see or realize the Brahman in their lifetime. Certain qualifications are absolutely necessary.

(1) **Mumuksha or intense desire to get free**. He, who thinks that he is bound and that he should get free from bondage and works earnestly and resolutely to that end; and who does not care for any other thinks, is qualified for the spiritual life.

(2) **Virakti or a feeling of disgust with the things of this world and the next**. Unless a man feels disgusted with the things, emoluments and honors, which his action would bring in this world and the next, he has no right to enter into the spiritual realm.

(3) **Antarmukhata (introversion)**. Our senses have been created by God with a tendency to move outward and so, man always looks outside himself and not inside. He, who wants self-realization and immortal life, must turn his gaze inwards and look to his inner Self.

(4) **Catharsis from (Purging of) sins**. Unless a man has turned away from wickedness, and stopped from doing wrong,

and has entirely composed himself and unless his mind is at rest, he cannot gain self-realization, even by means of knowledge.

(5) **Right Conduct**. Unless, a man leads a life of truth, penance and insight, a life of celibacy, he cannot get God-realization.

(6) **Preferring Shreyas, (the Good) to Preyas (the Pleasant)**. There are two sorts of things viz., the Good and the Pleasant; the former deals with spiritual affairs, and the latter with mundane matters. Both these approach man for acceptance. He has to think and choose one of them. The wise man prefers the Good to the Pleasant; but the unwise, through greed and attachment, chooses the Pleasant.

(7) **Control of the mind and the senses**. The body is the chariot and the Self is its master; intellect is the charioteer and the mind is the reins; the senses are the horses and sense-objects their paths. He who has no understanding and whose mind is unrestrained, his senses unmanageable like the vicious horses of a charioteer, does not reach his destination (get realization), but goes through the round of births and deaths; but he who has understanding and whose mind is restrained, his senses being under control, like the good horse of a charioteer, reaches that place, i.e., the state of self-realization, when he is not born again. The man, who has understanding as his charioteer (guide) and is able to rein his mind, reaches the end of the journey, which is the supreme abode of the all-pervading, Vishnu.

(8) **Purification of the mind**. Unless a man discharges satisfactorily and disinterestedly the duties of his station in life, his mind will not be purified and, unless his mind is purified, he cannot get self-realization. It is only in the purified mind that Viveka (discrimination between the Unreal and the Real), and Vairagya (Non-attachment to the unreal) crop up and lead on the self-realization. Unless egoism is dropped, avarice got rid of, and the mind made desire-less (pure), self-realization is not possible. The idea that 'I am the body' is a great delusion, and attachment to this idea is the cause of bondage. Leave off this idea and attachment therefore, if you want to get to the Self-realization.

(9) **The necessity of a Guru**. The knowledge of the self is so subtle and mystic, that no one could, by his own individual effort ever hope to attain it. So the help of another person-Teacher, who

has himself got self-realization, is absolutely necessary. What others cannot give with great labor and pains, can be easily gained with the help of such a Teacher; for he has walked on the path himself and can easily take the disciple, step by step on the ladder of spiritual progress.

(10) The **Lord's Grace**. When the Lord is pleased with any person, He gives him Viveka and Vairagya; and takes him safe beyond the ocean of mundane existence, "The Self cannot be gained by the study of Vedas, nor by intellect, or by much learning. He, whom the Self chooses, by him It is gained. To him the Self reveals Its nature", says the Katha Upanishad.

After the dissertation was over, Baba turned to the gentleman and said - "Well sir, there is in your pocket the Brahma (or Mammon) in the form of fifty-times five (Rs.250) rupees; please take that out." The gentleman took out from his pocket the bundle of currency notes and to his great surprise found, on counting them, that there were 25 notes of 10 rupees each, Seeing this omniscience of Baba, he was moved and fell at Baba's Feet and craved for His blessings. Then Baba said to him, "Roll up your bundle of Brahma, your Currency notes. Unless you get rid completely of your avarice or greed, you will not get the real Brahma. How can he, whose mind is engrossed in wealth, progeny and prosperity, expect to know the Brahma, without removing away his attachment for the same? The illusion of attachment or the love for money is a deep whirlpool of pain full of crocodiles in the form of conceit and jealousy. He, who is desire-less, can alone cross this whirlpool. Greed and Brahma are as poles asunder, they are eternally opposed to each other. Where there is greed, there is no room for thought or meditation of the Brahma. Then how can a greedy man get dis-passion and salvation? For a greedy man there is no peace, neither contentment nor certainty (steadiness).

If there be even a little trace of greed in mind, all the Sadhanas (spiritual endeavors) are of no avail. Even the knowledge of a well-read man, who is not free from the desire of the fruit or reward of his actions, and who has got no disgust for the same, is useless and can't help him in getting self-realization. The teachings of a Guru are of no use to a man, who is full of egoism, and who always thinks about the sense-objects. Purification of mind is absolutely necessary; without it, all our spiritual endeavors are nothing, but useless show and pomp. It is, therefore, better for one to take only what he can digest and assimilate. My treasury is full, and I can give anyone, what he wants, but I have to see whether he is qualified to receive what I give. If you listen to Me carefully, you will be certainly benefited. Sitting in this Masjid, I never speak any untruth."

When a guest is invited to a house, all the members of the household and other friends and relations that happen to be present, are entertained, along with the guest. So all those that were present in the Masjid at this time, could partake of the spiritual feast that was served by Baba for the rich gentleman. After getting Baba's blessings, one and all, including the gentleman left the place quite happy and contented.

Special Characteristic of Baba

There are many Saints, who leaving their houses, stay in forest, caves or hermitages and remaining in solitude, try to get liberation or salvation for themselves. They do not care for other people, and are always self-absorbed. Sai Baba was not of such a type. He had no home, no wife, no progeny, nor any relations, near or distant. Still, He lived in the world (society). He begged His bread from four or five houses, always lived at the foot of the (Neem) tree, carried on worldly dealings, and taught all the people how to act. and behave in this world. Rare are the Sadhus and Saints who, after attaining God Realization, strive for the welfare of the people. Sai Baba was the foremost of these and, therefore, says Hemadpant:

"Blessed is the country, blessed is the family, and blessed are the chaste parents where This extraordinary, transcendent, precious and pure jewel (Sai Baba) was born."

Bow to Shri Sai - Peace be to all

Chapters XVIII & XIX

How Hemadpant was Accepted and Blessed

Stories of Mr. Sathe and Mrs. Deshmukh - Encouraging Good
Thoughts to Fruition - Variety in Upadesh
Teachings Readings Slander, and Remuneration for Labor

In the last two Chapters, Hemadpant described, how a rich
gentleman, aspiring for quick Brahma-Jnana, was treated
by Baba, and now in these two Chapters, he describes how
Hemadpant, himself, was accepted and blessed by Baba,
how Baba encouraged good thoughts and fructified them;
and gives His teachings regarding Self-improvement,
slander and remuneration for labor.

Preliminary

It is a well-known fact that the Sadguru looks first to the qualifications of his disciples; and then gives them suitable instructions, without unsettling their minds in the least, and leads them
on towards the goal of self-realization. In this respect, some say
that what the Sadguru teaches or instructs, should not be divulged
to others. They think that their instructions become useless, if they
are published. This view is not correct. The Sadguru is like a
monsoon cloud. He pours down profusely, i.e., scatters widely his
nectar-like teachings. These, we should enjoy and assimilate to
our heart's content; and then serve others with them, without any
reserve. This rule should apply, not only to what he teaches in our
waking state, but to the visions he gives us in our dreams. To
quote an instance: Budhakowshik Rishi composed his celebrated
Ram-raksha stotra, which he had seen in his dream.

Like a loving mother forcing bitter but wholesome medicines
down the throats of her children for the sake of their health, Sai
Baba imparted spiritual instructions to His devotees. His method
was not veiled or secret, but quite open. The devotees who
followed His instructions got their object. Sadgurus like Sai Baba
open our intellect and show us the divine beauties of the Self, and

fulfill our tender longings of devotion. When this is done, our desire for sense-objects vanishes, twin fruits of Viveka (discrimination) and Vairagya (dis-passion or non-attachment) come to our hands; and knowledge sprouts up even in the sleep. All this we get, when we come in contact with Saints (Sadguru), serve them and secure their love. The Lord, who fulfills the desires of His devotees, comes to our aid, removes our troubles and sufferings, and makes us happy. This progress or development is entirely due to the help of the Sadguru, who is regarded as the Lord Himself. Therefore, we should always be after the Sadguru, hear His stories, fall at His Feet and serve Him. Now we come to our main story.

Mr. Sathe

There was a gentleman named Mr. Sathe, who had attained some publicity many year ago during Crawford Regime (Arthur Crawford, the first Municipal Commissioner of Bombay, between the years of 1865 and 1871) which was terminated by Lord Reay, the then Governor of Bombay. He suffered severe losses in trade. Other adverse circumstances gave him much trouble, and made him sad and dejected. Being restless, he thought of leaving home; and going out to a distant place. Man does not generally think of God, but when difficulties and calamities overtake him, he turns to Him and prays for relief. If his evil actions have come to an end, God arranges his meeting with a Saint, who gives him proper directions regarding his welfare. Mr. Sathe had similar experience. His friends advised him to go to Shirdi, where so many people were flocking to get Sai Baba's darshan, for getting peace of mind and the satisfaction of their wants. He liked the idea, and at once came to Shirdi in 1917.

Seeing Baba's Form, which was like Eternal Brahma, Self-luminous, Spotless and Pure, his mind lost its restlessness and became calm and composed. He thought that it was the accumulation of merits in his former births that brought him to the Holy Feet of Baba. He was a man of strong will. He at once started to make a parayana (study) of Guru-charitra. When the reading was finished in the saptaha (seven days), Baba gave him a vision that night. It was to this effect: Baba with Guru-charitra in

His hand was explaining its contents to Mr. Sathe, who was sitting in front and listening carefully.

When he woke up, he remembered the dream and felt very happy. He thought that it was extremely kind of Baba. Who awakens souls like his that are snoring in ignorance, and makes them taste the nectar of Guru-charitra. Next day, he informed Kakasaheb Dixit of this vision, and requested him to consult Sai Baba regarding its meaning or significance -- whether one saptah (week's) reading was sufficient or whether he should begin again. Kakasaheb Dixit, when got a suitable opportunity, asked Baba - "Deva (Oh God), what did you suggest to Mr. Sathe by this vision? Whether he should stop or continue the saptaha? He is a simple devotee, his desire should be fulfilled and the vision explained to him, and he should be blessed." Then Baba replied - "He should make one more saptah of the book; if the work be studied carefully, the devotee will become pure and will be bene-fited, the Lord will be pleased and will rescue him from the bond-age of the mundane existence."

At this time, Hemadpant was present there. He was shampoo-ing Baba's Legs. When he heard Baba's words, he thought in his mind as follows - "What! Mr. Sathe read for a week only and got a reward; and I am reading it for forty years with no result! His seven days' stay here becomes fruitful while my seven years' stay (1910 to 1917) goes for nothing. Like a Chatak bird I am ever waiting for the Merciful Cloud (Baba) to pour its nectar on me; and bless me with His instructions." No sooner did this thought cross his mind; Baba knew it then and there. It was the experience of the Bhaktas that Baba read and understood all their thoughts, and that He suppressed the evil thoughts and encouraged the good ones. Reading Hemadpant's mind Baba at once asked him to get up, go to Shama (Madhavrao Deshpande), get from him Rs. 15 as Dakshina, sit and chitchat with him for a while and then return. Mercy dawned in Baba's mind, and so he issued this order. And who could disobey Baba's order?

Hemadpant immediately left the Masjid and came to Shama's house. He had just bathed, and was wearing a dhotar. He came out and asked Hemadpant - "How is it that you are here now? It seems that you have come from the Masjid. Why do you look restless and dejected? Why are you alone? Please sit and rest, while I shall just do my worship and return: in the meanwhile you please take pan-vida (leaves and betel nuts etc...) let us then have a pleasant chat." After saying his, he went inside and Hemadpant sat alone in the front verandah. He saw in the window a well-known Marathi book named 'Nath-Bhagwat.' This is a commentary by the Saint Ekanath, on the eleventh Skandha (chapter) of the bigger Sanskrit work, the Bhagwat. At the suggestion or recommendation of Sai Baba, Messrs. Bapusaheb Jog and Kakasaheb Dixit read daily in Shirdi, Aggravate Gita with its Marathi commentary named Bhawartha-Deepika or Jnaneshwari (A dialogue between Krishna and His friend devotee Arjuna) and Nath Bhagwat (A dialogue between Krishna and His servant devotee Uddhava) and also Ekanath's other big work, viz. Bhawartha Ramayana. When devotees came to Baba and asked Him certain questions. He sometimes answered them in part, and asked them to go and listen to the readings of the above-mentioned works, which are the main treatises of Bhagwat Dharma. When the devotees went and listened, they got full and satisfactory replies to their questions. Hemadpant also used to read daily some portions of the book Nath-Bhagwat.

That day, he did not complete the daily portion of his reading, but had left it unfinished in order to accompany certain devotees, who were going to the Masjid. When he took up the book from Shama's window and casually opened, it, he found, to his surprise that the unfinished portion turned up. He thought that Baba sent him very kindly to Shama's house for enabling him to complete his daily reading. So he went through the unfinished portion and completed it. As soon as this was over, Shama, after doing his worship came out, and the following conversation took place between them:

Hemadpant: - "I have come with a message from Baba. He has asked me to return with Rs. 15 as Dakshina from you, also to sit with you for a while and have a pleasant chitchat and then return to the Masjid with you."

106

Shama (with surprise):- "I have no money to give. Take my 15 Namaskaras (bows) in lieu of rupees as Dakshina, to Baba."

Hemadpant: - "Alright, your Namaskaras are accepted. Now let us have some chitchat. tell me some stories and Leelas of Baba, which will destroy our sins."

Shama: - "Then sit here for a while. Wonderful is the sport (Leela) of this God (Baba). You know it already. I am a village rustic, while you are an enlightened citizen. You have seen some more Leelas since you're coming here. How should I describe them before you? Well, take these leaves, betel nut and chunam and eat the pan-vida; while I go in, dress myself and come out."

In a few minutes Shama come out and sat talking with Hemadpant. He said - "The Leela of this God (Baba) is inscrutable; there is no end to His Leelas. Who can see them? He plays or sports with His Leelas, still He is outside of (unaffected by) them. What do we rustics know? Why does not Baba Himself tell stories? Why does He send learned men like you to fools like me? His ways are inconceivable. I can only say that they are not human." With this preface Shama added, - "I now remember a story, which I shall relate to you. I know it personally. As a devotee is resolute and determined, so is Baba's immediate response. Sometimes Baba puts the devotees to severe test; and then gives them 'Upadesh' (instructions).

As soon as Hemadpant heard the word 'Upadesh', a flash of lightning crossed, through his mind. He at once remembered the story of Mr. Sathe's Guru-charitra reading and thought that Baba might have sent him to Shama, in order to give peace to his restless mind. However, he curbed this feeling, and began to listen to Shama's stories. They all showed how kind and affectionate Baba was to His devotees. Hemadpant began to feel a sort of joy while hearing them. Then Shama began to tell the following story:

Mrs. Radhabai Deshmukh

There was an old woman by name Radhabai; She was the mother of one Khashaba Deshmukh. Hearing Baba's fame, she came to Shirdi with the people of Sangamner. She took Baba's darshan and was much satisfied. She loved Baba intimately and resolved in her mind, that She should accept Baba as her Guru, and take some Upadesh from Him. She knew nothing else. She determined to fast herself unto death, so long as Baba did not accept her, and give her any Upadesh or Mantra. She stayed in her lodging and left off taking any food or water for three days. I was frightened by this ordeal of the old woman, and interceded with Baba on her behalf. I said, "Deva, what is this You have started? You drag so many persons here. You know that old lady. She is very obstinate and depends on You entirely, She has resolved to fast unto death, if You don't accept and instruct her. If anything worse happens, people will blame You, and say that Baba did not instruct her, and consequently she met her death. So take some mercy on her, bless her and instruct her." On seeing her determination, Baba sent for her, changed the turn of her mind by addressing her as follows:

"Oh mother, why are you subjecting yourself to unnecessary tortures and hastening your death? You are really My Mother and I am your child. Take pity on Me and hear Me through. I tell you My own story, which if you listen carefully, will do you good. I had a Guru. He was a great Saint and most merciful. I served him long, very long; still he would not blow any Mantra into My ears. I had a keen desire, never to leave him but to stay with and serve him; and at all costs receive some instructions from him. But he had his own way. He first got my head shaved and asked Me two pice as Dakshina. I gave the same at once. If you say that as My Guru was perfect, why should he ask for money and how should he be called desire-less? I replied plainly that he never cared for coins. What had he to do with them? His two pice were (1) Firm Faith and (2) Patience or perseverance. I gave these two pice or things to him, and he was pleased.

"I resorted to My Guru for twelve years. He brought Me up. There was no dearth of food and clothing. He was full of love nay, he was love incarnate. How can I describe it? He loved Me most. Rare is a Guru like him. When I looked at him, he seemed as if he was in deep meditation, and then we both were filled with Bliss. Night and day, I gazed at him with no thought of hunger and thirst. Without him, I felt restless. I had no other object to meditate, nor any other thing than My Guru to attend. He was My sole refuge. My mind was always fixed on him. This is one pice

Dakshina. Saburi (Patience or perseverance) is the other pice. I waited patiently and very long on My Guru and served him. This Saburi will ferry you across the sea of this mundane existence. Saburi is manliness in man, it removes all sins and afflictions, gets rid of calamities in various ways, and casts aside all fear, and ultimately gives you success. Saburi is the mine of virtues, consort of good thought. Nishtha (Faith) and Saburi (Patience) are like twin sisters, loving each other very intimately."

"My Guru never expected any other thing from Me. He never neglected Me, but protected Me at all times. I lived with him, and was sometimes away from him; still I never felt the want or absence of his love. He always protected Me by his glance, just as the tortoise feeds her young ones, whether they are near her or away from her on the other side of the river bank, by her loving looks. Oh mother, My Guru never taught Me any Mantra, then how shall I blow any Mantra in your ears? Just remember that Guru's tortoise-like loving glance gives us happiness. Do not try to get Mantra or Upadesh from anybody. Make Me the sole object of your thoughts and actions; and you will, no doubt, attain Paramartha (the spiritual goal of life). Look at Me whole-heartedly, and I in turn look at you similarly. Sitting in this Masjid, I speak the truth, nothing but the truth. No Sadhanas, nor proficiency in the six Shastras, are necessary. Have faith and confidence in your Guru. Believe fully, that Guru is the sole Actor or Doer. Blessed is he who knows the greatness of his Guru and thinks him to be Hari, Hara and Brahma (Trimurti) Incarnate."

Instructed in this way, the old lady was convinced; she bowed to Baba and gave up her fast. Hearing this story carefully and attentively, and marking its significance and appropriateness, Hemadpant was most agreeably surprised. Seeing this wonderful Leela of Baba, he was moved from top to toe, he was overflowing with joy, his throat was choked, and he was not able to utter a single word. Shama, on seeing him in this condition asked him, - "What is the matter with you, why are you silent? How many innumerable Leelas of Baba shall I describe?"

Just at that time the bell in the Masjid began to ring, proclaiming that the noon-worship and Arati ceremony (offering of lighted lamp) had begun. Therefore, Shama and Hemadpant hurried to the

Masjid. Bapusaheb Jog had just started the worship. Women were up in the Masjid, and men were standing below in the open court-yard and they were all loudly singing the Arati in chorus to the accompaniment of drums. Shama went up, pulling Hemadpant with him. He sat to the right and Hemadpant in front of Baba. On seeing them, Baba asked Hemadpant to give the Dakshina brought from Shama. He replied that Shama gave Namaskaras in lieu of Rupees and that he was there in person. Baba said, "Alright, now let Me know whether you both had chitchat, and if so, tell Me all that you talked about." Not minding the sounds of the bell, the drum and the chorus songs, Hemadpant was eager to tell what they had talked and started to narrate it. Baba was also anxious to hear, and so He left the bolster and leaned forward. Hemadpant said all that they talked about was very pleasant, and that especially the story of the old lady was most wonderful and that on hearing it, he thought that His Leela was inexplicable, and under the guise of that story, He really blessed him.

Baba then said - "Wonderful is the story. How were you blessed? I would like to know everything in detail from you, so tell Me all about it." Then Hemadpant related in full the story which he had heard a little while before, and which had made a lasting impression on his mind. Hearing this Baba was much pleased and asked him - "Did the story strike you and did you catch its significance?" He replied - "Yes, Baba the restlessness of my mind has vanished and I have got true peace and rest, and come to know the true path."

Then Baba spoke as follows: "My method is quite unique. Remember well, this one story, and it will be very useful. To get the knowledge (realization) of the Self, Dhyana (meditation) is necessary. If you practice it continuously, the Vrittis (thoughts) will be pacified. Being quite desire-less, you should meditate on the Lord, Who is in all the creatures, and when the mind is con-centrated, the goal will be achieved. Meditate always on My formless nature, which is knowledge incarnate, consciousness and bliss. If you cannot do this, meditate on My Form from top to toe as you see here night and day. As you go on doing this, your Vrittis will concentrate on one point and the distinction between the Dhyata (meditator), Dhyana (act of meditation), and Dhyeya (this meditated upon) will be lost and the meditator will be one with the Consciousness and be merged in the Brahman. The (mother) tortoise is on one bank of the river, and her young ones are on the other side. She gives neither milk, nor warmth to them. Her mere glance gives them nutrition. The young ones do nothing, but remember (meditate upon) their mother. The tortoise glance is, to the young ones, a down-pour of nectar, the only source of sustenance and happiness. Similar is the relation, between the Guru and disciples."

When Baba uttered these last words, the chorus of the Arati songs stopped and all cried out loudly in one voice: "Victory be to our Sadguru Sai Maharaj, Who is Existence, Knowledge and Bliss." Dear readers, let us imagine, that we are at this time, standing amongst the crowd in the Masjid; and let us join them in this Jayajayakar.

After the Arati ceremony was over, Prasad was distributed. Bapusaheb Jog advanced as usual, and after saluting Baba, gave into His hand a handful of sugar-candy. Baba pushed all this quantity into the hands of Hemadpant and said to him, "If you take this story to heart and remember it well, your state will be sweet as the sugar-candy, all your desires will be fulfilled and you will be happy." Hemadpant bowed before Baba and implored, "Do favor me like this, bless and protect me always." Baba replied - "Hear this story, meditate on it and assimilate its spirit. Then you will always remember and meditate on the Lord, Who will manifest Himself to you."

Dear readers! Hemadpant got Prasad of sugar-candy then; and we now get the Prasad of sugar-candy or nectar of this story. Let us drink it to out heart's content, meditate on it, and assimilate it, and be strong and happy by Baba's grace. Amen!

Towards the end of the 19th Chapter Hemapter Hemadpant had dealt with some other matters which are given below.

Baba's Advice Regarding our Behavior

The following words of Baba are general and invaluable. If they are kept in mind and acted upon, they will always do you good. "Unless there is some relationship or connection, nobody goes anywhere. If any men or creatures come to you, do not discourteously drive them away, but receive them well and treat them, with due respect. Shri Hari (God) will be certainly pleased, if you give water to the thirsty, bread to the hungry, clothes to the naked, and your verandah to strangers for sitting and resting. If anybody wants any money from you, and you are not inclined to give, do not give, but do not bark at him, like a dog. Let anybody speak hundreds of things against you, do not resent by giving any bitter reply. If you always tolerate such things, you will certainly be happy. Let the world go topsy-turvy, you remain where you are. Standing or staying in your own place, look on calmly at the show of all things passing before you. Demolish the wall of difference that separates you from Me; and then the road for our meeting will be clear and open. The sense of differentiation, as I and thou, is the barrier that keeps away the disciple from his Master, and unless that is destroyed the state of union or atonement is not possible, "Allah Malik" i.e. God is the sole Proprietor, nobody else is our Protector. His method of work is extraordinary, invaluable, and inscrutable. His will will be done and He will show us the way, and satisfy our heart's desires. It is on account of rnanubandha (relationships in past lives) that we have come together, let us love and serve each other and be happy. He, who attain the supreme goal of life, is immortal and happy; all others merely exist, i.e., live so long as they breathe".

Encouraging Good Thoughts of Fruition

It is interesting to note how Sai Baba encouraged good thoughts. You have to surrender yourself completely to Him with love, and devotion, and they you will see how, He helps you, off and on, in so many things. Some Saint has said, that when you get a good thought, immediately after awakening from sleep, and if you develop the same afterwards during the day, your intellect will be unfolded and your mind will attain calmness. Hemadpant wanted to try this. On one Wednesday night before going to bed, be thought - "Tomorrow is Thursday - an auspicious day and the place, viz. Shirdi, is so holy; so let me pass the whole day in remembering and chanting the Rama-Nama, and then he slept. Next morning when he got up he remembered without any effort the name of Rama and was much pleased. He then, after finishing his morning duties, went to see Baba with flowers. When he left Dixit's Wada, and was just passing Booty's Wada (present Samadhi-mandir) he heard a beautiful song that was being sung nicely by one Aurangabadkar, in the Masjid before Baba. The song was Guru - kripanjan payo mere bhai" etc... by Ekanath, in which he says that he got collyrium in the form of Guru's grace which opened his vision and made him see Rama, in and out, in sleep, dream, and waking state and everywhere. There were so many songs; and why was this song particularly chosen by Aurangabadkar, a devotee of Baba? Is this not a curious coincidence arranged by Baba to feed the determination of Hemadpant to sing unceasingly Rama-Nama, during the day?

All Saints agree on and lay stress upon the efficacy of uttering Rama's (God's) name, in fulfilling the ambitions of the Bhaktas and in protecting and saving them from all calamities.

Variety in Upadesh -- Slanderer Condemned

Sai Baba required no special place, nor any special time for giving instructions. Whenever any occasion demanded, He gave them freely. Once it so happened that a Bhakta of Baba, reviled another behind his back, before other people. On leaving aside merits, he dwelt on the faults of his brother, and spoke so sarcastically, that the hearers were disgusted. Generally, we see that people have a tendency to scandalize others, unnecessarily; and this brings on hatred and ill will. Saints see scandal, in another light. They say that there are various ways of cleansing or removing dirt, viz. by means of earth, water and soap etc.., but a scandal-monger has got a way of his own. He removes the dirt (faults) of others by his tongue; so in a way of obliges the person, whom he reviles and for this he is to be thanked. Sai Baba had his own method of correcting the scandal-monger. He knew by his omniscience what the slanderer had done and when He met him at noon near the Lendi, Baba pointed out to him a pig that was eating filth near the fence and said to him - "Behold how, with what relish it is gorging dung. Your conduct is similar. You go on reviling your own brethren to your heart's content. After performing many deeds of merit, you are born a man, and if you act like this, will Shirdi help you in any way?" Needless to say, that the Bhakta took the lesson to his heart, and went away.

In this way Baba went on giving instructions whenever necessary. If these are borne in our minds and acted upon, the spiritual goal (realization) is not far off. There is a proverb which says - "If there be my Hari (Lord), He will feed me on my cot." This proverb is only true in respect of food and clothing, but if anyone trusting in this sits quiet and does nothing in spiritual matters, he will be ruined. One has to exert himself to his utmost for attaining self-realization. The more he endeavors, the better for him.

Baba said that He was omnipresent, occupying land, air, country, world, light and heaven, and that He was not limited. To remove the misunderstanding of those, who thought that Baba was only His body - three cubits and a half in length, He incarnated Himself in this form and if any devotee meditated on Him day and night with complete self-surrender, he experienced complete union (without any difference) with Him like sweetness and sugar, waves and sea, eye and its lustre. He, who wants to get rid of the cycle of births and deaths, should lead a righteous life, with his mind calm and composed. He should always engage himself in good actions, should do his duties and surrender himself, heart and soul to Him. He need not then be afraid of anything. He, who trusts Him entirely, hears and expounds His Leelas and does not think of anything else, is sure to attain Self-realization. Baba asked many to remember His name and to surrender to Him, but to those, who wanted to know who they were ('Who am I' enquiry), He advised Shravanam (study) and Mananam (meditation). To some, He advised remembering God's name, to others hearing His Leelas; to some worship of His Feet, to others reading and studying Adhyatma Ramayan, Jnaneshwari and other sacred scriptures. Some He made sit near His Feet, some He sent to Khandoba's temple, and some He advised the repetition of the thousands names of Vishnu and some the study of Chhandogya Upanishad and Greta. There were no limit, nor restriction to His instructions. To some, He gave them in person. To others by visions in dreams. To one addicted to drink, He appeared in his dream, sat on his chest, pressed it and left him, after he gave a promise not to touch liquor any more. To some, He explained

114

some Mantras like 'Gurur Brahma' in dreams. To some devotee, who was practising HathaYoga, He sent word that he should leave off HathaYoga practices, sit quiet and wait (Saburi). It is impossible to describe all His ways and methods. In ordinary worldly dealings, He set examples by His actions, one of which is given below:

Remuneration for Labor

One day at noon, Baba came near Radha-Krishna-Mai's house and said - "Bring Me a ladder." Some men brought it and set it against a house as directed by Baba. He climbed up on the roof of Vaman Gondkar's house, passed the roof of Radha-Krishna-Mai's house and then got down from the other corner. What object Baba had, none could know. Radha-Krishna-Mai was, at that time, shivering with Malaria. It may be to drive off that fever that He may have gone there. Immediately after getting down, Baba paid two Rupees to the persons who brought the ladder. Somebody asked Baba, why he paid so much for this. He replied that nobody should take the labor of others, in vain. The worker should be paid, his dues promptly and liberally.

Bow to Shri Sai - Peace be to all

Chapter XX

Das Ganu's Problem Solved by Kaka's Maid Servant

In this Chapter, Hemadpant describes, how Das Ganu's problem was solved by Kakasaheb Dixit's maid servant.

Preliminary

Sai (Lord) was originally formless. he assumed a form for the sake of Bhaktas. With the help of the actress Maya, He played the part of the Actor in the big drama of the universe. Let us remember and visualize Shri Sai. Let us go to Shirdi, and see carefully the programs, after the noon-Arati. After the Arati ceremony was over, Sai used to come out of the Masjid, and standing on its edge, distribute Udi to the devotees with very kind and loving looks. The Bhaktas also got up with equal fervor, clasped His Feet, and standing and staring at Him, enjoyed the shower of Udi. Baba passed handfuls of Udi into the palms of the devotees and marked their foreheads with Udi with His fingers. The love He bore for them in His heart was boundless. Then He addressed the Bhaktas as follows: - "Oh Bhau, go to take your lunch; you Anna go to your lodgings; you Bapu enjoy your dishes". In this way He accosted each and every devotee and sent them home. Even now, you can enjoy these sights if you bring into play your imagination. You can visualize and enjoy them. Now bringing Sai before our mental vision, let us meditate on Him, from His Feet upwards to His face, and prostrating before Him humbly, lovingly and respectfully, revert to the story of this Chapter.

Ishavasya Upanishad

Das Ganu once started to write a Marathi commentary on the he Ishavasya Upanishad. Let us first give a brief idea of this Upanishad, before proceeding further. It is called a 'Mantropanishad', as it is embodied in the Mantras of the Vedic Samhita. It constitutes the last or the 40th Chapter of the Vajasaneyi Samhita (Yajurveda) and it is, therefore, called Vajasaneyi Samhitopanishad. Being embodied in Vedic Samhitas, this is regarded as superior to all other Upanishads, which occur in the Brahmanas and Aranyakas (explanatory treatises on Mantras and rituals). Not only this, other Upanishads are considered to be commentaries on the truths mentioned briefly in the Ishavasya Upanishad. For instance, the biggest of the Upanishads, viz., the Brihadaranyaka Upanishad, is considered by Pandit Satwalekar to be a running commentary on the Ishavasya Upanishad.

Professor R.D. Ranade says: - "The Ishopanishad is quite a small Upanishad; and yet it contains many hints which show an extraordinarily piercing insight. Within the short compass of 18 verses, it gives a valuable mystical description of the Atman, a description of the ideal sage, who stands unruffled in the minds of temptations and sorrows; and adumbration of the doctrine of Karma Yoga as later formulated, and finally a reconciliation of the claims of knowledge and works. The most valuable ideas that lies at the root of the Upanishad is that of a logical synthesis between the two opposites of knowledge; and work, which are both required according to the Upanishad to be annulled in a higher synthesis". In another place he says that "The poetry of the Ishopanishad is a Co-mixture of moral, mystical and metaphysical".

From the brief description given above about this Upanishad, anyone can see how difficult it is to translate this Upanishad in a vernacular language, and brief out its exact meaning. Das Ganu translated it in Marathi 'Ovi' metre, verse by verse, but as he did not comprehend the gist or essence of the Upanishad, he was not satisfied with his performance. He therefore consulted some learned men regarding his doubts and difficulties and discussed with them at great length. They did not solve them nor did they give him any rational and satisfactory explanation. So Das Ganu was a little restless over this matter.

SadGuru only competent and Qualified to Explain

As we have seen, this Upanishad is the quintessence of the Vedas. It is the science of self-realization, it is the scythe or weapon which can rend asunder the bondage of life and death, and make us free. Therefore, he thought, that he who has himself attained self-realization, can only give him the true or correct

117

interpretation of the Upanishad. When nobody could satisfy Das Ganu, he resolved to consult Sai Baba about this. When he got an opportunity to go to Shirdi, he saw Sai Baba, prostrated himself before Him, and mentioned his difficulties about the Ishavasya Upanishad and requested Him to give the correct solution. Sai Baba blessed him and said- "You need not be anxious, there is no difficulty about the matter, the mind-servant of Kaka (Kakasaheb Dixit) will solve your doubts at Vile Parle, on your way home". The people, who went present then and heard this, thought that Baba was joking and said, "How could an illiterate maid-servant solve the difficulties of this nature", but Das Garu thought otherwise. He was sure, that whatever Baba spoke, must come true, Baba's word was the decree of the Brahma (Almighty).

Kaka's Maid-Servant

On fully believing in Baba's words, he left Shirdi and came to Vile Parle (a suburb of Mumbai), and stayed with Kakasaheb Dixit. There the next day, when Das Ganu was enjoying his morning nap (some say when he was engaged in worship), he heard a poor girl singing a beautiful song in clear and melodious tones. The subject matter of the song was a crimson colored Sari, how nice it was, how fine was its embroidery, how beautiful were its ends and borders etc... He liked the song so much that he came out, and saw that it was being sung by a young girl, the sister of Namya, who was a servant of Kakasaheb. The girl was cleaning vessels, and had only a torn rag on her person.

On seeing her impoverished condition, and her jovial temperament, Das Ganu felt pity for her and when Rao Bahadur M.V. Pradhan next day gave him a pair of dhotars, he requested him to give a sari to the poor little girl also. Rao Bahadur bought a good Chirdi (small Sari) and presented it to her. Like a starving person getting luckily good dishes to eat, her joy knew to bounds. Next day she wore the new Sari, and out of great joy and merriment, whirled, danced round and played `Fugadi' with other girls and excelled them all.

The Day following, she kept the new Sari in her box at home and came with the old and torn rags, but she looked as merry as she did the previous day. On seeing this, Das Ganu's pity was transferred into admiration. He thought that the girl being poor had to wear a torn rag, but now she had a new Sari which she kept in reserve and putting on the old rag, strutted herself, showing no trace of sorrow or dejection. Thus he realized that all our feelings of pain and pleasure depend upon the attitude of our mind.

On thinking deeply over this incident, he realized that a man ought to enjoy whatever God has bestowed on him in the firm conviction that He besets everything, from behind and before, and on all sides and that whatever is bestowed on him by God must be for his good. In this particular case, the impoverished condition of the poor girl, her torn rag and the new Sari, the donor, the dance and the acceptance were all parts of the Lord and pervaded by Him. Hence, Das Ganu got a practical demonstration of the lesson of the Upanishad - the lesson of contentment with one's own lot in the belief that whatever happens is ordained by God, and is ultimately good for us.

Unique Method of Teaching

From the above incident, the reader will see that Baba's method was unique and varied. Though Baba never left Shirdi, He sent some to Machhindragad, some to Kolhapur or Sholapur for practising sadhanas. To some He appeared in His usual form, to some He appeared in waking or dreaming state, day or night and satisfied their desires. It is impossible to describe all the methods that Baba used in imparting instructions to His Bhaktas. In this particular case, He sent Das Ganu to Vile Parle, where he got his problem solved, through the maid servant. To those, who say that it was not necessary to send Das Ganu outside and that Baba could have personally taught him, we say that Baba followed the right or best course, or how else could Das Ganu have learnt a great lesson, that the poor maid servant and her Sari were pervaded by the Lord.

Now we close the Chapter with another beautiful extract about this Upanishad.

The Ethics of the Ishavasya Upanishad

"One of the main features of the Ishavasya Upanishad is the ethical advice it offers, and it is interesting to note that the ethics of the Upanishad are definitely based upon the meta-physical position advanced in it. The very opening words of the Upanishad tell us that God pervades everything. As a corollary from this metaphysical position, the ethical advice it offers is, that a man ought to enjoy whatever God bestows on him in the firm belief, that as He pervades everything, whatever is bestowed on him by God must be good. It follows naturally, that the Upanishad should forbid us from coveting another man's property. In fact, we are fittingly taught here a lesson of contentment with one's own lot in the belief that whatever happens, it is divinely ordained and it is hence good for us. Another moral advice is that man must spend his life-time always in doing action, specially the karmas enjoined in the Shastras, in a mood of believing resignation to His will.

Inactivity, according to this Upanishad, would be the canker of the soul. It is only when a man spends his life-time on doing actions in this manner that he can hope to attain the ideal of Naishkarmya. Finally, the text goes on to say that a man, who sees all beings in the Self and sees the Self as existing in all beings; in fact, for whom all beings and everything that exists have becomes the Self - how can such a man suffer infatuation? What ground would such a man have for grief? Loathfulness, infatuation and grief verily proceed from our not being able to see the Atman in all things. But a man, who realizes the oneness of all things, for whom everything has become the Self, must ipso facto, cease to be affected by the common foibles of humanity.

Bow to Shri Sai - Peace be to all

Chapter XXI

Stories of (1) V.H. Thakur (2) Anantrao Patankar
and (3) Pandharpur Pleader

In this Chapter, Hemadpant relates the stories of Vinayak
Harishchandra Thakur, B.A., Anantrao Patankar of Poona, and
a pleader from Pandharpur. All these stories are very interesting which if very carefully read and grasped, will lead the
readers on to the spiritual path.

Preliminary

It is a general rule, that it is our good luck in the form of
accumulation of merits in past births that enables us to seek the
company of Saints and profit thereby. In illustration of this rule,
Hemadpant gives his own instance. He was a resident Magistrate
of Bandra, A suburb of Bombay, for many years. A famous
Mohammedan Saint named Pir Moulana was living there and
many Hindus, Parsis and many others who followed different
religion used to go to him and take his darshan. His Mujavar
(priest) by name Inus pressed Hemadpant many a time, night and
day, for going to see him, but for some reason or other he was not
able to see him. After many years his turn came and he was called
to Shirdi where he was permanently enlisted in Sai Baba's Darbar.
Unfortunate fellows do not get this contact of the Saints. It is only
the fortunate ones that get it.

Institution of Saints

There have been institutions of Saints in this world, from time
immemorial. Various Saints appear (incarnate) themselves in various places to carry out the missions allotted to them, but though
they work in different places, they are, as it were, one. They work
in unison under the common authority of the Almighty Lord and
know full well what each of them is doing in his place, and
supplement his work where necessary. An instance illustrating this
is given below.

Mr. Thakur

Mr. V.H.Thakur, B.A., was a clerk in the Revenue Department and he once came to a town named Vadgaum near Belgaum (S.M. Country) along with a Survey party. There he saw a Kanarese Saint (Appa) and bowed before him. The Saint was explaining a portion from the book "Vichar-Sagar" of Nischaldas (a standard work on Vedanta) to the audience. When Thakur was taking his leave to go, he said to him, "you should study this book, and if you do so, your desires will be fulfilled, and when you go to the North in the discharge of your duties in future, you will come across a great Saint by your good luck, and then he will show you the future path, and give rest to your mind and make you happy".

Then, he was transferred to Junnar, where he had to go by crossing Nhane Ghat. This Ghat was very steep and impassible, and no other conveyance, than a buffalo was of use in crossing it. So he had to take a buffalo-ride through the Ghat, which inconvenienced and pained him much. Thereafter, he was transferred to Kalyan on higher post, and there he became acquainted with Nanasaheb Chandorkar. He heard much about Sai Baba from him and wished to see Him.

Next day, Nanasaheb had to go to Shirdi, and he asked Thakur to accompany him. He could not do so as he had to attend the Thana Civil Court for a civil case. So Nanasaheb went alone. Thakur went to Thana, but there the case was postponed. Then, he repented for not accompanying Nanasaheb. Still he left for Shirdi and when he went there, he found that Nanasaheb had left the place the previous day.

Some of his other friends, whom he met there, took him to Baba. He saw Baba, fell at His Feet and was overjoyed. His eyes were full of tears of joy and his hair stood on end. Then after a while the omniscient Baba said to him - "The path of this place is not so easy as the teaching of the Kanarese Saint Appa or even as the buffalo-ride in the Nhane Ghat. In this spiritual path, you have to put in your best exertion as it is very difficult". When Thakur heard these significant signs and words, which none else than he knew, he was overwhelmed with joy. He came to know, that the word of the Kanarese Saint had turned true. Then joining both hands and placing his head on Baba's Feet, he prayed that he should be accepted and blessed. Then Baba said - "What Appa told you was all right, but these things have to be practiced and lived. Mere reading won't do. You have to think and carry out what you read; otherwise, it is of no use. Mere book-learning, without the grace of the Guru, and self-realization is of no avail". The theoretical portion was read from the work 'Vichar Sagar' by Thakur, but the practical way was shown to him at Shirdi.

Another story given below will bring out this truth more forcibly.

Anantrao Patankar

One gentleman from Poona, by name Anantrao Patankar wished to see Baba. He came to Shirdi, and took Baba's darshan. His eyes were appeased, he was much pleased. He fell at Baba's Feet; and after performing proper worship said to Baba - "I have read a lot, studied Vedas, Vedanta and Upanishads and heard all the Puranas, but still I have not got any peace of mind; so I think that all my reading was useless. Simple ignorant devout persons are better than myself. Unless the mind becomes calm, all book-learning is of no avail. I have heard, from many people, that you easily give peace of mind to so many people by your mere glance, and playful word; so I have come here; please take pity on me and bless me". Then Baba told him a parable, which was as follows:

Parable of Nine Balls of Stool (Nava-vidha Bhakti)

"Once a Soudagar (merchant) came here. Before him a mare passed her stool (nine balls of stool). The merchant, intent on his quest, spread the end of his dhotar and gathered all the nine balls in it, and thus he got concentration (peace) of mind".

Mr. Patankar could not make out the meaning of this story; so he asked Ganesh Damodar, alias Dada Kelkar, "What does Baba mean by this?" He replied - "I too do not know all that Baba says and means, but at His inspiration I say, what I come to know. The mare is God's grace and the nine balls excreted are the nine forms or types of Bhakti, (1) Shravana (Hearing); (2) Kirtana (Praying); (3) Smarana (Remembering); (4) Padasevana (resorting to the feet); (5) Archana (Worship); (6) Namaskara (Bowing); (7) Dasya

123

(Service); (8) Sakhyatva (Friendship); (9) Atmanivedana (surrender of the self). These are the nine types of Bhakti. If any of these is faithfully followed, Lord Hari will be pleased, and manifest Himself in the home of the devotee. All the sadhanas, Japa (vocal worship), Tapas (penance), Yoga practice and studying the scriptures and expounding them are quite useless unless they are accompanied by Bhakti, i.e., devotion. Knowledge of the Vedas or fame as a great Jnani, and mere formal Bhajan (worship) are of no avail. What is wanted is Loving Devotion. Consider yourself as the merchant or seeker after the truth and be anxious and eager like him to collect or cultivate the nine types of devotion. Then you will attain stability and peace of mind".

Next day, when Patankar went to Baba for salutation, he was asked whether he collected the 'nine balls of stool'. Then he said that he, being a poor fellow, should first be graced by Baba, and then they will be easily collected. Then Baba blessed and comforted him, saying that he would attain peace and welfare. After hearing this, Patankar became overjoyed and happy.

The Pandharpur Pleader

We shall close this Chapter with short story showing Baba's omniscience and His using it for correcting people and setting them on the right path. Once a pleader from Pandharpur came to Shirdi, went to the Masjid, saw Sai Baba, fell at His Feet and, without being asked, offered some Dakshina, and sat in a corner eager to hear the talk that was going on. Then Baba turned His face towards him and said - "How cunning the people are! They fall at the feet, offer Dakshina, but inwardly give abuses behind the back. Is not this wonderful?" This cap (remark) fitted the pleader and he had to wear (take) it. None understood the remark. The pleader grasped it, but kept silent.

When they returned to the Wada, the pleader said to Kakasaheb Dixit - "What Baba remarked was perfectly right. The dart (remark) was aimed at me; it was a hint to me that I should not indulge in reviling or scandalizing others (calling by names). When the sub-judge or munsiff of Pandharput (Mr. Noolkar) came and stayed here for the improvement of his health, a discussion about this matter was going on in the bar-room at Pandharpur (as it ever happens in many a bar-room). It was said or discussed there whether the ailments, from which the sub-judge suffered were, ever likely to be got rid of without medicines, by merely going after Sai Baba, and whether it was proper for an educated man, like the sub-judge, to have recourse to such methods. The sub-judge was taken to task, i.e. he was criticized, as also Sai Baba. I also took some part in this affair; and now Sai Baba showed the impropriety of my conduct. This is not a rebuke to me, but a favor, an advice that I should not indulge in any scandal or slander of others; and not interfere unnecessarily in others' affairs".

Shirdi is about 100 Koss (One Koss equals about 3 miles) distant from Pandharpur; still Baba by His omniscience knew what transpired there in the bar-room. The intervening places -- rivers, jungles and mountains - were not a bar to His all-perceiving sight and He could see or read the hearts of all. There was nothing secret or veiled from Him. Everything, far or near, was plain and clear to Him as broad as daylight. Let a man be far or near, he cannot avoid the all-pervading gaze of Sai Baba. From this incident, the pleader took the lesson that he should never speak ill of others, nor unnecessarily criticize them. This, his evil tendency was completely got rid of, and he was set on the right path.

Though the story refers to a pleader, still it is applicable to all. All should, therefore, take this lesson to heart and profit thereby.

Sai Baba's greatness is unfathomable, so are His wonderful Leelas. His life is also such; for He is Para-Brahman (Lord God) incarnate.

Bow to Shri Sai - Peace be to all

Chapter XXII

Rescues from Serpent-bites - (1) Balasaheb Mirikar
(2) Bapusaheb Booty (3) Amir Shakkar (4) Hemadpant
Baba's Opinion Regarding Killing of Serpents

Preliminary

How to meditate on Baba? No one has been able to fathom the nature or the form of the Almighty. Even the Vedas and the thousand-tongued Shesha are not able to describe it fully; but the devotees cannot but know and look at the form of the Lord, for they know that His Feet are the only means of their happiness. They know no other method of attaining the supreme goal of life, except meditating on the Holy Feet. Hemadpant suggests an easy way of devotion and meditation as follows:

As the dark fortnight of every month wears out gradually, the moonlight also wanes in the same degree and on the new moon day, we do not see the moon at all, nor do we get her light. Therefore, when the bright fortnight begins, people are very anxious to see the moon. On the first day, the moon is not seen and on the second day also she is not clearly visible. Then the people are asked to see the moon through an opening between the two branches of a tree, and when they begin to see through this aperture eagerly and after concentration, the distant small crescent of the moon comes, to their great delight, within their ken. Following this clue, let us try to see Baba's Light. Look at Baba's posture, how fine it is! He is sitting with His legs folded, the right leg held across the left knee. The fingers of His left hand are spread on the right-foot. On the right toe are spread His two fingers-the index and middle ones. By this posture Baba means to say, as it were- if you want to see My Light, be ego-less and most humble and meditate on My toe through the opening between the two branches-index and middle fingers-and then you will be able to see My Light. This is the easiest means of attaining devotion.

Now let us turn for a moment to Baba's life. Shirdi had become a place of pilgrimage on account of Baba's stay. People from all quarters began to flock there, and both the rich and the poor began to be benefited in more ways than one and in some form or other. Who can describe Baba's boundless love and His wonderful natural knowledge and His all-pervasiveness? Blessed is he, who could experience one or all of these.

Sometimes Baba observed long silence which was, in a way, His dissertation on Brahman; at other times He was Consciousness-Bliss Incarnate, surrounded by His devotees. Sometimes He spoke in parables, and at other times indulged in wit and humor. At times, He was quite unambiguous (clear) and at times He seemed enraged. Sometimes He gave His teachings in a nut-shell, at other times He argued at length. Many a time He was very plain. In this way, He gave varied instructions to many, according to their requirements. His life was, therefore, inscrutable, beyond the ken of our mind, beyond our intellect and speech. Our longing to see His face, to talk with Him and hear His Leelas was never satisfied; still we were overflowing with joy. We can count the showers of rain, encircle (tie) the wind in a leather bag, but who can gauge or measure His Leelas? Now we deal here with one aspect of them, viz. how He anticipated or forestalled the calamities of His devotees and warded them off in time.

Balasaheb Mirikar

Balasaheb Mirikar, son of Sirdar Kakasaheb Mirikar was Mamlatdar of Kopergaon. He was going on tour to Chitali. On the way he came to Shirdi to see Sai Baba. When he went to the Masjid and prostrated himself before Baba, usual conversation regarding health and other matters commenced, when Baba sounded a note of warning as follows:- "Do you know our Dwarkamai?" As Balasaheb did not understand he kept quiet, Baba continued - "This is our Dwarkamai, where you are sitting. She wards off all dangers and anxieties of the children, who sit on her lap. This Masjidmayi (its presiding Deity) is very merciful; she is the mother of the simple devotees, whom she will save in calamities. Once a person sits on her lap, all his troubles are over. He, who rests in her shade, gets Bliss". Then Baba gave him Udi, and placed His protecting hand on his head. When Balasaheb was about to depart, He again said- "Do you know the "Lamba Bava" (long gentleman), Viz... serpent?" And then closing the left arm like fist He brought it near the right elbow, and moving His left arm like the hood of a serpent, He said- "He is so terrible, but what can he do to the children of Dwarkamai: When the Dwarkamai (its presiding deity) protects, what can the serpent do?"

All who were present there were curious to know the meaning of all this and its reference to Mirikar, but none had the courage to ask Baba about this. Then Balasaheb saluted Baba and left the Masjid with Shama. Baba called Shama back and asked him to accompany Balasaheb, and enjoy the Chitali trip. Shama came to Balasaheb, and told him that he would go with him according to Baba's wish. Balasaheb replied that he need not come as it would be inconvenient. Shama returned to Baba and told Him what Balasaheb said to him. Baba said, "Alright, do not go. We should mean well and do well. Whatever is destined to happen, will happen".

In the meanwhile Balasaheb thought over again, and calling Shama asked him to accompany him. Then Shama going again to Baba and taking His leave started with Balasaheb in the tanga. They reached Chitali at 9 P.M. and encamped in the Maruti temple. The office-people had not come; so they sat quiet in the temple, talking and chitchatting. Balasaheb was sitting on a mat reading a newspaper. His Uparani (upper dhotar) was spread across his waist and on a part of it a snake was sitting unobserved. It began to move with a rustling sound which was heard by the peon. He brought a lantern, saw the snake and raised an alarm- 'serpent, serpent'. Balasaheb was frightened and began to quiver. Shama was also amazed. Then he and others moved noiselessly and took sticks and clubs in their hands. The snake got down slowly from the waist and it moved away from Balasaheb; it was immediately done to death. Thus this calamity, which was prophesied by Baba, was averted and Balasaheb's love for Baba was deeply confirmed.

Bapusaheb Booty

A great astrologer named Nanasaheb Dengale told one day Bapusaheb Booty, who was then in Shirdi, "Today is an inauspicious day for you, there is a danger to your life". This made

Bapusaheb restless. When they, as usual, came to Masjid, Baba said to Bapusaheb- "What does this Nana say? He foretells death for you. Well, you need not be afraid. Tell him boldly "Let us see how death kills." Then later in the evening Bapusaheb went to his privy for easing himself where he saw a snake. His servant saw it and lifted a stone to strike at it. Bapusaheb asked him to get a big stick, but before the servant returned with the stick, the snake was seen moving away and soon disappeared. Bapusaheb remembered with joy Baba's words of fearlessness.

Amir Shankar

Amir Shankar was a native of the village Korale, in Kopergaon Taluka. he belonged to the butcher caste. He worked as a commission agent in Bandra, and was well-known there. He once suffered from Rheumatism, which gave him much pain. He was then reminded of God, and so, he left his business and went to Shirdi, and prayed to Baba to relieve him from his malady. Baba then stationed him in the Chavadi, which was then a damp unhealthy place, unfit for such a patient. Any other place in the village, or Korale itself would have been better for Amir, but Baba's word was the deciding factor and the chief medicine.

Baba did not allow him to come to the Masjid, but fixed him in the Chavadi, where he got very great advantage. Baba passed via Chavadi every morning and evening; and every alternate day Baba went to the Chavadi in a procession and slept there. So Amir got Baba's contact very often easily. Amir stayed there for full nine months, and then, somehow or other, he got a disgust for the place. So one night he stealthily left the place and came to Kopergaon and stayed in a Dharmashala. There he saw an old dying Fakir, who asked him for water. Amir brought it and gave it to him. As soon as he drank it, he passed away.

Then Amir was in a fix. He thought that if he went and informed the authorities, he would be held responsible for the death as he was the first and sole informant, and knew something about it. He repented for his action, viz. leaving Shirdi without Baba's leave, and prayed to Baba. He then determined to return to Shirdi, and that same night he ran back, remembering and muttering Baba's name on the way, and reached Shirdi before day-break, and became free from anxiety. Then he lived in the Chavadi in perfect accordance with Baba's wishes and orders, and got himself cured.

One night it so happened that Baba cried at midnight- "Oh Abdul, some devilish creature is dashing against the side of My bed". Abdul came with a lantern, examined Baba's bed but found nothing, Baba asked him to examine carefully all the place and began to strike ground with His satka. Seeing this Leela of Baba, Amir thought that Baba might have suspected some serpent had come there. Amir could know by close and long contact the meaning of Baba's words and actions. Baba then saw near Amir's cushion something moving. He asked Abdul to bring in the light, and when he brought it, he saw the coil of a serpent there, moving its head up and down. Thereupon the serpent was immediately beaten to death. Thus Baba gave timely warning and saved Amir.

Hemadpant (Scorpion and Serpent)

(1) At Baba's recommendation Kakasaheb Dixit was daily reading the two works of Shri Eknath Maharaj, viz., Bhagwat and Bhawartha Ramayana and Hemadpant had the good fortune to be one of the audience when the reading of the works was going on. Once when a portion from the Ramayana relating to Hanuman's testing Rama's greatness, according to his mother's instructions, was being read, all the listeners were spell-bound. Hemadpant was one of them. A big scorpion (none knew where it came from), jumped and sat on the right shoulder of Hemadpant, on his Uparani (upper dhotar). First it was not noticed, but as the Lord protects those, who are intent on hearing His stories, he casually cast a glance over his right shoulder and noticed it. It was dead silence, not a bit moved here or there. It seemed as if, it also enjoyed the reading. Then by the Lord's grace, Hemadpant without disturbing the audience, took the two ends of his dhotar, folded them, and brought them together, enclosing the scorpion within. Then he went out, and threw it in the garden.

(2) On another occasion some persons were sitting in the upper floor of Kakasaheb's Wada, just before nightfall, when a serpent crept through a hole in the window frame and sat coiled up. A light was brought. Though it was first dazzled, yet it sat still

and only moved its head up and down. Then many persons rushed there with sticks and cudgels, but as it sat in an awkward place, no blow could be dealt. But hearing the noises of men, the serpent went out hastily through the same hole. Then all the persons there felt relieved.

Baba's Opinion

One devotee named Muktaram, then said that it was good that the poor creature escaped. Hemadpant challenged him saying that serpents should better be killed. There was a hot discussion between them - the former contending that serpents, and such creatures, should not be killed, the latter that they should be. As night came on, the discussion came to an end, without any decision being arrived at. Next day, the question was referred to Baba, who gave His settled opinion as follows: - "God lives in all beings and creatures, whether they be serpents or scorpions. He is the Great Wire-puller of the world, and all beings, serpents, scorpions etc.., obey His command. Unless He will it, nobody can do any harm to others. The world is all dependent on Him, and no one is independent. So we should take pity and love all creatures, leave off adventurous fights and killings and be patient. The Lord (God) is the Protector of all.

Bow to Shri Sai - Peace be to all

Chapter XXIII

Yoga and Onion - Shama Cured of Snake-Bite
Cholera Ordinance Broken - Ordeal of Guru-Bhakti

Preliminary

Really this Jiva (human soul) transcends the three qualities, viz. Sattva, Rajas and Tamas, but being deluded by Maya, he forgets his nature which is 'Existence-knowledge-bliss', and thinks that he is the doer and enjoyer and thus entangles himself in endless miseries and does not know the way of deliverance. The only way of deliverance is Loving Devotion towards the Guru's feet. The great Player or Actor Lord Sai has delighted His Bhaktas and transformed them into Himself (His nature).

We regard Sai Baba as an incarnation of God for reasons already stated, but He always said that He was an obedient servant of God. Though an incarnation He showed the people the way, how to behave satisfactorily and carry out the duties of their respective stations (Varnas or Castes) in this life. He never emulated others in any way, nor asked others to have something done for Him. For Him, Who saw the Lord in all movable and immovable things of this world, humility was the most proper thing. None He disregarded or disrespected; for He saw Narayan (Lord) in all beings, He never said, "I am God," but that He was a humble servant and He always remembered Him and always uttered - "Allah Malik" (God is the sole proprietor or Owner).

We do not know the various kinds of Saints, how they behave, what they do and eat etc... We only know that by God's grace they manifest themselves in this world to liberate the ignorant and bound souls. If there be any store of merits on our account, we get a desire in listening to the stories and Leelas of the Saints, otherwise not. Let us now turn to the main stories of this Chapter.

Yoga and Onion

Once it so happened, that a sadhak of Yoga came to Shirdi with Nanasaheb Chandorkar. He had studied all the works on Yoga, including the Yoga Sutras of Patanjali, but had no practical experience. He could not concentrate his mind and attain samadhi even for a short time. He thought that if Sai Baba be pleased with him, He will show him the way to attain samadhi for a long time. With this object in view he came to Shirdi, and when he went to the Masjid he saw Sai Baba eating bread with onion. On seeing this, a thought arose in his mind - 'how can this man, eating stale bread with raw onion, solve my difficulties and help me?' Sai Baba read his mind and said to Nanasaheb - "Oh Nana, he who has the power to digest onion, should eat it and none else". Hearing this remark, the yogi was wonder-struck and then he fell at Baba's Feet with complete surrender. With pure and open mind, he asked his difficulties and got their solution from Baba. Thus being satisfied and happy, he left Shirdi with Baba's Udi and blessings.

Shama Cured of Snake-Bite

Before Hemadpant begins the story, he says about the Jiva that it can be very well compared with a parrot, and that they both are bound, the one in the body and the other in a cage. Both think that their present bound state is good for them. It is only when a Helper, i.e., Guru comes and by God's grace opens their eyes and liberates them from their bondage that their eyes are opened to a greater and larger life compared to which their former limited life is nothing.

In the last Chapter, it was shown how Baba anticipated the calamity, that was to befall on Mr. Mirikar and rescued him from it. Now let the readers hear a story grander than that. Once Shama was bitten by a poisonous snake, his little finger of the hand was stung and the poison began to spread into the body. The pain was also severe and Shama thought that he would pass off soon.

His friends wanted to take him to the God Viroba, where such cases were often sent, but Shama ran to the Masjid -- to His Viroba (Sai Baba). When Baba saw him, He began to scold and abuse. He got enraged and said - "Oh vile Bhaturdya (Priest) do not climb up. Beware if you do so" and then roared - "Go, Get away, Come down." Seeing Baba thus red with wrath, Shama was greatly puzzled and disappointed. He thought that the Masjid was his home and Sai Baba his sole Refuge, but if he was driven away like this, where should he go? He lost all hope of life and kept silent. After a time Baba became normal and calm when Shama went up and sat near.

Then Baba said to him - "Don't be afraid, don't care a jot, the Merciful Fakir will save you, go and sit quiet at home, don't go out, believe in Me and remain fearless and have no anxiety". Then he was sent home. Immediately afterwards, Baba sent Tatya Patil and Kakasaheb Dixit to him with instructions to the effect, that he should eat what he liked, should move in the home, but should never lie down and sleep. Needless to say that these instructions were acted upon and Shama was healed in a short time.

The only thing to be remembered in this connection is this - the words of Baba (or the five syllable Mantra, viz., 'Go, Get away, Come down') were not addressed to Shama- as it apparently looked - but they were a direct order to the snake and its poison not to go up and circulate through Shama's body. Like others well-versed in Mantrashastra, He had not to use any incantation, charged rice or water etc... His words only were most efficacious in saving the life of Shama. Any one, hearing this story and other similar ones, will get firm faith in the Feet of Sai Baba, and the only way to cross the ocean of Maya is to remember ever the Feet of Baba in the heart.

Cholera Epidemic

Once, Cholera was raging virulently in Shirdi. The residents were much frightened and they stopped all communication with the outside people. The panchas of the village assembled together and decided upon two ordinances as a remedy to check and put down the Epidemic. They were (1) No fuel-cart should be allowed to come in the village, and (2) No goat should be killed there. If anybody disobeyed these ordinances, they were to be fined by the village authorities and panchas.

Baba knew that all this was mere superstition, and therefore, He cared two pence for the Cholera-ordinances. While the ordinances were in force, a fuel-cart came there, and wanted to enter the village. Everybody knew that there was dearth of fuel in the village; still the people began to drive away the fuel-cart. Baba came to know of this. He came to the spot and asked the cart-man to take the fuel-cart to the Masjid. None dared to raise his voice against this action of Baba. He wanted fuel for His Dhuni and so He purchased it.

Like an Agnihotri keeping his sacred fire alive throughout his life, Baba kept His Dhuni ever burning all day and night; and for this He always stocked fuel. Baba's home, i.e. the Masjid was free and open to all. It had no lock and key; and some poor people removed some wood from there for their use. Baba did not grumble about this. Baba saw that the whole universe was pervaded by the Almighty, and so He never bore enmity or ill will to anybody. Though perfectly detached, He behaved like an ordinary householder to set an example to the people.

Ordeal of Guru-Bhakti

Let us now see, how the second Cholera Ordinance fared with Baba. While it was in force, somebody brought a goat to the Masjid. It was weak, old and about to die. At this time Fakir Pir Mohamed of Malegaon alias Bade Baba was near. Sai Baba asked him to behead it with one stroke, and offer it as an oblation.

This Bade Baba was much respected by Sai Baba. He always sat on the right hand of Sai Baba. After the chillum (pipe) was first smoked by him, it was then offered to Baba and others. After the dishes were served, at the time of taking meals at noon, Baba respectfully called Bade Baba and made him sit on His left side, and then all partook of food. Baba paid him also daily Rs.50 out of the amount collected as Dakshina. Baba accompanied him hundred paces whenever he was going away. Such was his position with Baba. But when Baba asked him to behead the goat, he flatly refused, saying "Why it should be killed for nothing?"

Then Baba asked Shama to kill it. He went to Radha-Krishna-Mai and brought a knife from her and placed it before Baba. Knowing the purpose for which the knife was taken, she recalled it. Then Shama went to bring another knife, but stayed in the Wada, and did not return soon.

Then came the turn of Kakasaheb Dixit. He was 'good gold' no doubt, but had to be tested. Baba asked him to get a knife and kill the goat. He went to Sathe's Wada and returned with a knife. He was ready to kill it at Baba's bidding. He was born in a pure

Brahmin family and never in his life knew killing. Though quite averse to do any act of violence, he made himself bold to kill the goat. All the people wondered to see that Bade Baba, a Mohammedan was unwilling to kill it while this pure Brahmin was making preparations to do so.

He tightened his dhotar and with a semicircular motion raised his hand with the knife and looked at Baba for the final signal. Baba said - "What are you thinking of? Go on, strike". Then, when the hand was just about to come down, Baba said - "Stop, how cruel you are! Being a Brahmin, you are killing a goat?"

Kakasaheb obeyed and put the knife down and said to Baba - "Your nectar-like word is law unto us, we do not know any other ordinance. We remember You always, meditate on Your Form and obey You day and night, we do not know or consider whether it is right or wrong to kill, we do not want to reason or discuss things, but implicit and prompt compliance with Guru's orders, is our duty and dharma".

Then Baba said to Kakasaheb, that He would Himself do the offering and killing business. It was settled that the goat should be disposed of near a place called Takkya, where fakirs used to sit. When the goat was being removed to that place, it fell dead on the way.

Hemadpant closes the Chapter with a classification of disciples. He says that they are of three kinds: (1) First or best (2) Second or middling and (3) Third or ordinary. The best kind of disciples are those who guess what their Gurus want and immediately carry it out and serve them without waiting for an order from them. The average disciples are those who carry out the orders of their Masters to a letter, without any delay, and the third kind of disciples are those, who go on postponing the carrying out of their orders and making mistakes at every step.

The disciples should have firm faith, backed up by intelligence and if they and patience to these, their spiritual goal will not be distant. Control of breath -- ingoing and outgoing, or HathaYoga or other difficult practices are not at all necessary. When the disciples get the above-mentioned qualities, they become ready for further instructions and the Masters then appear and lead them on, in their spiritual path to perfection.

In the next Chapter we will deal with Baba's interesting wit and humor.

Bow to Shri Sai - Peace be to all

Chapter XXIV

Baba's Wit and Humor - Chanak Leela - (1) Hemadpant
(2) Sudama (3) Anna Chinchanikar vs. Mavsibai

Preliminary

To say that, we shall state such and such in the next or this Chapter, is a sort of egoism. Unless, we surrender our ego to the feet of our Sadguru, we will not succeed in our undertaking. If we become ego-less, then our success is assured.

By worshipping Sai Baba, we attain both the objects, worldly and spiritual, and are fixed in our true Nature, and get peace and happiness. Therefore, those who want to gain their welfare should respectfully hear Sai Baba's Leelas or stories and meditate on them. If they do this, they will easily attain the object of their life and get Bliss.

Generally, all people like wit and humor, but they do not like that jokes should be cut at their expense. But Baba's method was peculiar; when it was accompanied with gestures, it was very interesting and instructive, and the people, therefore, did not mind, if they were held up to the ridicule. Hemadpant gives his own instance below.

Chanak-Leela

In Shirdi, the open market was held every Sunday, and people from the neighboring villages came there, erected booths and stalls on the street, and sold their wares and commodities. Every noon, the Masjid was crowded more or less; but on Sunday, it was crowded to suffocation. On one such Sunday, Hemadpant sat in front of Baba, shampooing His Legs and muttering God's name. Shama was on Baba's left, Vamanrao to His right - Shriman Booty and Kakasaheb Dixit and others were also present there. Then Shama laughed and said to Annasaheb - "See that some grains seem to have stuck to the sleeve of your coat". So saying he touched the sleeve and found that there were some grains. Hemadpant straightened his left fore-arm to see what the matter was, when to the surprise of all, some grains of gram come rolling

138

down and were picked up by the people who were sitting there.

This incident furnished a subject matter for joke. Everybody present began to wonder and said something or other as to how the grains found their way into the sleeve of the coat and lodged there so long. Hemadpant also could not guess how they found an entrance and stayed there. When nobody could give any satisfactory explanation in this matter, and everybody was wondering about this mystery, Baba said as follows:

Baba - "This fellow (Annasaheb) has got the bad habit of eating alone. Today is a bazaar-day and he was here chewing grams. I know his habit and these grams are a proof of it. What wonder is there is this matter?"

Hemadpant - "Baba, I never know of eating things alone; then why do you thrust this bad habit on me? I have never yet seen Shirdi bazaar. I never went to the bazaar today, then how could I buy grams, and how could I eat them if I had not bought them? I never eat anything unless I share it with others present near me".

Baba - "It is true that you give to the persons present; but if none be near-by, what could you or I do But do you remember Me before eating? Am I not always with you? Then do you offer Me anything before you eat?"

Moral

Let us mark and note carefully, what Baba has taught us, by this incident. He has advised us that before the senses, mind and intellect enjoy their objects, he should first be remembered, and if this be done, it is in a way an offering to Him. The senses etc... can never remain without their objects, but if those objects are first offered to the Guru, the attachment for them will naturally vanish. In this way, all the Vrittis (thoughts) regarding Desire, Anger, and Avarice etc..., should first be offered and directed to the Guru and if this practice be followed, the Lord will help you in eradicating all the Vrittis. When before enjoyment of the objects, you think that Baba is close by, the question whether the object is fit to be enjoyed or not will at once arise. Then the object that is not fit to be enjoyed will be shunned and in this way our vicious habits or vices will disappear and our character will improve. Then love for the Guru will grow and pure knowledge will sprout up. When this knowledge grows, the bondage of body-consciousness (we are the body) will snap and our intellect will be merged in spirit-consciousness (we are the spirit). Then we shall get Bliss and contentment.

There is no difference between Guru and God. He, who sees any difference in them, sees God nowhere. So leaving aside all ideas of difference, we should regard Guru and God as one, and if we serve our Guru as stated above, Lord (God) will be certainly pleased and purifying our minds He will give us self-realization. To put the matter in a nut-shell, we should not enjoy any object with our senses etc..., without first remembering our Guru. When the mind is trained in this way, we will be always reminded of Baba, and our meditation on Baba will grow apace. The Sagun Form of Baba will ever be before our eyes and then devotion, non-attachment and salvation will all be ours. When Baba's Form is thus fixed before our mental vision, we forget hunger, thirst, and this samsar; the consciousness of worldly pleasures will disappear and our mind shall attain peace and happiness.

Sudama's Story

When the above story was being narrated, Hemadpant was reminded of similar story of Sudama, which illustrates the same principle and, therefore, it is given here.

Shri Krishna and His elder brother, Balaram, were living with a co-student, named Sudama, in the ashram of their Guru, Sandipani. Once Krishna and Balaram were sent to the forest for bringing fuel, then the wife of Sandipani sent also Sudama for the same purpose with some quantity of grams for the three. When Krishna met Sudama in the forest, he said to him - "Dada, I want water as I am thirsty". Sudama replied - "No water should be drunk on an empty stomach, so it is better to rest a while". He did not say that he had got grams with him and that He should take some. As Krishna was tired, He lay down for rest on the lap of Sudama and was snoring. Seeing this, Sudama took out the grams and began to eat. Then Krishna suddenly asked him - "Dada, what are you eating, whence is the sound?" He replied - "What is there to eat? I am shivering with cold and my teeth are chattering. I can't even repeat distinctly Vishnu-Sahastra-Nama". Hearing this, the Omniscient Krishna said - "I just dreamt a dream, in which I saw a man, eating things of another, and when asked about this, he said - "What earth (dust) should he eat?" meaning thereby that he had nothing to eat? The other man said - "Let it be so". Dada, this is only a dream. I know that you won't eat anything without Me; under the influence of the dream I asked you what you were eating?" If Sudama had known a bit of the Omniscient, Shri Krishna and His Leelas, he would not have acted, as he did. Therefore, he had to suffer for what he did. Though he was a close friend of Shri Krishna he had to pass his later life in utter poverty. But when he later offered Krishna a handful of parched rice, earned by his wife with her own labor, Krishna was pleased and gave him a golden city to enjoy.

This story should be remembered by those who have the habit of eating things alone without partaking them with others.

The Shruti also emphasizes this lesson, and asks us to offer things first to God and then enjoy them after they are renounced by Him. Baba also has taught us the same lesson in His inimitable and humorous way.

Anna Chinchanikar vs. Mavsibai

Hemadpant now describes another witty incident, in which Baba played a peace maker's part. There was one devotee by name Damodar Ghanashyama Babare alias Anna Chinchanikar. He was simple, rough and straightforward. He cared for nobody, always spoke plainly and carried all dealings in cash. Though he looked outwardly harsh and uncompromising, he was good natured and guileless. So Sai Baba loved him.

One day, like others serving Baba in their own way, this Anna was, one noon standing prone and was shampooing the left arm of Baba, which rested on the kathada (railing). On the right side, one old widow named Venubai Koujalgi whom Baba called mother and all others Mavsibai, was serving Baba in her own way. This Mavsibai was an elderly woman of pure heart. She clasped the fingers of both her hands round the trunk of Baba and was at this time kneading Baba's abdomen. She did this so forcibly that Baba's back and abdomen became flat (one) and Baba moved from side to side. Anna on the other side was steady, but Mavsibai's face moved up and down with her strokes. Once it so happened that her face came very close to Anna's. Being of a witty disposition she remarked - "Oh, this Anna is a lewd fellow, he wants to kiss me. Even being so old with grey hair he feels no shame in kissing me."

These words enraged Anna and he pulled up his sleeves and said - "You say that I am an old bad fellow, am I quite a fool? It is you that have picked up a quarrel and are quarrelling with me". All the persons, present there were enjoying this encounter between them. Baba Who loved both of them equally and wanted to pacify them, managed the affair very skillfully. Lovingly He said - "Oh Anna, why are you unnecessarily raising this hue and cry? I do not understand what harm or impropriety is there, when the mother is kissed?" Hearing these words of Baba, both of them were satisfied and all the persons laughed merrily and enjoyed Baba's wit to their heart's content.

Baba's Characteristics -- His Dependency on Bhaktas

Baba allowed His devotees to serve Him in their own way, and did not like any other persons interfering in this. To quote an instance, the same Mavsibai was on another occasion, kneading Baba's abdomen. Seeing the fury and force used by her, all the other devotees felt nervous and anxious. They said, "Oh mother, be more considerate and moderate, otherwise you will break Baba's arteries and nerves".

At this Baba got up at once from His seat, dashed His satka on the ground. He got enraged and His eyes became red like a live charcoal. None dared to stand before or face Baba. Then He took hold of one end of the Satka with both hands and pressed it in the hollow of his abdomen. The other end He fixed to the post and began to press His abdomen against it. The satka which was about two or three feet in length seemed all to go into the abdomen and the people feared that the abdomen would be ruptured in a short time. The post was fixed and immovable and Baba began to go closer and closer to it and clasped the post firmly. Every moment the rupture was expected, and they were all dismayed, did not know what to do, and stood dumb with wonder and fear. Baba suffered this ordeal for the sake of His Bhakta. The other devotees wanted only to give a hint to the Mavsibai to be moderate in her service and not cause any trouble or pain to Baba. This they did with good intention, but Baba did not brook even this. They were surprised to see that their well-intentioned effort had resulted in this catastrophe; and they could do nothing but to wait and see.

Fortunately, Baba's rage soon cooled down. He left the satka and resumed His seat. From this time onward, the devotees took the lesson that they should not meddle with anybody but allow him to serve Baba as the chooses, as He was capable to gauge the merits and worth of the service rendered unto Him.

Bow to Shri Sai - Peace be to all

Chapter XXV

Damu Anna Kasar of Ahmednagar (1) Speculations
(2) Amra-Leela

Preliminary

We begin this Chapter with a bow with all our eight limbs to Sai Baba, Who is an ocean of mercy, the God incarnate, who is Para-Brahman and the great Yogeshwara (Lord of Yoga). Victory be unto Sai Baba, Who is the crest-jewel of the Saints, who is the home of all auspicious things, who is our Atmaram (Dear Self), and who is the able refuge of the devotees. We prostrate ourselves before Him, Who has attained the aim and end of life.

Sai Baba is always full of mercy. What is wanted on our part is whole-hearted devotion to Him. When a devotee has got firm faith and devotion, his wishes are soon fulfilled. When the desire arose in the mind of Hemadpant to write the life and Leelas of Sai Baba, He immediately got it written by him. When the order 'to keep the memos' was given, Hemadpant was inspired and his intellect got strength and boldness to undertake and finish the work. He was not, he say, qualified to write the work, but the gracious blessings of Baba enabled him to complete the undertaking; and thus you have this Satcharita which is a Somakant jewel, from which nectar in the form of Sai Leelas oozes out for the readers to drink to their hearts' content.

Whenever, a devotee had complete and whole-hearted devotion to Sai Baba, all his calamities and dangers were warded off and his welfare attended to by Baba. The story of Damodar Savalaram Resane, Kasar of Ahmednagar (now of Poona) alias Damu Anna illustrating the above statement, is given below.

Damu Anna

The readers are aware that a mention of this gentleman was made in the 6th Chapter, regarding the celebration of Rama-Navami festival in Shirdi. He went to Shirdi about the year 1895, when the Rama-Navami Utsava celebration began and from that time he has been providing an ornamental flag for that occasion every year. He also feeds the poor and the fakirs that come there for the festival.

144

His Speculations: (1) Cotton

A Bombay friend of Damu Anna wrote to him, that they should do some cotton speculation business in partnership which would bring them about two lacs of rupees as profit. (Damu Anna says in his statement made about the year 1936 to Mr. B.V.Narasimha Swami that the proposal about speculating at Bombay in cotton was from a broker who was not to be a partner, and that he (Damu Anna) was to be the sole adventurer: - vide P.75 of the Devotees' Experiences Part II). The broker wrote that the business was good and involved no risks and that the opportunity should not be lost. Damu Anna was oscillating in his mind. He could not at once determine to venture in the speculation. He thought about this and as he was a devotee of Baba, he wrote a detailed letter to Shama giving all the facts and requested him to consult Baba and take His advice in the matter.

Shama got the letter next day and when he came with it at noon to the Masjid and placed it before Baba. He asked Shama what the matter was, and what the paper (letter) was about. He replied that Damu Anna of Nagar wanted to consult Him about something. Then Baba said - "What does he write, and what does he plan? It seems that he wants to catch the sky and that he is not content with what God has given him; read his letter". Shama than said, "The letter contains what you have just said now. Oh, Deva you sit here calm and composed and agitate the devotees and when they get restless, you draw them here, some in person and others through letters. If you know the contents of the latter, why do you then press me to read it?" Baba said - "Oh Shama, read it please. I speak at random and who believes Me."

Then Shama read the letter and Baba heard it attentively and said feelingly - "The Shet (Damu Anna) has gone mad; write to him in reply that nothing is wanting in his house. Let him be content with the half loaf (bread) he has now and let him not bother himself about lacs." Shama sent the reply which Damu Anna was anxiously waiting for. Reading it, he found that all his hopes and prospects about lacs of rupees as profit were dashed to the ground. He thought that he had done a mistake in consulting Baba. But as Shama had hinted in the reply that there was always much difference between seeing and hearing, and that therefore, he should come to Shirdi personally and see Baba.

He thought it advisable to go to Shirdi and consult Baba personally about the affair. So he went to Shirdi, saw Baba, prostrated himself before Him and sat shampooing His legs. He had no courage to ask Baba openly about the speculation, but he thought in his mind, that it would be better if some share in the business should be assigned to Baba and said in his mind, that if Baba were to help him in this transaction, he would surrender some share of profits to Him. Damu Anna was thus thinking secretly in his mind, but nothing was veiled from Baba; everything past, present and future were clear to Him as an Amalaka fruit in hand. A child wants sweets, but its mother gives bitter pills; the former spoil its health, while the latter improve it. So the mother looking to the welfare of her infant coaxes it and gives it bitter pills. Baba, kind mother as He was, knew the present and future prospects of His devotees, and therefore reading Damu Anna's mind, He openly spoke to him - "Bapu, I do not want to be entangled in any such worldly things (sharing profits)." Seeing Baba's disapproval Damu Anna dropped the enterprise.

(2)   Grain-Dealing

Then he thought of trading in grain, rice, wheat and other groceries. Baba read also this thought and said to him, "You will be buying at five seers and selling at seven seers a rupee". So this business was also given up. The rice in the prices of grains was kept up for some time, and Baba's prophecy seemed to be falsified, but in a month or two there was abundant rain everywhere and the prices suddenly fell down; and, therefore, those who stored grains suffered a severe loss. Damu Anna was saved from this fate. Needless to say, that the cotton speculation which was conducted by the broker with the help of another merchant also collapsed with a severe loss to the adventurers. After seeing that Baba had saved him from two severe losses in cotton and grain speculations, Damu Anna's faith in Baba grew strong and he remained a true devotee of Baba till His passing away and even now.

Amra-Leela (Mango miracle)

Once a parcel of about 300 good mangoes was received at Shirdi, it was sent from Goa by one Mamlatdar named Rale to Sai Baba in the name of Shama. When it was opened, all the mangoes were found to be in a good condition. They were given in Shama's charge and only four were retained and placed in the kolamba (pot) by Baba. He said that, "These four fruits are for Damu Anna, let them lie there".

This Damu Anna had three wives. According to his statement mentioned above, he had not three but two wives only. He had no issue. He consulted many astrologers and himself studied astrology to some extent and found that as there was a 'papi' (inauspicious) planet in his horoscope, there was no prospect of any issue to him in this life. But he had great faith in Baba. When he went to Shirdi, two hours after the receipt of the mango parcel, for worshipping Baba, He said, "Though other people are looking for the mangoes, they are Dammya's. He whose they are, should 'eat and die'." Damu Anna on hearing these words was first shocked, but on Mhalsapati (a prominent Shirdi devotees) explaining to him that death meant the death of the little self or egos, and to have it at Baba's Feet was a blessing, he said that he would accept the fruits and eat them. But Baba said to him. "Do not eat yourself, but give them to your junior wife. This Amra-Leela (mango miracle of 4 mangoes) will give her four sons and four daughters. This was done and ultimately in due course it was found Baba's words turned out true and not those of the astrologers.

Baba's speech established its efficacy or greatness while He was living in the flesh, but wonder of wonders! It did the same even after His passing away. Baba said - "Believe Me, though I pass away, My bones in My tomb will give you hope and confidence. Not only Myself but My tomb would be speaking, moving and communicating with those who would surrender themselves wholeheartedly to Me. Do not be anxious that I would be absent from you. You will hear My bones speaking and discussing your welfare. But remember Me always, believe in Me heart and soul and then you will be most benefited.

SHRI SAI SATCHARITRA

Prayer

Hemadpant closes this Chapter with a prayer.

"Oh Sai Sadguru, the wish fulfilling tree of the Bhaktas, Let us never forget and lose sight of Your Feet; we have been troubled with the ins and outs (births and deaths) in this samsar; now free us from this cycle of births and deaths. Restrain us from the outgoing of our senses to their objects and introvert us and bring us face to face with the Atma (Self). As long as this outgoing tendency of the senses and the mind is not checked, there is no prospect of self-realization. Neither son, nor wife nor friend will be of any use in the end. It is only You, Who will give us salvation and happiness. Destroy completely our tendency for discussions and other evil matters, let out tongue get a passion for chanting Your name. Drive out our thoughts, good or otherwise and make us forget our bodies and houses, and do away with our egoism. Make us ever remember Your name and forget all other things. Remove the restlessness of our mind, and make it steady and calm. If you just clasp us, the darkness of night of our ignorance will vanish and we shall live happily in Your light. That You made us drink the nectar of Your Leelas and awakened us from our slumber is due to Your grace and our store of merits in past births".

Note: In this connection the following extract from Damu Anna's statement mentioned above, is worth perusal:

"Once when I sat at His Feet along with many others, I had two questions in my mind and He gave answers to both."

(1) There are so many crowding to Sai Baba. Do they all get benefit from Him?

To this, He replied orally - "Look at the mango tree in blossom. If all the flowers brought fruit, what a splendid crop it would be. But do they? Most fall off (either as flowers or as unripe fruits) by wind etc... Very few remain".

148

(2) The second question was about myself. If Baba were to pass away, how hopelessly adrift I would be and how am I to fare then?

To this Baba answered that He would be with me when and wherever I thought of Him. That promise He had kept up before 1918 and has been keeping up after 1918. He is still with me. He is still guiding me. This was about 1910-11, when brothers separated from me and my sister died, and there was a theft and police enquiry, all of which incidents upset me very much.

When my sister died, my mind was much upset. I did not care for life and enjoyments. When I went to Baba, He pacified me with His Upadesh and made me eat a feast of Pooran Poli at Appa Kulkarni's house and get pasted with sandal.

There was a theft in my house. A thirty year's friend of mine stole my wife's jewel-box, including her auspicious Nathi (nose-ring). I wept before Baba's photo. The next day, the man returned the jewel-box and prayed for pardon.

Bow to Shri Sai - Peace be to all

Chapter XXVI

Stories of (1) Bhakata Pant (2) Harishchandra Pitale
and (3) Gopal Ambadekar

Preliminary

All the things that we see in the universe are nothing but a play of Maya -- the creative power of the Lord. These things do not really exist. What really exists is the Real Absolute. Just as we mistake a rope of a garland or a stick for a serpent on account of darkness, we always see the phenomena, i.e. things as they outwardly appear, and not that which underlies all the visible things. It is only the SadGuru that opens the eyes of our understanding and enables us to see things in their true light and not as they appear. Let us, therefore, worship the Sadguru and pray to him to give us the true vision, which is nothing but God-Vision.

Inner Worship

Hemadpant has given us a novel form of worship. Let us, he says, use hot water in the form of tears of joy to wash the Sadguru's feet, let us besmear His body with sandal paste of pure love, let us cover His body with the cloth of true faith, let us offer eight lotuses in the form of our eight Gatwick emotions and fruit in the form of our concentrated mind; let us apply to His head bukka (black-powder) in the form of devotion and tie the waistband of Bhakti and place our head on his toes.

After decorating the Sadguru with all jewelry in this way, let us offer our all to Him and wave chamar (a handmade fan) of devotion to ward off heat. After such blissful worship, let us pray thus: - "Introvert our mind, turn it inward, give us discrimination between the Unreal and the Real and non-attachment for all worldly things and thus enable us to get Self-realization. We surrender ourselves, body and soul (body-consciousness and ego). Make our eyes Yours, so that we should never feel pleasure and pain. Control our body and mind as You will and wish. Let our mind get rest in Your Feet".

Now let us turn to the stories of this Chapter.

Bhakta Pant

Once it so happened that a devotee by name Pant, a disciple of another Sadguru had the good fortune of visiting Shirdi. He had no mind to go to Shirdi, but man proposes one way and God disposes the other. He was travelling in a B.B. & C.I. Rly. train where he met many friends and relations bound for Shirdi. They all asked him to accompany them and he could not say nay. They alighted at Bombay while pant got down at Virar.

There he took the permission of his Sadguru for the Shirdi trip and after arranging for the expenses, left with the party for Shirdi. They all reached the place in the morning and went to the Masjid at about 11 A.M. Seeing the concourse of the devotees assembled for Baba's worship, they were all pleased, but Pant suddenly got a fit and fell senseless. They were all frightened; still they tried their best to bring him to his senses. With Baba's grace and with pitchers of water which they poured over his head, he regained his consciousness and sat upright as if he was just awakened from sleep. The omniscient Baba knowing that he was a disciple of another Guru, assured him fearlessness and confirmed his faith in his own Guru, by addressing him as follows:- "Come what may, leave not, but stick to your Bolster(support, i.e. Guru) and ever remain steady, always at-one (in union) with him." Pant at once knew the significance of this remark and thus he was reminded of his Sadguru. This kindness of Baba he never forgot in his life.

Harishchandra Pitale

There was a gentleman by name Harishchandra Pital in Bombay. He had a son, who suffered from epilepsy. He tried many allopathic and ayurvedic doctors, but there was no cure. There remained only one way of remedy, viz. resorting to the Saints. It has been stated in Chapter XV that Das Ganu by his inimitable and splendid kirtans spread the fame of Sai Baba in the Bombay Presidency. Mr. Pitale heard some of these kirtans in 1910 and learnt there-from and from others that Baba, by His touch and mere glance, cured many incurable diseases. Then a desire arose in his mind to see Sai Baba. Making all preparations and taking presents and fruit-baskets, Mr. Pitale came to Shirdi with family, wife and children.

He then went to the Masjid with them, prostrated before Baba and placed his sick son on Baba's Feet. No sooner Baba saw the child than an untoward thing happened. The son immediately revolved his eyes and fell down senseless. His mouth began to foam and his whole body began to perspire profusely and it seemed as if he breathed himself out. Seeing this, the parents became very nervous and excited. The boy used to get such fits very often, but this fit seemed to persist long. Tears began to flow ceaselessly from the mother's eyes and she began to wail, crying that her condition was like that of a person, who being afraid of the robbers ran into a house which collapsed on him, or like a cow fearing a tiger, ran into the hands of a butcher, or like a traveler, who being tormented by the heat of the sun went to take refuge under a tree, which fell upon him, or like a devout person going for worship into a temple which collapsed upon him.

Then Baba comforted her saying - "Do not wail like this, wait a bit, have patience, take the boy to your lodging, he will come to his senses within half an hour." They did as directed by Baba and found that His words came true. As soon as he was taken into the Wada, the boy recovered and all the Pitale family, husband, wife and others were very delighted and all their doubts disappeared. Then Mr. Pitale came with his wife to see Baba and prostrated himself before Him very humbly and respectfully and sat shampooing His legs and mentally thanking Baba for His help. Baba then smilingly said - "Are not all your thoughts, doubts and apprehensions calmed down now? Hari (Lord) will protect him, who has got faith and patience".

Mr. Pitale was a rich and well-to-do gentleman. He distributed sweets on a large scale and gave Baba excellent fruits and pan (betel-leaves). Mrs. Pitale was a very Sattvic lady, simple, loving and faithful. She used to sit near the post staring at Baba with tears of joy flowing down from her eyes. Seeing her of an amicable and loving nature, Baba was much pleased with her. Like Gods, Saints are always dependent on their devotees who surrender and worship them with their heart and soul. After passing some happy days in Baba's company, the Pitale family came to the Masjid to take Baba's leave to depart. Baba gave them Udi and blessings and called Mr. Pitale close by and said to him - "Bapu, I had given you before, Rs. two, now I give you Rs. three; keep these in your shrine for worship and you will be benefited." Mr. Pitale accepted these as Prasad, prostrated himself again before Baba and prayed for His blessings.

A thought arose in his mind, that as that was his first trip to Shirdi, he could not understand what Baba meant, when He said that He had given Rs. two previously. He was curious to have this mystery solves, but Baba kept silent. When Mr. Pitale returned to Bombay, he narrated to his old mother all that had happened at Shirdi and the mystery about Baba's giving him Rs. two formerly. The mother also did not understand the mystery, but, thinking seriously about that, she was reminded of an old incident, which solved the mystery.

She said to her son - "As you now went to Sai Baba with your son, so had your father done when he took you to Akkalkot, for the darshan of the Maharaj there many years ago. That Maharaj was also a Siddha, Perfect Yogi, omniscient and liberal. Your father was pure, devout and his worship was accepted. He then gave your father two rupees for him to keep in the shrine and worship. Your father worshipped them accordingly till his death, but thereafter the worship was neglected and the rupees were lost. After some years the memory of these two rupees also disappeared and now, as you are very fortunate, the Akkalkotkar Maharaj has appeared to you in the form of Sai Baba just to remind you to your duties and worship, and to ward off all dangers. Now beware henceforth, leave off all doubts and bad thoughts, follow your ancestors and behave well; go on worshipping the family gods and the rupees, appraise properly and take pride in the blessing of the Saints.

Sai Samartha has kindly revived the spirit of Bhakti in you; cultivate it for your benefit." Hearing the remarks of the mother, Mr. Pitale was very much delighted. He came to know, and was convinced about the all-pervasiveness of Baba and the significance of His Darshan. From that time he became very careful about his behavior.

Mr. Ambadekar

Mr. Gopal Narayan Ambadekar of Poona was a devotee of Baba. He served for ten years in the Abkari department in the Thana District and in Javhar state, from where he had to retire. He tried to get some other job, but he did not succeed. He was over-taken by other calamities and his condition grew from bad to worse. He passed seven years in this condition, visiting Shirdi every year and placing his grievance before Baba. In 1916 his plight became worst and be decided to commit suicide in Shirdi. So he came there with his wife and stayed for two months. One night while sitting in a bullock cart in front of Dixit's Wada, he resolved to end his life by throwing himself into a well close by. He proposed to do one way but Baba wished to do something else.

A few paces from this place, there was a hotel and its proprietor Mr. Sagun, a devotee of Baba, came out and accosted him thus - "Did you ever read this Akkalkotkar Maharaja's life?" Ambadekar took that book from Sagun and began to read it. Cas-ually, or we may say providentially he came across a story which was to this effect. - During the life time of Akkalkotkar Maharaj a certain devotee suffered very much from an incurable disease and when he could endure the agony and pain no longer be became desperate and to end his miseries threw himself one night into a well. Immediately the Maharaj came there and took him out with his own hands and advised him thus - "You must enjoy the fruit - good or bad - of your past actions; if the enjoyment be incomplete, suicide won't help you. You have to take another birth and suffer again; so instead of killing yourself, why not suffer for some time and finish up your store of the fruit of your past deeds and be done with it once and for all?"

Reading this appropriate and timely story, Ambadekar was much surprised, and moved. Had he not got Baba's hint through the story, he would have been no more. On seeing Baba's all-pervasiveness and benevolence, his faith in Him was confirmed, and he became a staunch devotee. His father was a devotee of Akkalkotkar Maharaj and Sai Baba wanted him to walk into his father's footsteps and continue his devotion to Him. He then got Sai Baba's blessings and his prospects began to improve.

He studied astrology and gained proficiency in it and thereby improved his lot. He was able to earn sufficient money and passed the remainder of his life in ease and comfort.

Bow to Shri Sai - Peace be to all

Chapter XXVII

Favor Shown by Giving Bhagwat and Vishnu-Sahasra Nam
Dixit's Vitthal Vision - Gita Rahasya - Khapardes

This Chapter describes how Sai Baba favored His devotees by
granting them religious books after he had touched and
consecrated them, for parayana (reading regularly) and certain
other matters.

Preliminary

When a man takes a plunge into the sea, he gets the merit of
bathing in all the Tirthas and sacred rivers. Similarly when a man
takes refuge at the feet of the Sadguru, he gets the merit of
bowing to the Trinity, i.e. Brahma, Vishnu and Mahesh and also
Para-Brahma. Victory be unto Shri Sai the wish-fulfilling tree and
the ocean of knowledge, who gives us self-realization. Oh Sai,
create in us regard for Your stories. Let the readers and audience
devour them with the same relish with which the chatak bird
drinks the water from the clouds and becomes happy. While
listening to Your stories, let them and their families get all the
sattvic emotions, viz. let their bodies perspire, let their eyes be
full of tears, let their prana be steady, let their minds be
composed, let their hair stand on end, let them cry, sob and shake,
let their hostilities and their distinctions, great and small vanish. If
these things happen, that is a sign of the grace of the Guru
dawning upon them. When these emotions develop in you, the
Guru is most pleased and will certainly lead you on to the goal of
self-realization. The best way, therefore, to get free from the
shackles of Maya is our complete and whole-hearted surrender to
Baba. The Vedas cannot take you across the ocean of Maya. It is
only the Sadguru, who can do so and make you, see the Lord in
all creatures.

Granting Consecrated Book

The variety of imparting instructions followed by Baba has already been noticed in the previous Chapters. In this, we shall deal

with one aspect of it. It was the habit of some devotees to take some religious books, of which they wanted to make a special study, to Baba and to receive the same back from Him, after they were touched and consecrated by Him. While reading daily such books, they felt that Baba was with them. Once, Kaka Mahajani came to Shirdi with a copy of Ekanath Bhagwat. Shama took that book to read and taking it with him went to the Masjid. There Baba took it from him; touched it and turning some pages here and there gave it back to Shama and asked him to keep it with him. Then Shama said that it belonged to Kaka and had to be returned to him. "No, no", said Baba. "As I have given it to you, better keep it with you for safe custody; it will be of use to you." In this way many books were entrusted to Shama. Kaka Mahajani after a some days came again with another copy of the same Bhagwat and gave it in Baba's hand. Then Baba gave it back as Prasad and asked him to preserve it well and assured him that it would stand him in good stead. Kaka accepted it with a bow.

Shama and Vishnu-Sahasra-Nam

Shama was a very intimate devotee of Baba and Baba wanted to favor him in a particular way by giving him a copy of Vishnu-Sahasra-Nam as Prasad. This was done in the following way. Once a Ramadasi (follower of Saint Ramadas) came to Shirdi and stayed for some time. The routine he followed daily was as follows: He got up early in the morning, washed his face, bathed and then after wearing saffron-colored clothes and besmearing himself with sacred ashes, read the Vishnu-Sahasra-Nam (a book giving a thousand names in praise of Vishnu, and held second in importance to Bhagavad Gita) and Adhyatma-Ramayana (Esoteric version of Rama's story) with faith. He read these books often and often and then after some days Baba thought of favoring and initiating Shama with Vishnu-Sahasra-Nam.

He, therefore, called the Ramadasi to Him and said to him that, He was suffering from intense stomach-pain, and unless He took Senna-pods (Sonamukhi, a mild purgative drug) the pain would not stop; so he should please go to the bazaar and bring the drug. The Ramadasi closed his reading and went to the bazaar.

Then Baba descended from His seat, came to the Ramadasi's place of reading, took out the copy of Vishnu-Sahasra- Nam, and coming to His seat said to Shama- "Oh Shama, this book is very valuable and efficacious, so I present it to you, you read it. Once I suffered intensely and My heart began to palpitate and My life was in danger. At that critical time, I hugged this book to My heart and then, Shama, what a relief it gave me! I thought that Allah Himself came down and saved Me. So I give this to you, read it slowly, little by little, read daily one name at least and it will do you good." Shama replied that he did not want it, and that the owner of it, the Ramadasi who was a mad, obstinate and irritable fellow would certainly pick up a quarrel with him, besides, being a rustic himself, he could not read distinctly the Sanskrit (Devanagari) letters of the book.

Shama thought that Baba wanted to set him up against the Ramadasi by this act of His, but he had no idea of what Baba felt for him. Baba must have thought to tie this necklace of Vishu-Sahasra-Nam round the neck of Shama, as he was an intimate devotee, though a rustic, and thus save him from the miseries of the worldly existence. The efficacy of God's Name is well-known. It saves us from all sins and bad tendencies, frees us from the cycle of births and deaths. There is no easier sadhana than this. It is the best purifier of our mind. It requires no paraphernalia and no restrictions. It is so easy and so effective. This sadhana, Baba wanted Shama to practice, though he did not crave for it. So Baba forced this on him. It is also reported that long ago, Eknath Maharaj, similarly, forced this Vishnu-Sahasra-Nam on a poor Brahmin neighbor, and thus saved him. The reading and study of this Vishnu-Sahasra-Nam is a broad open way of purifying the mind, and hence Baba thrust this on His Shama.

The Ramadasi returned soon with the Seena-pods. Anna Chinchanikar, who was then present and who wanted to play the part of Narada (the Celestial Rishi who was well-known for setting up quarrels between Gods and demons and vice versa), informed him of what had happened. The Ramadasi at once flared up. He came down at once on Shama with all fury. He said that it was Shama who set Baba to send him away under the pretext of stomach ache for bringing the medicine and thus got the book. He began to scold and abuse Shama and remarked that if the book be not returned, he would dash his head before him. Shama calmly remonstrated with him, but in vain.

Then Baba spoke kindly to him as follows - "Oh Ramadasi, what is the matter with you? Why are you so turbulent? Is not Shama our boy? Why do you scold him unnecessarily? How is it that you are so quarrelsome? Can you not speak soft and sweet words? You read daily these sacred books and still your mind is impure and your passions uncontrolled. What sort of a Ramadasi you are! You ought to be indifferent to all things. Is it not strange that you should covet this book so strongly? A true Ramadasi should have no 'mamata' (attachment) but have 'samata' (equality) towards all. You are now quarrelling with the boy Shama for a mere book. Go, take your seat, books can be had in plenty for money, but not men; think well and be considerate. What worth is your book? Shama had no concern with it. I took it up Myself and gave it to him. You know it by heart. I thought Shama might read it and profit thereby, and so I gave to it him."

How sweet were these words of Baba, soft, tender and nectar-like! Their effect was wonderful. The Ramadasi calmed down and said to Shama that he would take 'Panch-ratni' Gita in return. Shama was much pleased and said - "Why one, I shall give ten copies in return".

So the matter was ultimately compromised. The question for consideration is "Why should the Ramadasi press for Panch-ratni Gita, the God in which he never cared to know, and why should he, who daily read religious books in the Masjid in front of Baba, quarrel with Shama before Him?" We do not know how to appor-tion the blame and whom to blame. We only say that, had this procedure been not gone through, the importance of the subject, the efficacy of God's name and the study of Vishnu-Sahasra-Nam would not have been brought home to Shama. So we see that Baba's method, of teaching and initiating was unique. In this cas-es Shama did gradually study the book and mastered its contents to such an extent, that he was able to explain it to Professor G.G. Narke, M.A. of the College of Engineering, Poona, the son-in-law of Shriman Booty and a devotee of Baba.

Vitthal-Vision

One day, while Kakasaheb Dixit was in mediation after his morning bath in his Wada at Shirdi he saw a vision of Vitthal. When he went to see Baba afterwards, Baba asked him - "Did Vitthal Patil come? did you not see Him? He is very elusive, hold Him fast, otherwise He will give you the slip and run away". Then at noon a certain hawker came there, with 20 or 25 pictures of Vitthal of Pandharpur for sale. Mr. Dixit was surprised to see that the form of Vithal he saw in his mediation exactly tallied with that in the picture and he was also reminded of Baba's words. He therefore, bought one picture most willingly and kept it in his shrine for worship.

Greta-Rahasya

Baba always loved those who studied Brahma-vidya (metaphysics) and encouraged them. To give an instance - Once Bapusaheb Jog received a post-parcel. It contained a copy of Greta-Rahasya by Lokamanya Tilak. Taking it under his armpit he came to the Masjid and prostrated himself before Baba, when the parcel fell at Baba's Feet. Baba enquired what it was. It was opened then and there and the book was placed in Baba's hand. He turned some pages here and there for a few minutes and took out a rupee from His pocket placed it on the book and handed the same with the rupee to Jog and said to him - "Read this completely and you will be benefited".

Mr. and Mrs. Khaparde

Let us close this Chapter with a description of the Khapardes. Once Dadasaheb Khaparde came with his family and lived in Shirdi for some months. (The diary of his stay has been published in English in the Shri Sai Leela Magazine first Volume.) Dadasaheb was not an ordinary man. He was the richest and the most famous advocate of Amraoti (Berar) and was a member of the Council of State, Delhi. He was very intelligent and a very good speaker. Still he dared not open his mouth before Baba. Most devotees spoke and argued with Baba off and on, but only

160

three, viz. Khaparde, Noolkar and Booty kept always silent. They were meek, modest, humble and good-natured.

Dadasaheb, who was able to expound Panchadashi (A well-known Sanskrit treatise on the Adwaita Philosophy by the famous Vidyaranya) to others, said nothing or uttered no word when he came to the Masjid before Baba. Really a man however learned he may be even in Vedas, fades away before one, who was realized Brahman and become one with it. Learning cannot shine before Self-realization.

Dadasaheb stayed for four months, but Mrs. Khaparde stayed for seven. Both were highly pleased with their Shirdi stay. Mrs. Khaparde was faithful and devout, and loved Baba deeply. Every noon she brought naivedya herself to the Masjid, and after it was accepted by Baba, she used to return and take her meals. Seeing her steady and firm devotion, Baba wanted to exhibit it to others.

One noon she brought a dish containing Sanza (wheat-pudding), purees, rice, soup, and kheer (sweet rice pudding) and other sundry articles to the Masjid. Baba, who usually waited for hours, got up at once, went up to His dining seat and removing the outer covering from the dish, began to partake of the things zealously. Shama then asked Him - "Why this partiality? You throw away dishes of others and do not care to look at them, but this You draw to You earnestly and do justice to it. Why is the dish of this woman so sweet? This is a problem to us."

Baba then explained - "This food is really extraordinary. In former birth this lady was a merchant's fat cow yielding much milk. Then she disappeared and took birth in a gardener's family, then in a Kshatriya family, and married a merchant. Then she was born in a Brahmin family. I saw her after a very long time; let Me take some sweet morsels of love from her dish." Saying this, Baba did full justice to her dish, washed his mouth and hands, gave out some belches as a mark of satisfaction, and resumed His seat. Then she made a bow and began to shampoo Baba's legs and Baba began to talk with her and knead her arms which were shampooing His Legs.

On seeing this reciprocal service Shama began to joke and said, "It is going on well, it is a wonderful sight to see God and His Bhakta serving each other." After being pleased with her sincere service, Baba asked her in low and fascinating tone to chant 'Rajarama, Rajarama' then and always, and said - "If you do this, your life's object will be gained, your mind will attain peace and you will be immensely benefited." To persons unfamiliar with spiritual matters, this might appear as affair, but really it was not so. It was a case of, what in technically called, 'Shakti-pat', i.e. transference of power from the Guru to the disciple. How forcible and effective were Baba's words! In an instant, they pierced her heart and found lodgment there.

This case illustrates the nature of the relations that should subsist between the Guru and the disciple. Both should love and serve each other as One. There is no distinction nor any difference between them. Both are One, and one cannot live without the other. The disciple placing his head on the Guru's feet is a gross or outward vision; really and internally they are both one and the same. Those who see any difference between them are yet unripe and not perfect.

Bow to Shri Sai - Peace be to all

Chapter XXVIII

Sparrows Drawn To Shirdi
(1) Lakhamichand - (2) Burhanpore Lady - (3) Megha

Preliminary

Sai is not finite or limited. He dwells in all beings, from ants and insects to the God Brahma. He pervades all. Sai was well-versed in the knowledge of the Vedas, as well as in the science of Self-realization. As He was proficient in both these, He was well-fitted to be the Sadguru. Any one, though learned, but not able to awaken the disciples and establish them in Self-realization, does not deserve to be called a Sadguru. Generally the father gives birth to the body, and death invariably follows life; but Sadguru does away with both life and death, and so he is more kind and merciful, than anybody.

Sai Baba often said that let His man (Devotee) be at any distance, a thousand koss away from Him, he will be drawn to Shirdi like a sparrow, with a thread tied to its feet. This Chapter describes the stories of three such sparrows.

Lala Lakhamichand

This gentleman was first serving in the Railways and afterwards in Shri Venkateshwar Press in Bombay and thereafter in the firm of Messrs. Ralli Brothers as a munshi (clerk). He got the contact of Baba in 1910. One or two months before Christmas he saw in his dream at Santacruz (a suburb of Bombay) an old man with a beard, standing and surrounded by his Bhaktas. Some days later he went to the house of his friend, Mr. Dattatreya Manjunath Bijur to hear the kirtan by Das Ganu. It was always the practice of Das Ganu to keep Baba's picture in front of the audience while making the kirtan. Lakhamichand was surprised to see that the features of the old man he saw in his dream, tallied exactly with those in the picture and thus he came to the conclusion, that the old man, he saw in his dream was Sai Baba himself.

The sight of this picture, Das Ganu's kirtan and the life of the Saint Tukaram on which Das Ganu discoursed, all these things made a deep impression on his mind and he pined to go to Shirdi. It is always the experience of the Bhaktas that God always helps them in their search for Sadguru and other spiritual endeavors. That very night at 8:00 p.m. a friend named Shankarrao knocked at his door and asked him whether he would accompany him to Shirdi. His joy knew no bounds and he at once decided to go to Shirdi. He borrowed Rs.15 from his cousin and after making due preparations left for Shirdi.

In the train, he and his friend Shankar Rao did some Bhajan (sang religious songs) and enquired about Sai Baba with some fellow passengers, four Mohammedans, who were returning to their place near Shirdi. They all told them that Sai baa was a great Saint living in Shirdi for many years. Then when they reached Kopergaon he wanted to buy some good guavas for offering to Baba, but he was so much enraptured with the scenery and sights there that he forgot to purchase them. When they were nearing Shirdi, he was reminded of the guavas; just then he saw an old woman with a guava-basket on her head, running after the tanga. The tanga was stopped and he gladly purchased some select fruits, when the woman said - "Take all the rest and offer them on my behalf to Baba".

The facts viz. that he had intended to purchase guavas, but that he had forgotten to do so, the old woman's encounter and her devotion to Baba, all these were a surprise to both the friends; and Lakhamichand thought in his mind, that the old woman might be some relation of the old man he saw in his dream. Then they drove on and came near Shirdi and seeing the flags on the Masjid they saluted them. With Puja materials in hand, they then went to the Masjid and worshipped Baba with due formality. Lakhamichand was much moved and was extremely happy to see Baba. He was enraptured with Baba's Feet as a bee with a sweet smelling lotus. Then Baba spoke as follows:

"Cunning fellow, he does bhajan on the way and enquires from others. Why ask others? Everything we should see with our own eyes; where is the necessity to question others? Just think for yourself whether your dream is true or not? Where was the necessity of the darshan by taking a loan from a Marwari? Is the heart's desire now satisfied?"

Hearing these words Lakhamichand was wonder-struck at Baba's omniscience. He was at a loss to know how Baba came to know about all the things that had happened en route from his house to Shirdi. The chief thing to note in this respect is that Baba never liked people to run into debt for taking His darshan, or celebrating any holiday or making any pilgrimage.

Sanza

At noon when Lakhamichand was sitting for meals he got some sanza (wheat-pudding) from a devotee as Prasad. He was pleased to have it. Next day also he expected it, but got nothing. So, he was anxious to get it again. Then on the third day at the noon Arati time, Bapusaheb Jog asked Baba, what naivedya he should bring. Baba told him to bring sanza. Then the Bhaktas brought two big potfuls of sanza. Lakhamichand was very hungry and there was some pain in his back. Then Baba said to him - "It is good that you are hungry, take sanza and some medicine for the pain in the back." He was again wonder-struck to see that Baba again read his mind and spoke out what was passing therein. How omniscient was He!

Evil Eye

On this occasion, he once witnessed one night the procession to the Chavadi. Baba then suffered much from cough. He thought that this suffering of Baba might be due to somebody's evil eye. Next morning when he went to the Masjid Baba spoke to Shama as follows - "I suffered last night from cough; is it due to some evil eye? I think that somebody's evil eye has worked on me and so I am suffering". In this case Baba spoke out what was passing in Lakhamichand's mind.

On seeing these proofs of Baba's omniscience and kindness to His Bhaktas, he fell prostrate at Baba's Feet and said - "I am much pleased with your darshan. Ever be kind and merciful to me and protect me always. There is no other God to me in this world except Your Feet. Let my mind be ever rapt in Your Bhajan and Feet. Let Your grace protect me from the miseries of the world and let me ever chant Your name and be happy".

After getting Baba' Udi and blessing he returned home with

165

his friend, much pleased and contented and singing Baba's glory on the way. He remained a staunch devotee of Baba afterwards and always sent garlands of flowers, camphor and Dakshina with any person of his acquaintance bound for Shirdi.

Burhanpore Lady

Now let us turn to another sparrow (Baba's word meaning devotee). One lady in Burhanpore saw in her dream Sai Baba coming to her door and begging khichadi (rice cooked with dal and salt) for His meals. On awakening she saw nobody at her door. However, she was pleased with the vision and told it to all including her husband.

He was employed in the Postal Department and when he was transferred to Akola, both husband and wife, who were devout, decided to go to Shirdi. Then on a suitable day they left for Shirdi and after visiting Gomati Tirth on the way, reached Shirdi and stayed there for two months. Every day they went to the Masjid, performed Baba's worship and passed their time happily. The couple came to Shirdi to offer Chadwick as naivedya but for the first 14 days, somehow or other, it could not be offered. The lady did not like this delay. Then on the 15th day she came at noon to the Masjid with her khichadi. There she found that Baba and others were already sitting for meals, and that the curtain was down. Nobody dared enter in when the curtain was let down, but the lady could not wait. She threw up the curtain with her hand and entered. Strange to say that Baba seemed that day, hungry for khichadi and wanted that thing first and when the lady came in with the dish, Baba was delighted, and began to eat morsel after morsel of khichadi. On seeing the earnestness of Baba in this respect, everybody was wonder-struck and those, who heard the story of khichadi, were convinced about His extraordinary love for His devotees.

Megha

Now let us go to the third and bigger 'sparrow'. Megha of Viramgaon was a simple and illiterate Brahmin cook of Rao Bahadur H. V. Sathe. He was a devotee of Shiva and always chanted the five syllable mantra 'Namah Shivaya'. He did not know the Sandhya nor its chief mantra, the Gayatri. Rao Bahadur Sathe was interested in him, got him taught the Sandhya and the Gayatri. Sathe told him that Sai Baba of Shirdi was the embodied form of the God Shiva and made him start for Shirdi. At the Broach Railway station he learnt that Sai Baba was a Muslim and his simple and orthodox mind was much perturbed at the prospect of bowing to a Muslim, and he prayed to his master not to send him there. His master, however, insisted on his going there and gave him a letter of introduction to his (Sathe's) father-in-law, Ganesh Domodar, alias Dada Kelkar at Shirdi, to introduce him to Sai Baba.

When he reached Shirdi and went to the Masjid, Baba was very indignant and would not allow him to enter. "Kick out the rascal" roared Baba, and then said to Megha - "You are a high caste Brahmin and I am a low Muslim; you will lose your caste by coming here. So get away." Hearing these words Megha began to tremble. He was wondering as to how Baba had come to know about what was passing in his mind. He stayed there for some days, serving Baba in his own way, but was not convinced. Then he went home. After that he went to Tryambak (Nasik District) and stayed there for a year and a half.

Then again he returned to Shirdi. This time, at the intercession of Dada Kelkar, he was allowed to enter the Masjid and stay in Shirdi. Sai Baba's help to Megha was not through any oral instruction. He worked upon Megha internally, through his mind, with the result that he was considerably changed and benefited. Then Megha began to look upon Sai Baba as an incarnation of Shiva.

In order to worship Shiva, bela leaves are required and Megha used to go miles and miles every day to bring them and worship his Shiva (Baba). His practice was to worship all the Gods in the village and then come to the Masjid and after saluting Baba's gadi (asan) he worshipped Baba and after doing some service (shampooing His Legs) drank the washings (Tirth) of Baba's Feet. Once it so happened that he came to the Masjid without worshipping God Khandoba, as the door of the temple was closed. Baba did not accept his worship and sent him again, saying that the door was open then. Megha went, found the door open, worshipped the

Deity, and then returned to Baba as usual.

Ganges-Bath

On one Makar-Sankranti day (harvest festival celebrated Jan. 14th each year), Megha wanted to besmear the body of Baba with sandal-paste and bathe Him with Ganges water. Baba was first unwilling to undergo this operation, but at his repeated requests, He consented. Megha had to traverse a distance of eight koss (going and returning) to bring the sacred water from the Gomati river. He brought the water, made all preparations for the bath at noon and asked Baba to get ready for the same. Then Baba again asked him to be freed from his bath saying that, as a Fakir He had nothing to do (or gain) with Ganges water; but Megha did not listen. He knew that Shiva is pleased with a bath of Ganges water and that he must give his Shiva (Baba) that bath on that auspicious day. Baba then consented, came down and sat on a pat (wooden board) and protruding his head said - "Oh Megha, do at least this favor; head is the most important organ of the body, so pour the water over that only it is equivalent to the full or whole bath." "Alright" said Megha and lifting the water pot up, began to pour it on the head but in doing this he was so much overwhelmed with love that he cried out 'Har Gange' and emptied the pot on the whole body. He kept the pot aside and began to look at Baba, but to his surprise and amazement he found that Baba's head was only drenched but the body quite dry.

Trident and Pindi

Megha worshipped Baba in two places; in the Masjid he worshipped Baba in person and in the Wada, Baba's big picture, given by Nanasaheb Chandorkar. This he did for twelve months. Then in order to appreciate his devotion and confirm his faith, Baba gave him a vision. Early one morning when Megha was still lying down on his bed with eyes closed but internally awake, he saw clearly Baba's Form. Baba knowing him to be awake threw Akshata (rice-grains marked red with Kumar) and said, "Megha, draw a Trident" and disappeared. Hearing Baba's words, he eagerly opened his eyes but did not see Baba, but saw only rice grains spread here and there. He then went to Baba, told Him about the vision and asked permission to draw Trident.

Baba said - "Did you not hear My words asking you to draw Trident? It was no vision but direct order and My words are always pregnant with meaning and never hollow." Megha said - "I thought you woke me up, but all the doors were closed, so I thought it was a vision". Baba rejoined - "I require no door to enter. I have no form nor any extension; I always live everywhere. I carry on, as a wire-puller, all the actions of the man who trusts Me and merges in Me."

Megha returned to the Wada, and drew a red Trident on the wall near Baba's picture. Next day a Ramadasi Bhakta came from Poona, saluted Baba and offered Him Pindi (an image of Shiva). At this time Megha also turned up there. Baba said to him - "See, Shankar has come, protect (i.e., worship) Him now." Megha was surprised to see Pindi following Trident immediately. Then also in the Wada, Kakasaheb Dixit was standing with a towel on his head after having taken his bath, and was remembering Sai, when he saw a Pindi before his mental vision. While he was wondering about this, Megha came and showed him the Pindi presented to him by Baba. Dixit was happy to know that the Pindi exactly tallied with the One he saw a few minutes before in his vision. In a few days after the drawing of the Trident was complete, Baba installed the Pindi near the big picture which Megha was worshipping. The worship of Shiva was dear to Megha and by arranging the drawing of the Trident and the installation of the Pindi, Baba confirmed his faith therein.

After continuous service of Baba for many years, doing regular worship and Arati every noon and evening, Megha passed away in 1912. Then Baba passed His hands over his corpse and said - "This was a true devotee of Mine." Baba also ordered that at His own expense the usual funeral dinner should be given to the Brahmins, and this order was carried out by Kakasaheb Dixit.

Bow to Shri Sai - Peace be to all

Chapter XXIX

Stories of (1) Madrasi Bhajani Mela - (2) Tendulkars (Father and son) - (3) Dr. Captain Hate - (4) Waman Narvekar

This Chapter describes other wonderful stories of Sai Baba.

(1)   Madrasi Bhajani Mela

It was in the year 1916 that a Madrasi Bhajani Mela (Party of the Ramadasi Panth) started on a Pilgrimage to the holy city of Banaras. The Party consisted of a man, his wife, daughter and sister-in-law. Unfortunately their names are not mentioned. On their way, the party heard that there lived at Shirdi in Kopergaon Taluka, Ahmednagar District a great sage named Sai Baba, who was calm and composed, and who was very liberal and who distributed money every day to His Bhaktas and to skillful persons, who went and showed their skill there.

A lot of money in the form of Dakshina was collected daily by Sai Baba and out of this amount, He gave daily one rupee to a three year old girl Amani, the daughter of a Bhakta Kondaji and Rs. 2 to 5 to some, Rs. 6 to Jamali, the mother of Amani and Rs. 10 to 20 and even Rs. 50 to other Bhaktas as He pleased. On hearing all this the party came to Shirdi and stayed there.

The Mela did very good bhajan and sang very good songs, but inwardly they craved for money. Three of the party were full of avarice, but the chief lady or mistress was of a very different nature. She had a regard and love for Baba. Once it so happened, that when the noon-day Arati was going on, Baba was much pleased with her faith and devotion, and was pleased to give her darshan of her Ishtam (Beloved Deity). To her Baba appeared as Sitanath (Rama) while to all the others the usual Sainath. On seeing her beloved Deity, she was very much moved. Tears began to flow from her eyes and she clapped her hands in joy. The people began to wonder at her joyful mood; but were not able to guess its cause. Late in the afternoon she disclosed everything to her husband. She told him how she saw Shri Rama in Sai Baba. He thought that she was very simple and devout, and her seeing

Rama might be a hallucination of her mind. He pooh-poohed her, saying that it was not possible, that she alone should see Rama while they all saw Sai Baba. She did not resent this remark, as she was fortunate enough to get Ramadarshan now and then, when her mind was calm and composed and free from avarice.

Wonderful Vision

Things were going on like this, when the husband got a wonderful vision in his dream one night as follows: He was in a big city; the police there had arrested him, tied his hands with a rope, and put him up in a lock-up. As the police were tightening the grip, he saw Sai Baba standing quiet outside, near the cage. On seeing Baba so near, he said in a plaintive tone - "Hearing Your fame I came to Your Feet and why should a calamity befall me when You are standing here in person?" Baba said - "You must suffer the consequences of your action" He said - "I have not done anything in this life which would bring such a misfortune on me." Baba said - "If not in this life, you must have committed some sin in your past life." He replied, "I do not know anything of my past life, but assuming that I did commit some sin then, why should it not be burnt and destroyed in Your presence, as dry grass before fire?" Baba - "Have you got such faith?" He - "Yes." Baba then asked him to close his eyes.

No sooner did he shut them than he heard a thumping sound of something falling down, and opening his eyes, he saw that he was free and the police had fallen down, bleeding. Being much frightened he began to look at Baba who said - "Now you are well caught, officers will now come and arrest you." Then he begged - "There is no other savior except You, save me anyhow." Then Baba again asked him to close his eyes. He did so and when he opened them, he saw that he was free, out of the cage and that Baba was by his side. He then fell at Baba's Feet. Baba then asked him - "Is there any difference between this namaskar and your previous ones? Think well and reply." He said, "There is a lot of difference; my former namaskaras were offered with the object of getting money from You, but the present namaskar is one offered to You as God; besides, formerly I thought resentfully that you, being a Mohammedan, were spoiling us, the Hindus". Baba "Do you not believe in your mind in Mohammedan Gods?" He said "No". Then Baba said - "Have you not got a Panja (Emblem of Hand) in your house and do you not worship the same in Tabut, i.e. Moharum festival? Also there is in your house another Mohammedan Deity by name Kadbibi, whom you propitiate and appease on your marriage and other festivals. Is it not so?" He admitted all this. Then Baba said, "What more do you want?" Then a desire arose in his mind to get the darshan of his Guru Ramdas, when Baba asked him to turn back and see. And when he turned, lo, Ramadas was in front of him. No sooner did he begin to fall at His Feet, Ramadas vanished. Then he inquisitively asked Baba, "You look old. Do You know Your age?" Baba - "What! Do you say I am old! just run a race with Me and see." Saying this Baba began to run and he too followed. Baba disappeared in the dust raised by His foot-steps while running and the man was awakened.

After awakening he began to think seriously about the dream - vision. His mental attitude was completely changed and he realized the greatness of Baba. After this, his grabbing and doubting tendencies disappeared and true devotion to Baba's Feet sprang in his mind. The vision was a mere dream, but the questions and answers therein were most significant and interesting. Next morning when all the persons assembled in the Masjid for the Arati, Baba gave him as prasad two rupees' worth sweets and also two rupees from His pocket and blessed him. He made him stay there for a few more days and gave him His blessing, saying, "Allah (God) will give you plenty and He will do you all good". He did not get more money there, but he got far better things viz. Baba's blessing which stood him in good stead all along. The party got plenty of money afterwards and their pilgrimage was successful as they had not to suffer any trouble or inconvenience during their journey. They all returned home safe and sound, thinking of Baba's words and blessings and the Ananda (Bliss) they experienced by His grace.

This story illustrates one of the methods, which Baba followed (and is following even now) in some cases to improve and reform His devotees.

(2)   Tendulkar Family

There lived in Bandra (a suburb of Bombay) a family named Tendalkar, all the members of which were devoted to Baba. Mrs. Savitribai Tendulkar has published a Marathi book named "Shri Sainath Bhajan Mala" containing 800 abhangas and padas describing the Leelas of Baba. It is a book worth reading by those who are interested in Baba. The son, Babu Tendulkar was studying hard day and night and wanted to appear for the medical examination. He consulted some astrologers. Examining his horoscope they told him that the stars were not favorable that year and that he should appear for the examination next year, when he would be certainly successful. This cast a gloom over him and made him restless. A few days afterwards his mother went to Shirdi and saw Baba. Amongst other things she mentioned the gloomy and morose condition of her son, who was to appear for the examination in a few days.

Hearing this Baba said to her, "Tell your son to believe in Me, to throw aside horoscopes and predictions of astrologers and palmists and go on with his studies. Let him appear for the examination with a calm mind, he is sure to pass this year. Ask him to trust in Me and not to get disappointed". The mother returned home and communicated Baba's message to her son. Then he studied hard and in due course appeared for the examination. In the written papers he did well, but being overwhelmed by doubts he thought that he would not secure sufficient marks for passing. So he did not care to appear for the oral examination. But the examiner was after him. He sent word through a fellow student, stating that he had passed the written examination and that he should appear for the oral part. The son being thus encouraged appeared for the oral examination and was successful in both. Thus he got through the examination that year successfully by Baba's grace, though the stars were against him. It is to be noted here that doubts and difficulties surround us just to move us and confirm our faith. We are tested as it were. If we only hold on steadily to Baba with full faith and continue our endeavors, our efforts will be ultimately crowned with success.

The father of this boy, Raghunathrao was serving in some foreign mercantile firm in Bombay. As he grew old, he was not able to attend to his work properly and so he had to take leave and rest. As he did not improve during the period of leave a further extension of leave or retirement from service was inevitable. The Chief Manager of the firm decided to retire him on pension as he was an old and a reliable servant. The question regarding the amount of pension to be given was under consideration. He was getting Rs.150 per month and his pension i.e. half the amount viz. Rs.75 would not be enough to meet the expenses of the family. So they were all anxious about this matter. Fifteen days before the final settlement, Baba appeared to Mrs. Tendulkar in her dream and said, "I wish that Rs.100 should be paid (settled) as pension, will this satisfy you?" She replied "Baba, why ask me this? We fully trust in You". Though Baba said Rs.100 still he was given ten Rupees more i.e. Rs.110 as a special case. Such wonderful love and care did Baba exhibit for His Bhaktas.

(3) Captain Hate

Captain Hate, who was staying in Bikaner, was a great devotee of Baba. Once Baba appeared to him in his dream and said "Did you forget Me?" Hate then immediately held Baba's Feet and replied, "If a child forgets his mother, how could it be saved?" Then he went into the garden and took out fresh valor-papadi (flat beans), and made 'shidha' (ghee, flour & dal) and Dakshina, was about to offer all this to Baba when he was awakened and came to know that the whole thing was a dream. Then he decided to send all these things to Baba at Shirdi. When he came to Gwalior some days afterwards, he sent Rs.12 by moneyorder to a friend, with instructions that Rs.2 should be spent in buying shidha articles and walpapadi vegetables, and those should be offered to Baba with Rs.10 as Dakshina. The friend went to Shirdi and purchased the items, but walpapadi was not available. In a short time a woman turned up with a basket on her head, which of course contained the vegetables. It was purchased and then all the things were offered to Baba on behalf of Captain Hate. Mr. Nimonkar prepared the 'naivedya' next day and offered the same to Baba. All the people were surprised to see that Baba while dining, took and ate walpapadi, and did not touch rice and other things. Hate's joy knew no bounds when he heard of this from his friend.

Consecrated Rupee

At another time Captain Hate wished that he should have in his house a coin of rupee consecrated by Baba with His touch. He came across a friend who was bound for Shirdi. With him Hate sent his rupee. The friend went to Shirdi and after the usual salutation gave first his Dakshina which Baba pocketed. Then he gave Hate's rupee, which Baba took in His hand and began to stare at it. He held it in front, tossed it up with His right thumb and played with it. Then He said to the friend, "Return this to its owner with the Prasad of Udi, tell him that I want nothing from him, ask him to live in peace and contentment." The friend returned to Gwalior, handed over the consecrated rupee to Hate, and told him all that happened at Shirdi. This time Hate was much pleased and realized that Baba always encouraged good thoughts, and as he wished intently, Baba fulfilled the same accordingly.

(4) Waman Narvekar

Now let the readers hear a different story. A gentleman, named Waman Narvekar loved Baba very much. He once brought a rupee. On one side (obverse) of it were engraved the figures of Rama, Laxman and Sita and on the other (reverse) side was engraved the figure of Maruti, with folded hands. He offered it to Baba with a hope that He should consecrate it with His touch and return it to him with udi. But Baba immediately pocketed it. Then Shama spoke to Baba, regarding Womanrao's intention and requested Him to return it. Then Baba spoke in the presence of Wamanrao as follows: "Why should it be returned to him? We should keep it ourselves. If he gives Rs.25 for it, it will be returned." Then, for the sake of that rupee, Wamanrao collected Rs.25 and placed them before Baba. Then Baba said, "The value of that rupee far exceeds 25 Rupees. Shama, take this rupee, let us have it in our store, keep this in your shrine and worship it." No one had the courage to ask Baba why He followed this particular action. He only knows what is best and most suitable to each and all.

Bow to Shri Sai - Peace be to all

Chapter XXX

Drawn To Shirdi
(1) Kakaji Vaidya of Vani (2) Punjabi Ramalal of Bombay

In this Chapter the story of two more devotees that were drawn to Shirdi, is narrated.

Preliminary

Bow to the Kind Sai Who is the Abode of Mercy and Who is affectionate towards His devotees. By His mere darshan, He does away with their fear of this 'bhava' (samsar) and destroys their calamities. He was first Nirgun (formless), but on account of the devotion of His Bhaktas, He was obliged to take a form. To give liberation - self-realization to the Bhaktas is the mission of the saints, and for Sai - the Chief of them, that mission is inevitable. Those who take refuge in His Feet have all their sins destroyed and their progress is certain. Remembering His Feet, Brahmins from holy places come to Him and read scriptures and chant the Gayatri mantra in His presence. We, who are weak and without any merits, do not know what Bhakti is but we know this much, that though all others may leave us, Sai won't forsake us. Those whom He favors get enormous strength, discrimination between the Unreal and the Real and knowledge.

Sai knows fully the desire of His devotees and fulfills the same. Hence they get what they want and are grateful. So we invoke Him and prostrate ourselves before Him. Forgetting all our faults let Him free us from all anxieties. He who being overcome with calamities remembers and prays Sai thus, will get his mind calmed and pacified through His grace.

This Sai - the ocean of mercy, says Hemadpant, favored him and the result of this, is the present work - Sai-Satcharita. Otherwise what qualifications had he and who would undertake this enterprise? But as Sai took all the responsibility, Hemadpant felt no burden, nor any care about this. When the powerful Light of knowledge was there to inspire his speech and pen, why should he entertain any doubt or feel any anxiety? Sai got the service in the form of this book done by him; this is due to the accumulation of his merits in the past births and, therefore, he thinks himself fortunate and blessed.

The following story is not a mere tale, but pure nectar. He who drinks it will realize Sai's greatness and all-pervasiveness. Those who want to argue and criticize should not go in for these stories. What is wanted here is not discussion but unlimited love and devotion. Learned, devout and faithful believers or those, who consider themselves as servants of the Saints, will like and appreciate these stories; others will take them to be fables. The fortunate Bhaktas of Sai will find the Sai-leelas as the Kalpataru (Wish Fulfilling Tree). Drinking this nectar of Sai-leelas, will give liberation to the ignorant Jivas, satisfaction to the house-holders and a sadhana to the aspirants. Now to the story of this Chapter.

Kakaji Vaidya

There lived in Vani, Nasik District, a man named Kakaji Vaidya, he was the priest of the Goodness Sapta-Shringi there. He was so much overwhelmed with adverse circumstances and calamities that he lost peace of mind and became quite restless. Under such circumstances one evening he went into the Temple of the Goddess and prayed unto Her from the bottom of his heart and invoked Her aid to free him from anxiety. The Goddess was pleased with his devotion and the same night appeared to him in his dream and said to him, "You go to Baba and then your mind will become calm and composed". Kakaji was anxious to know from Her who that Baba was, but before he could get any explanation, he was awakened. Then he began to think as to who might be that Baba, to whom the Goddess has asked him to go. After some thinking, he resolved that this Baba might be 'Tryambakeshwar' (Lord Shiva). So he went to the holy place 'Tryambak' (Nasik District) and stayed there for ten days. During this period, he bathed early in the morning, chanted the 'Rudra' (Shiva) hymns, did the 'Abhishek' (pouring unceasingly fresh cold water over the Pindi (stones "dressed" as Gods) and did other religious rites; but with all that, he was as restless as before. Then he returned to his place and again invoked the Goddess most pitifully. They night She again appeared in his dream and said -

177

"Why did you go to Tryambakeshwar in vain? I mean by Baba - Shri Sai Samarth of Shirdi."

The question before Kakaji now was 'How and when to go to Shirdi and how to see Baba? If anybody is in real earnest to see a Saint, not only the Saint but God also, fulfills his wish. In fact the 'Sant' (Saint) and the 'Anant' (God) are one and the same; there is not the least difference between them. If anybody thinks that he will go himself and see a Saint, that will be a mere boast. Unless the Saint wills it, who is able to go and see him? Even the leaf of the tree won't move without his bidding. The more anxious a Bhakta is for the saint's visit, the more devout and faithful he is, then the more speedily and effectively is his wish satisfied to his heart's content. He who invites anybody for a visit, also arranges everything for his reception, and so it happened with Kakaji.

Shama's Vows

When Kakaji was thinking his visit to Shirdi, a guest came to him at his place to take him to Shirdi. He was no other than Shama, a very close and intimate devotee of Baba. How he came to Vani at this juncture, we shall just see. Shama was severely ill when he was very young and his mother had taken a vow to her family Goddess Sapta-Shringi at Vani, that if the son got well, she would bring and dedicate him at Her feet. Then after some years the mother herself suffered much from ring-worms on her breasts. At that time she again took another vow to her Deity that if she got all right, she would offer Her two silver breasts. These two vows remained unfulfilled. At her death-bed she called her son Shama to her and drew his attention to the vows and after taking a promise from him that he would fulfills them, she breathed her last.

After some time, Shama quite forgot about these vows and thus 30 years elapsed. About this time a famous astrologer had come to Shirdi and stayed there for a month. His predictions in the case of Shriman Booty and others came true and everybody was satisfied. Shama's younger brother Bapaji consulted him and was told that his mother's vows, which his elder brother promised to fulfill at her death-bed, were not yet fulfilled; hence the Goddess was displeased with them and bringing troubles on them.

Bapaji told this to his brother Shama who was then reminded of the unfulfilled vows. Thinking that any further delay would be dangerous, he called a goldsmith and got a pair of silver breast prepared. Then he went to the Masjid, prostrated himself before Baba and, placing before Him the two silver breath, requested Him to accept them and free him from the vows as He was to him his Sapta-Shringi Goddess. Then Baba insisted upon him to go himself to the temple of Sapta-Shringi and offer them in person at the feet of the Goddess. Then after taking Baba's permission and Udi, he left for Vani and searching for the priest came to Kakaji's house. Kakaji was then very anxious to visit Baba and Shama went there to see him at that very time. What a wonderful coincidence is this!

Kakaji asked him who he was and whence he had come, and on learning that he came from Shirdi, he at once embraced him. So overpowered was he with love! Then they talked about Sai-leelas and after finishing the rites of Shama's vows, they both started for Shirdi. On reaching the place, Kakaji went to the Masjid, and fell at Baba's Feet. His eyes were soon be-dewed with tears, and his mind attained calmness. According to the vision of the Goddess, no sooner did he see Baba, that his mind lost all its restlessness and it became calm and composed. Kakaji began to think, in his mind, "What a wonderful power is this! Baba spoke nothing, there was no question and answer, no benediction pronounced; the mere darshan itself was so conducive to happiness; the restlessness of my mind disappeared by His mere darshan, consciousness of joy came upon me - this is what is called 'the greatness of darshan'." His vision was fixed on Sai's feet and he could utter no word. Hearing Baba's Leelas, his joy knew no bounds. He surrendered himself completely to Baba, forgot his anxiety and cares and got undiluted happiness. He lived happily there for twelve days and after taking Baba's leave, Udi and blessings returned home.

Khushalchand of Rahata

It is said that a dream, which we get in the small hours of the morning, generally comes out true in the walking state. This may be so, but regarding Baba's dreams there is no restriction of time.

To quote an instance: - Baba told Kakasaheb Dixit one afternoon to go to Rahata and fetch Khushalchand to Shirdi, as He had not seen him since long. Kakasaheb accordingly took a tanga and went to Rahata. He saw Khushalchand and gave him Baba's message. Hearing it, Khushalchand was surprised and said that he was taking a noon nap after meals when Baba appeared in his dream and asked him to come to Shirdi immediately and that he was anxious to go. As he had no horse of his own nearby, he had sent his son to inform Baba; when his son was just outside of the village-border, Dixit's tanga turned up. Dixit then said that he was sent specially to bring him. Then they both went in the tanga back to Shirdi. Khushalchand saw Baba and all were pleased. Seeing this Leela of Baba, Khushalchand was much moved.

Punjabi Ramalal of Bombay

Once a Punjabi Brahmin of Bombay named Ramalal had a dream in which Baba appeared and asked him to come to Shirdi. Baba appeared to him as a Mahant (Saint), but he did not know His whereabouts. He thought that he should go and see Him, but as he knew not His address, he did not know what to do. But He Who calls anybody for an interview makes the necessary arrangements for the same. The same happened in this case. The same afternoon when he was strolling in the streets, he saw a picture of Baba in a shop. The features of the Mahant, he saw in the dream, exactly tallied with those of the picture. Then making enquiries, he came to know that the picture was of Sai Baba of Shirdi. He then went soon after to Shirdi and stayed there till his death.

In this way Baba brought His devotees to Shirdi for darshan and satisfied their wants, material as well as spiritual.

Bow to Shri Sai - Peace be to all

Chapter XXXI

The Passing Away In Baba's Presence of –
(1) Sannyasi Vijayanand (2) Balaram Mankar (3) Noolkar
(4) Megha (5) the Tiger

In this Chapter Hemadpant describes the passing away of certain persons and a tiger in Baba's presence.

Preliminary

The last wish or thought that a man has at the hour of death, determines his future course. Shri Krishna has said in Gita (VIII-5-6) that "he, who remembers Me in his last moments, comes verily to Me, and he that meditates otherwise at that time goes to what he looks for." We cannot be certain that we can entertain a particular good thought at our last moment, for, more often than not, we are more likely to be frightened and terrified by many causes. Hence constant practice is necessary for enabling us to fix our mind on any desired good thought at any or the last moment. All Saints, therefore, recommended us to always remember God and chant His name always, so that we may not be puzzled when the time for departure comes. The devotees on their part surrender themselves completely to the Saints, fully believing that the all-knowing Saints would guide and help them in their last moments. A few such cases will be noted here.

(1) Vijayanand

A Madrasi Sannyasi named Vijayanand started on a pilgrimage to Manasarovar. En route, hearing Baba's fame, he halted at Shirdi. There he met one Somadevaji Swami of Hardwar and enquired of him about the particulars of the Manasarovar trip. The Swami told him that the Manasarovar was 500 miles above the Gangotri and described to him the difficulties of the journey, viz. plenty of snow and the change of dialect every 50 koss and the suspicious nature of the people of Bhutan who give a lot of trouble to the pilgrims on the way. Hearing this, the Sannyasi was dejected and cancelled the trip. Then when he went to Baba and prostrated himself before Him, Baba got enraged and said, "Drive out this useless Sannyasi, his company is of no use". The Sannyasi did not know Baba's nature. He felt discomforted, but sat there watching things that were going on. It was the morning Darbar and the Masjid was overcrowded. Baba was being worshipped in various ways. Some were washing His Feet, some taking the Tirth (holy water) from His toe and drinking it heartily and some touching their eyes with it, some were applying sandal-paste, and some scents to His body. And all were doing these things forgetting the distinction of caste and creed. Though Baba got enraged with him, he was filled with affection for Baba and he did not like to leave the place.

He stayed in Shirdi for two days when he got a letter from Madras stating that his mother was very ill. He felt very dejected and wanted to be by his mother's side; but he could not leave without Baba's permission. So he saw Baba with the letter in hand and asked for His permission to return home. The omniscient Baba knowing the future said to him - "If you so loved your mother, why did you take Sannayasa? Fondness or attachment ill becomes an ochre garb. Go and sit quiet at your lodging, wait with patience for a few days. In the Wada there are many robbers, bolt your doors, be very vigilant, the thieves will carry everything. Wealth and prosperity are transient and the body is subject to decay and death. Knowing this, do your duty, leaving all attachment to the things of this world and next. He who does this and surrenders himself to the Feet of Hari (Lord) will get free from all troubles and attain bliss. The Lord runs and helps him who remembers and meditates on Him with love and affection. Your store of past merits is considerable, so you have come here. Now attend to what I say and realize the end of your life. Being desire-less, begin from tomorrow the study of Bhagwat. Do three 'saptahas' i.e. three reading during three weeks, conscientiously. The Lord will be pleased with you and destroy your sorrows, your illusions will vanish and you will get peace."

Seeing that his end was approaching, Baba prescribed that remedy and made him read 'Ramavijaya' which pleases Yama (the God of death). Next morning after bathing and other purifying rites he commenced to read Bhagwat in a secluded part in the

Lendi garden. He completed two readings and thereafter felt much exhausted. He returned to the Wada and stayed in his lodging for two days and on the third day he breathed his last on Fakir (Bade) Baba's lap. Baba asked the people to preserve the body for a day for a good reason.

The police afterwards came and on making proper enquiries gave permission for the disposal of the body. It was buried in a proper place with due rites. In this way Baba helped the Sannyasi and ensured him Sadgati (salvation).

(2)   Balaram Mankar

There was a householder devotee of Baba by name Balaram Mankar. When his wife passed away, he got dejected and entrusting his household to his son, left his home and came to Shirdi and lived with Baba. Being pleased with his devotion, Baba wanted to give a good turn to his life and He did this in this wise. He gave him Rs.12 and asked him to go and live in Macchindragad (District Satara). Mankar was first unwilling to go and stay away from Baba, but Baba convinced him that he was giving the best course for him and asked him to practice mediation thrice a day on the Gad. Believing in Baba's words, Mankar came to the Gad. He was much pleased with the lovely sight, pure water, healthy air and the surroundings of the place, and began to practice assiduously the meditations as recommended by Baba.

After some days he got a revelation. Generally Bhaktas get revelation in their Samadhi or trance states, but in Mankar's case he got it, when he came down to his ordinary consciousness from his trance. Baba appeared to him in person. Not only that Mankar saw Him, but he also asked Him why he was sent there. Baba replied - "In Shirdi many thoughts and ideas began to rise in your mind and I sent you here to rest your unsteady mind. You thought that I was in Shirdi with a body composed of the five elements and three and a half cubits in length, and not outside of it. Now you see and determine for yourself whether the person you see here now is the same you saw at Shirdi. It is for this reason that I sent you here."

Then after the period was over, Mankar left the Gada and proceeded to his native place Bandra. He wanted to travel by rail from Poona to Dadar, but when he went to the booking office to get a ticket, he found it very much crowded. He could not get his ticket soon, when, a villager with a langoti (piece of cloth) on his waist and kambali on his shoulder turned up and said - "Where are you going?" "To Dadar." replied Mankar. Then he said - "Please take this Dadar ticket of mine; as I have some urgent business here, I have cancelled my Dadar trip." Mankar was very glad to receive the ticket and was just taking out money from his pocket, when the rustic disappeared in the crowd. Mankar tried to find him out in the crowd, but it was in vain. He waited for him till the train left the station but found no trace of him. This was the second revelation Mankar got in a strange form. Then Mankar after visiting his home again returned to Shirdi and remained there at Baba's feet, always following His biddings and advice. In the end, he was very fortunate to leave this world in the presence, and with the blessings of Baba.

(3)   Tatyasaheb Noolkar

Hemadpant gives no particulars regarding Tatyasaheb Noolkar, except the bare mention of the fact that he up his ghost in Shirdi. A brief summary of his account that appeared in the Sai Leela magazine is given here.

Tatyasaheb was a Sub-Judge at Pandharpur in 1909, when Nanasaheb Chandorkar was Mamalatdar there. Both met often and exchanged talks. Tatyasaheb did not believe in saints, while Nanasaheb loved them. Nanasaheb often told him the Leelas of Sai Baba and pressed him to go to Shirdi and see Baba. He finally agreed to go to Shirdi on two conditions: - (1) he must get a Brahmin cook, and (2) must get good Nagpur oranges for the presentation. Both these conditions were providentially fulfilled. A Brahmin came to Nanasaheb for service and he was sent to Tatyasaheb and a fruit parcel containing 100 beautiful oranges was received by Tatyasaheb, the consigner being not known. As the conditions were fulfilled, Tatyasaheb had to go to Shirdi. At first Baba was much enraged with him. But by and by Tatyasaheb got such experiences that he was convinced that Baba was God incarnate. So he was enamored of Baba and stayed there till his death. As his end was approaching, sacred literature was read out to him and at the last hour Baba's Pada-tirth was brought and given to him for drinking. Baba on hearing of his death, said, "Oh, Tatya went ahead of us, he won't be reborn."

(4) Megha

The story of Megha has been already described in Chapter 28. When Megha died, all the villagers followed the funeral procession. Baba also accompanied them and showered flowers on Megha's body. After the obsequies were performed, tears flowed from Baba's eyes and like an ordinary mortal, Baba showed Himself overcome with grief and sorrow. Then covering the body with flowers and crying like a near relation, Baba returned to the Masjid.

Many Saints have been seen giving Sadgati to men, but Baba's greatness is unique. Even a cruel animal like a tiger came to Baba's feet for being saved. It is this story which will be narrated now.

(5) Tiger

Seven days before Baba passed away, a wonderful incident occurred at Shirdi. There came a country cart and stopped in front of the Masjid. A tiger was on the cart, fastened with iron chains, with its fierce face turned to the rear. It was suffering from some pain or agony. Its keepers - three Dervishes - were taking it from place to place and making money by exhibiting it. It was the means of their subsistence. They tried all sorts of remedies to cure it from the malady it was suffering from, but all was in vain. Then they heard of Baba's fame and came to Him with the animal. They got it down the chains in their hands and made it stand at the door. It was naturally fierce, besides, disease ridden. So it was restless. The people began to look at it with fear and amazement. The Dervishes went in, told Baba everything about the animal and with His consent, brought it before Him. As it approached the steps, it was taken aback on account of the lustre of Baba and hung its head down. When both saw each other, the tiger got on the step and looked at Baba with affection. Immediately it moved the tuft of its tail and dashed it thrice against the ground and then fell down senseless. On seeing it dead the Dervishes were first much dejected and full of sorrow, but on mature thought they came to their senses. They considered that as the animal was diseased and nearing its end, it was very meritorious on its part that it should meet its death at the feet and in the presence of Baba. It was their debtor, and when the debt was paid off it was free and met its end at Sai's Feet. When any creatures bow down their heads at saints' feet and meet death, they are saved; and unless they have got a good store of merit on their account, How could they get such a happy end?

Bow to Shri Sai - Peace be to all

Chapter XXXII

In Quest of Guru and God - Fasting Disapprove

In this Chapter Hemadpant describes two things: - (1) How Baba met His Guru in the woods, and through him God; and (2) How Baba made one Mrs. Ghokhale, who had made up her mind to fast for three days, eat Puran-Polis.

Preliminary

In the beginning, Hemadpant describes the samsara (visible world) by the allegory of Ashvattha (Banyan) tree which has, in the phraseology of the Gita, roots above and branches below. Its branches are spread downwards and upwards and are nourished by the gunas (qualities), and its sprouts are the objects of the senses. Its roots, leading to actions, are extended downwards to this world of men. Its form cannot be known in this world, nor its end, its beginning nor its support. Cutting this Ashvattha tree of strong roots with the sharp weapon of non-attachment; one should seek the path beyond, treading which there is no return.

For traversing this path, the help of a good guide (Guru) is absolutely necessary. However learned a man may be, or however deep his study of Vedas and Vedangas (sacred literature) may be, he cannot go to his destination safely. If the guide be there to help him and show him the right way, he would avoid the pitfalls and the wild beasts on the journey, and everything will be smooth sailing.

Baba's experience in this matter, the story which He gave out Himself, is really wonderful, which, when attended to, will give you faith, devotion and salvation.

The Quest

Once four of us were studying religious scriptures and other books and, being thus enlightened, we began to discuss the nature of the Brahman. One of us said that we should raise the self by the Self and not depend on others. To this the second replied that he who controls his mind is blessed; we should be free from thoughts and ideas and there is nothing in the world without us. The third said that the world (phenomenon) is always changing, the formless is eternal; so we should discriminate between the Unreal and the Real. And the fourth (Baba Himself) urged that bookish knowledge is worthless and added, "Let us do our prescribed duty and surrender our body, mind and five pranas (life) to the Guru's feet. Guru is God, all pervading. To get this conviction, strong unbounded faith is necessary."

Discussing in this wise, we four learned men began to ramble through the woods in the quest of God. The three wanted to make the quest with their free and unaided intellect. On the way a Vanjari (a man who trades in certain things, such as grain etc... by carrying them on bullock) met us and asked us, "It is hot now, where and how far are you going?" "To search the woods", we replied. He enquired, "On what quest are you bound?" We gave him an ambiguous and evasive reply. Seeing us rambling aimlessly, he was moved and said, "Without knowing the woods fully, you should not wander at random. If you want to walk through forests and jungles, you should take a guide with you. Why do you exert yourselves unnecessarily at this sultry noon-time? You may not give out to me your secret quest; still you can sit down, eat bread, drink water, take rest and then go. Be always patient at heart."

Though he spoke so tenderly, we discarded his request and marched on. We thought that we were self-contained men and needed nobody's help. The woods were vast and trackless; the trees therein grew so close and tall, that the sun's rays could not penetrate through them; so we lost our way and wandered here and there for a long time. Ultimately through sheer good luck, we came back to the place from where we started. The Vanjari met us again and said, "Relying on your own cleverness you missed your way; a guide is always necessary to show us the right way in small or great matters; and no quest can be successfully carried out on an empty stomach. Unless God wills it, no one meets us on the way. Do not discard offers of food; served dish should not be thrust away. Offers of bread and food should be regarded as auspicious signs of success." Saying this he again offered us food and asked us to be calm and patient.

Again we did not like this good hospitality and discarded his offer and went away. Without doing any quest and without taking any food, the three began to move out. So obstinate were they. I was hungry and thirsty and I was moved with the Vanjari's extraordinary love; we thought ourselves very learned but were quite strangers to pity and kindness. The Vanjari was a quite illiterate and unqualified fellow and belonged to a low caste. Still he had love in his heart and asked us to eat the bread. In this way he who loves others disinterestedly is really enlightened and I thought acceptance of his hospitality was the best beginning of getting knowledge. So very respectfully I accepted the loaf of bread offered, ate it and drank water.

Then, The Guru at once came and stood before us, "What was the dispute about?" He asked and I told him everything that had happened. Then he said, "Would you like to come with me? I will show you what you want; but he alone, who believes in what I say, will be successful." The others did not agree to what he said and left him; but I bowed to him reverently and accepted his dictum. Then he took me to a well, tied my feet with a rope and hung me - head downwards and feet up - from a tree near the well. I was suspended three feet above the water, which I could not reach with My hands, nor which could go into my mouth.

Suspending me in this manner he went away, no one knew where. After 10 or 12 ghatakas (4 or 5 hours) he returned and taking me out quickly asked me how I fared. "In Bliss supreme, I was. How can a fool like me describe the joy I experienced?" I replied. On hearing my answer the Guru was much pleased with me, drew me near him and stroking my body with his hand kept me with him. He took care of me as tenderly as a mother-bird does of her young ones.

He put me into his school; how beautiful it was! There I forgot my parents, all my attachment was snapped and I was liberated easily. I thought that I should embrace his neck and remain staring at him always. If his image were not fixed in my pupils, I would like better to be blind. Such was the school! No one, who entered it once, could return empty-handed. My Guru became my all-in-all, my home and property, mother and father, everything. All my senses left their places and concentrated themselves in my eyes, and my sight was centered on him. Thus was my Guru, the sole object of my meditation and I was conscious of none else. While meditating on him my mind and intellect were stunned and I had thus to keep quiet and bow to him in silence.

There are other schools where you see an altogether different spectacle. The disciples go there to seek knowledge and spend their money, time and labor; but ultimately they have to repent. The Guru there boasts of his secret knowledge and his straight-forwardness. He makes a show of his sacredness and holiness, but he is not tender at heart. He speaks a lot and sings his own glory; but his own words do not touch the disciples' hearts and they are not convinced. So far as Self-realization is concerned, he has none. How can such schools be of any use to the disciples and how can they be benefited? The master (Guru) mentioned above was of different type. By his grace, realization flashed upon me of itself, without effort or study. I had not to seek anything, but everything became clear to me as broad day-light. The Guru alone knows how the topsy-turvy Suspension, 'with head down and feet up' can give happiness!

Among the four, one was a Karmatha (Ritualistic) who only knew how to observe, and abstain from, certain rites; the second was a Jnani, who was puffed up with pride of knowledge and the third was a Bhakta who surrendered himself completely to God, believing that he was the sole Doer. When they were discussing and arguing, the question of God turned up, and they, depending on their unaided knowledge, went in search of Him. Sai, who was Discrimination and Dispassion incarnate, was one of the four. Being Himself Brahman Incarnate, some may ask, "Why did He mix with them and act foolishly?" He did this for attaining the good of the public, and setting them an example to follow. Though an incarnation Himself, He respected a low Vanjari, by accepting his food with the firm belief that "Food is Brahman" and showed how those who rejected Vanjari's hospitable offer suffered and how it was impossible to get Jnana without a Guru.

The Shruti (Taittiriya Upanishad) exhorts us to honor and worship mother, father and preceptor, and to study (learn and teach) the sacred scriptures. These are the means of purifying our minds and unless this purification is effected, self-realization is not possible. Neither the senses, nor the mind and intellect reach the Self. Modes of proof, such as Perception and Inference will not help us in the matter. It is the grace of the Guru that counts. The objects of our life such as Dharma, Artha and Kama are attainable with our effort, but the fourth object, Moksha (liberation) can only he had with the help of the Guru.

In the Darbar of Shri Sai, many personalities appear and play their part; astrologers come and give out their predictions; princes, noblemen, ordinary and poor men, Sannyasis, Yogis songsters and others come for darshan. Even a mahar (out-caste) comes and, making a Johar (his salutation), says this Sai is the Mai-Baap (True parents - the mother/father), Who will do away with our rounds of births and deaths. So many others such as Jugglers, Gondhalis, the blind and the lame, nathpanthis, dancers and other players come and are given suitable reception. Biding his own time, the Vanjari also appeared, and played the part assigned to him. Let us now revert to the other story.

Fasting and Mrs. Gokhale

Baba never fasted Himself, nor did He allow others to do so. The mind of the faster is never at ease, then how could he attain his Paramartha (goal of life)? God is not attained on an empty stomach; first the soul has to be appeased. If there is no moisture of food in the stomach and nutrition, with what eyes should we see God, with what tongue should we describe His greatness and with what ears should we hear the same? In short, when all our organs get their proper nutrition and are sound, we can practice devotion and other sadhanas to attain God. Therefore, neither fasting nor overeating is good. Moderation in diet is really wholesome both to the body and mind.

One Mrs. Gokhale came to Shirdi with an introductory letter from Mrs. Kashibai Kanitkar (a devotee of Baba) to Dada Kelkar. She came to Baba with a determination to sit at Baba's Feet observing a three days fast. The day previous, Baba said to Dada Kelkar, that He would not allow his children to starve during the Shimga, i.e., Holi holidays, and that if they had to starve, why was He there? Next day when the woman went with Dada Kelkar and sat at Baba's Feet, Baba at once said to her, "Where is the necessity of fasting? Go to Dadabhat's house, prepare the dish of Puran Polis (wheat rotis with gram-flour and jaggery (a type of sugar), feed his children and yourself too." Shimga holidays were on. Mrs. Kelkar was then in her menses and there was nobody to cook in Dadabhat's house. So Baba's advice was very timely. Then Mrs. Gokhale had to go to Dadabhat's house and prepare the dish as directed. She cooked that day, fed others and herself. What a good story and how beautiful its import!

Baba's Sircar (Master)

Baba gave a story of his boyhood as follows: - "When I was a youngster, I was in search of bread and went to Beedgaum. There I got embroidery work. I worked hard, sparing no pains. The employer was very much pleased with Me. Three other boys worked before Me. The first got Rs. 50 the second Rs. 100 and the third Rs. 150. And I was given twice the whole of this amount, viz. Rs. 600. After seeing my cleverness, the employer loved me, praised me and honored me with a full dress, a turban for the head and a shell a for the body, etc... I kept this dress intact without using it. I thought that what a man might give does not last long and it is always imperfect. But what My Sircar (God) gives, lasts to the end of time. No other gift from any man can be compared to His. My Sircar says "Take, take," but everybody comes to me and says 'Give, give.' Nobody attends carefully to the meaning of what I say. My Sircar's treasury (spiritual wealth) is full, it is overflowing. I say, "Dig out and take away this wealth in cart-loads, the blessed son of a true mother should fill himself with this wealth. The skill of my Fakir, the Leela of my Bhagwan, and the aptitude of my Sircar is quite unique. What about Me? Body (earth) will mix with earth, breath with air. This time won't come again. I go somewhere, sit somewhere; the hard Maya troubles Me much; still I feel always anxiety for My men. He who does anything (spiritual endeavor) will reap its fruit and he who remembers these words of Mine will get invaluable happiness."

Bow to Shri Sai - Peace be to all

Chapter XXXIII

Greatness of Udi

Scorpion Sting and Plague Cases Cured - Jamner Miracle
Narayanarao's Sickness - Balabuva Sutar - Appasaheb Kulkarni
Haribhau Karnik

In the last Chapter we described the greatness of the Guru;
now in this we will describe the greatness of Udi.

Preliminary

Let us bow now before the great saints. Their merciful glances
will destroy mountains of sins and do away with all the evil taints
of our character. Their casual talk gives us good teachings and
confers on us imperishable happiness. Their minds do not know
any difference such as 'This is ours and that is yours.' Such differentiation never arises in their minds. Their debts (obligations) will
never be repaid by us in this birth as well as in many future births.

Udi

It is well-known that Baba took Dakshina from all, and out of
the amount thus collected, He spent a lot on charity and purchased
fuel with the balance left with Him. This fuel He threw in the
Dhuni - the sacred fire, which he kept ever burning. The ash from
this fire was called Udi and it was freely distributed to the
devotees at the time of their departure from Shirdi.

What did Baba teach or hint by this Udi? Baba taught by His
Udi that all the visible phenomena in the universe are as transient
as the ash. Our bodies composed of wood or matter of the five
elements, will fall down, after all their enjoyments are over, and
be reduced to ashes. In order to remind the devotees of the fact
that their bodies will be reduced to ashes, Baba distributed Udi to
them. Baba also taught by the Udi that the Brahman is the only
Reality and the universe is ephemeral and that no one in this
world, be he a son, father or wife, is really ours. We come here (in
this world) alone and we have to go out alone. It was found and is

even now found out, that the Udi cured many physical and mental maladies, but Baba wanted to din into the devotee's ears the principles of discrimination between the Unreal and the Real, non-attachment for the Unreal, by His Udi and Dakshina. The former (Udi) taught us discrimination and the latter (Dakshina) taught us non-attachment. Unless we have these two things, it is not possible for us to cross over the sea of the mundane existence. So Baba asked for and took Dakshina, and while the devotees took leave, He gave Udi as Prasad, besmeared some of it on the Bhaktas' foreheads and placed His boon conferring hand on their heads. When Baba was in a cheerful mood, He used to sing merrily. One such song was about Udi. The burden of the Udi song was this, "OH, playful Rama, come, come, and bring with you sacks of Udi." Baba used to sing in very clear and sweet tones.

So much about the spiritual implication of Udi, it had also its material significance. It conferred health, prosperity, freedom from anxiety, and many other worldly gains. So the Udi has helped us to gain both our ends - material as well as spiritual. We shall now begin with the stories about the Udi.

Scorpion-Sting

Narayan Motiram Jani of Nasik was a devotee of Baba. He was serving under another devotee of Baba, by name Ramachandra Vaman Modak. Once he went to Shirdi with his mother and saw Baba. Then Baba Himself told her that he (her son) should serve no more, but start independent business. Some days after, this prophecy turned true. Narayan Jani left service and started a boarding house 'Anandashram' which thrived well. Once a friend of this Narayanrao was stung by a scorpion and the pain caused by it, was severe and unbearable. Udi is most efficacious in such cases; it is to be applied on the seat of pain, and so Narayanrao searched for it, but found none. Then he stood before Baba's picture and invoked Baba's aid, chanted Baba's name and taking out a pinch of the ashes of the joss-stick burning in front of Baba's picture and thinking it to be Baba's Udi, applied it on the seat of pain and the sting. As soon as he took out his fingers, the pain vanished and both the person were moved and felt delighted.

Bubonic Plague Case

Once a devotee in Bandra came to know that his daughter, who was staying in another place was down with bubonic plague. He had no Udi with him; so he sent word to Nanasaheb Chandorkar to send the same. Nanasaheb got this message on a road near the Thana Railway Station when he was travelling with his wife to Kalyan. He had no Udi with him at that time. He, therefore, took up some earth from the road, meditated upon Sai Baba, invoked His aid and applied it on the forehead of his wife. The devotee saw all this and when he went to his daughter's house he was very glad to learn that his daughter, who was suffering for three days, began to improve from the very moment Nanasaheb invoked Baba's aid near the Thana Railway Station.

The Jamner Miracle

About 1904-05 Nanasaheb Chandorkar was Mamlatdar at Jamner, in the Khandesh District, which is more than 100 miles distant from Shirdi. His daughter Mainatai was pregnant and was about to deliver. Her case was very serious and she was suffering from labor pains for the last two or three days. Nanasaheb tried all remedies but they proved in vain; he then remembered Baba and invoked His aid.

There in Shirdi, one Ramgirbuva, whom Baba called Bapugirbuva, wanted at this time to go to his native place in Khandesh. Baba called him and told him to take a little rest and stop at Jamner on his way home and give the Udi and Arati to Nanasaheb. Ramgirbuva said that he had only two rupees with him and that amount was barely sufficient for the railway fare up to Jalgaon and it was not possible for him to go from Jalgaon to Jamner, a distance of about 30 miles. Baba assured him that he need not worry, as everything would be provided for him.

Then Baba asked Shama to write the well- known Arati composed by Madhav Adkar (a translation of this is given at the end of this work) and give a copy of it with Udi to Ramgirbuva to be delivered to Nanasaheb. Then relying on Baba's words, Ramgirbuva left Shirdi and reached Jalgaon at about 2:45 a.m., he had only two annas left with him and was in a hard plight. To his great relief he heard somebody calling out "Who is Bapugirbuva of Shirdi?" He went to him and told him that he was the person Bapugirbuva. Then the peon, professing to be sent by Nanasaheb, took him out to an excellent tanga with a good pair of horses. They both drove in it. The tanga ran fast and early in the morning they came to a brooklet. The drive took the horses for watering them and the peon asked Ramgirbuva to partake of some food.

On seeing the beard, moustache and the livery of the peon, Rangirbuva suspected him to be a Muslim and was unwilling to take any refreshments from him, but the peon satisfied him by saying that he was a Hindu, a Kshatriya of Garhwal and that Nanasaheb had sent these refreshments and that there should be no difficulty, nor any doubt about acceptance. Then both of them took the refreshments and started again. They reached Jamner at dawn. Ramgirbuva alighted to attend a call of nature (passing urine) and returned within a few minutes, but found that there was no tanga, no driver and no peon. He was dumbfounded.

Then he went to the neighboring Katcheri and making enquiries, learnt that the Mamlatdar was at home. He went to Nanasaheb's house, and announced himself and gave to Nanasaheb, Baba's Udi and Arati. At this time, Mainatai's case was most serious and all were in deep anxiety about her. Nanasaheb called out his wife and asked her to give the Udi, mixed with water, to their daughter to drink, and sing Baba's Arati. He thought that Baba's help was most opportune. In a few minutes came the news that the delivery was safe and that the crisis had passed away. When Ramgirbuva thanked Nanasaheb for the peon, tanga and the refreshments etc... the latter was greatly surprised as he had sent none to the station, and was not aware of any person coming from Shirdi.

Mr. B.V. Deo of Thana, Retired Mamlatdar, made enquiries about this matter with Bapurao Chandorkar, son of Nanasaheb and Ramgirbuva of Shirdi and after satisfying himself wrote an elaborate article - part prose and part poetry - in Shri Sai Leela magazine (Vol.. 13 Nos. 11, 12 and 13). Brother B.V. Narsimhswami has also taken down the statements of (1) Mainatai (No. V page 14) and (2) Bapusaheb Chandorkar (No. XX page 50) and (3) Ramgirbuva (No. XXVII, Page 83) dated 1st June 1936, 16th September 1936 and December 1936 respectively and published them in his "Devotees' Experiences, Part III." The following is quoted from Ramgirbuva's statement.

"One day Baba called me to him and gave me a packet of Udi and a copy of Baba's Arati. I had to go to Khandesh at the time. Baba directed me to go to Jamner and told me to deliver the Arati and Udi to Nanasaheb Chandorkar, at Jamner. I said to Baba that all I had was Rs. 2, and asked Him how that could take me by train from Kopergaon to Jalgaon and next by cart from Jalgaon to Jamner. Baba said, "God will give." That was Friday and I started at once. I reached Manmad at 7:30 p.m. and Jalgaon at 2:45 a.m. At that time plague regulations were enforced and I had much trouble. I was to discover what I should do to get to Jamner. At about 3 a.m. a peon in boots, turban and well equipped with other details of good dress came to me and took me to a tanga and drove me on. I was in terror. On the way at Bhaghoor, I took refreshments. We reached Jamner early in the morning and by the time I attended my call of nature the tanga (horse carriage) and its driver had disappeared."

Narayanarao

Bhakta Narayanrao (father's name and surname are not given) had the good fortune to see Baba twice during the Latter's lifetime. Three years after the passing away of Baba in 1918, he wanted to come to Shirdi, but he could not come. Within a year of Baba's Mahasamadhi he fell sick and suffered much. All ordinary remedies gave him no relief. So he meditated on Baba day and night. One night he had a vision in his dream. Baba coming to him through a cellar, comforted him saying, "Don't be anxious, you will be improving from tomorrow, and within a week you will be on your legs." Narayanrao got perfectly well within the time mentioned in the vision.

Now the point for consideration is this: - Was Baba living because he had the body, and was He dead because He left it? No, Baba is ever alive, for He transcends both life and death. He who loved Him once wholeheartedly gets response from Him at any time and at any place. He is always by our side and will take any form and appear before the devout Bhakta and satisfy him.

Appasaheb Kulkarni

In 1917 the chance of one Appasaheb Kulkarni came. He was transferred to Thana and began to worship Baba's picture presented to him by Balasaheb Bhate. In real earnest he did the worship. He offered flowers, sandal-paste, and naivedya daily to Baba in the picture and longed intently to see Him. In this connection it may be remarked that seeing Baba's picture earnestly is equivalent to seeing Him in person. The following story illustrates this statement.

Balabuva Sutar

A Saint of Bombay named Balabuva Sutar, who on account of his piety, devotion and bhajan, was called "Modern Tukaram", came to Shirdi for the first time in 1917. When he bowed before Baba, the latter said "I know this man since four years". Balabuva wondered and thought, how could that be, as that was his first trip to Shirdi. But thinking about it seriously he recollected that he had prostrated himself four years ago before Baba's portrait at Bombay and was convinced about the significance of Baba's words. He said to himself, "How omniscient and all-pervading are the Saints and how kind are they to their Bhaktas! I merely bowed to His photo, this fact was noticed by Baba and in due time He made me realize that seeing His photo is equivalent to seeing Him in person!"

Appasaheb Kulkarni

To return to Appasaheb's story. While he was in Thana, he had to go on tour to Bhivandi and was not expected to return within a week. In his absence, the following wonderful thing took place on the third day. At noon a fakir turned up at Appasaheb's house. His features resembled exactly those of Baba's photo. Mrs. Kulkarni and the children all asked him whether he was Sai Baba of Shirdi. He said 'No', but that he was an obedient servant of His and came there at His order to enquire after the health of the family. Then he asked for Dakshina. The lady gave him a rupee. He gave her a small packet of Udi, and asked her to keep this in the shrine along with the photo for worship. Then he left the house and went away. Now hear the wonderful Leela of Sai.

Appasaheb could not proceed with his tour as his horse fell sick at Bhivandi. He returned home that afternoon and learnt from his wife about fakir's visit. He smarted in his mind as he did not get the darshan of the fakir and he did not like that only one rupee was paid as Dakshina. He said that had he been present, he would have offered not less than 10 rupees. Then he immediately started in quest of the fakir and searched for him in the Masjid and other places, without taking any food. His search was in vain. He then returned home and took his food. The reader may remember here Baba's dictum in Chapter 32 that God's quest should not be made on an empty belly. Appasaheb got a lesson, here about this. Then after meals he went out for a walk with a friend Mr. Chitre. Going some distance they saw a man approaching them rapidly.

Appasaheb thought that he must be the fakir that came to his house at noon, as his features tallied with those of baa in the photo. The fakir immediately put forth his hand and asked for Dakshina. Appasaheb gave him a rupee. He demanded again and again and so Appasaheb gave him two more. Still he was not satisfied. Then he borrowed Rs. three from Mr. Chitre and gave them to him. He wanted still more. Appasaheb asked him to accompany him to his home. Then they all returned home and Appasaheb then gave him again three rupees, in all nine. He looked unsatisfied and demanded again. Then he told him that he had a ten rupee note. The fakir asked for the same and took it and returned the nine rupees in cash and went away. Appasaheb had said that he would pay ten rupees and that sum was taken from him and nine rupees, consecrated by Baba's touch, were returned to him. The figure 9 is significant. It denotes the nine types of devotion (vide Chapter 21). It may also be noted here that Baba gave 9 rupees to Laxmibai Shinde at His last moment.

Appasaheb examined the Udi-packet and found that it contained some flower-petals and Akshata (consecrated rice). Then some time afterwards he got hair from Baba when he saw Him at Shirdi. He put the Udi-packet and the hair in a talisman and always wore it on his arm. Appasaheb realized the power of the Udi. Though he was very clever he got Rs. 40 as pay in the beginning, but after he secured Baba's photo and His Udi, he got many times forty rupees per month and also got much power and influence; and along with these temporal benefits, his spiritual progress was also rapid. So those who are fortune enough to get Baba's Udi should, after bath, apply it on the forehead and take some little of it mixed with water in the mouth as holy Tirth (sacred water).

Haribhau Karnik

In 1917 Haribhau Karnik of Dahanu (Thana District) came to Shirdi on Guru Purnima day (in the month of Ashadha) and worshipped Baba with all formality. He offered clothes and Dakshina, and after taking Baba's leave through Shama, went down the steps of the Masjid. Then he thought that he should offer one more rupee to Baba and was just turning to get up when Shama informed him by signs that as he had got Baba's leave, he should go and not return. So he started home. On his way, when he went into the temple of Kala Rama at Nasik for darshan, the Saint Narsing Maharaj who used to sit just inside the big door of the temple, left his Bhaktas there came to Haribhau, caught his wrist and said, "Give me my one rupee". Karnik was surprised.

He paid the rupee most willingly and thought that Sai Baba recovered the rupee, which he intended in his mind to give, through saint Narsing Maharaj. This shows how the saints work in unison.

This story illustrates the fact that all saints are one and shows how they work in unison.

Bow to Shri Sai - Peace be to all

Chapter XXXIV

Greatness of Udi (continued)

(1) Doctor's Nephew - (2) Dr. Pillay - (3) Shama's Sister-in-Law
(4) Irani Girl - (5) Harda Gentleman - (6) Bombay Lady

This Chapter continues the subject "Greatness of Udi" and describes cases in which the application of Udi was most efficacious.

Doctor's Nephew

At Malegaon (Dr. Nasik) there lived a Medical Doctor. His nephew suffered from an incurable disease - Tubercular bone-abscess. The doctor himself and his brothers, all medical practitioners, tried all sorts of remedies and even an operation. There was no relief and there was no end to the little boy's suffering. Friends and relations advised the parents of the boy to seek Divine aid and recommended them to try Sai Baba, who was known to have cured such incurable cases by His mere glance. The parents, therefore, came to Shirdi. They prostrated themselves before Baba, placed the boy before Him and pleaded humbly and respectfully, and implored Him to save their son. The merciful Baba comforted them saying "Those who resort to this Masjid shall never suffer anything in this life and to the end of time. Be now carefree. Apply Udi on the abscess and within one week he will recover. Believe in God. This is no Masjid, but Dwarawati. He who steps here will soon get health and happiness and his sufferings will come to an end". The boy was made to sit before Baba, Who moved his hands on the affected part and cast His loving glances on him. The patient was pleased and with the application of the Udi, he began to recover, and was all right after some days. The parents then left Shirdi with their son, thanking Baba for the cure, which was effected by Udi and Baba's gracious looks.

After knowing this, the doctor, the uncle of the boy became wonder struck and desired to see Baba while he was on his way to Bombay for some business; but at Malegaon and Manmad somebody spoke to him against Baba and poisoned his ears. He therefore, dropped the idea of visiting Shirdi and went to Bombay directly. He wanted to spend the rest of his leave at Alibag, but at Bombay he heard three successive nights, a voice crying out, "Still you disbelieve me?" Then the doctor changed his mind and resolved to go to Shirdi. He had to attend in Bombay to a case of Infectious Fever, which showed no signs of abatement soon. So he thought that his Shirdi trip would be postponed. He however proposed a test in his mind and said, "If the patient gets all right today, I start for Shirdi tomorrow." The wonder is that exactly at the time when the determination was taken, the fever began to abate and the temperature became normal. Then he went to Shirdi as per his determination, took Baba's darshan and prostrated himself before Him. Baba gave him such experiences that he became His devotee. He stayed there for four days and returned home with Baba's Udi and blessings. Within a fortnight he was transferred on promotion to Bijapur. His nephew's case gave him an opportunity for seeing Baba and this visit engendered in him a never failing love for the Saint's feet.

Dr. Pillay

One Dr. Pillay was an intimate Bhakta of Baba. He was much liked by Baba, Who always called him Bhau (brother). Baba talked with him off and on and consulted him in all matters and wanted him always at His side. This Pillay suffered once very badly from guinea worms. He said to Kakasaheb Dixit, "The pain is most excruciating and unbearable. I prefer death to it. This pain, I know, is for repaying past Karma, but go to Baba and tell Him to stop the pain and transfer the working of my past Karma to ten future births of mine." Mr. Dixit went to Baba and told Him his request. Then Baba, being moved by his request, said to Dixit, "Tell him to be fearless. Why should he suffer for ten births? In ten days he can work out the sufferings and consequences of his past Karma. While I am here to give him temporal and spiritual welfare, why should he pray for death? Bring him here on somebody's back and let us work and finish his sufferings once for all."

The doctor was brought in that condition and was seated on

Baba's right side, where Fakir Baba always sat. Baba gave him His bolster and said, "Lie calmly here and be at ease. The true remedy is that the result of past actions has to be suffered and got over. Our Karma is the cause of our happiness and sorrow; therefore put up with whatever comes to you. Allah (God) is the sole Dispenser and Protector, always think of Him. He will take care of you. Surrender to His feet with body, mind, wealth and speech, i.e. completely and then see what He does." Dr. Pillay said in return that Nanasaheb had put a bandage over the leg, but he found no relief. "Nana is a fool" replied Baba. "Take off that bandage or else you will die. Now a crow will come and peck you, and then you will recover."

While this conversation was going on, one Abdul, who always cleaned the Masjid and trimmed the lamps, turned up. While he was attending to his work of training, his foot accidentally fell upon the stretched leg of Dr. Pillay. The leg was already swollen and when Abdul's foot fell upon it and pressed it, all the seven guinea worms were squeezed out at once. The pain was unbearable and Dr. Pillay bawled out loudly. After some time, he calmed down and began to sing and cry alternately. Then Pillay enquired when the crow was coming and peeking. Baba said, "Did you not see the crow? He won't come again. Abdul was the crow. Now go and rest yourself in the Wada and you will be soon all right."

By application of the Udi and by taking it in the stomach with water, and without taking any other treatment or medicine, the disease was completely cured in ten days as predicted by Baba.

Shama's Sister-in-law

Shama's younger brother Bapaji was staying near Sawool well. Once his wife was attacked with Bubonic plague, she had high fever and two buboes (swollen lymph nodes) in her groin. Bapaji rushed to Shama at Shirdi and asked him to come and help. Shama was frightened, but according to his wont, he went to Baba, prostrated himself before Him, invoked His aid, and requested Him to cure the case. He also asked His permission to go to his brother's house. Then Baba said, "Don't go there at this late hour (night), send her Udi. Why care for the fever and buboes? God is our father and master; she will be alright easily.

Do not go now, but go there in the morning and return immediately."

Shama had full faith in Baba's Udi. It was sent with Bapaji. It was applied on the buboes and some of it was mixed with water and was given to the patient for drinking. No sooner was it taken in, than perspiration set in profusely, the fever abated and the patient had a good sleep. Next morning Bapaji was surprised to see his wife alright and refreshed with no fever and buboes. When Shama went there next morning with Baba's permission he was also surprised to see her at the hearth and preparing tea. On questioning his brother, he learnt that Baba's Udi cured her completely in one night. Then Shama realized the significance of Baba's words. "Go there in the morning and return immediately".

After taking tea, Shama returned and after saluting Baba said, "Deva, what is this play of Yours? You first raise a storm and make us restless and then calm it down and ease us". Baba replied "You see mysterious is the path of action. Though I do nothing, they hold Me responsible for the actions which take place on account of Adrista (destiny). I am only their witness. The Lord is the sole Doer and Inspirer. He is also most merciful. Neither I am God nor Lord. I am His obedient servant and remember Him often. He, who casts aside his egoism, thanks Him and he, who trusts Him entirely, will have his shackles removed and will obtain liberation".

Irani's Daughter

Now read the experience of an Irani gentleman. His young daughter got fits every hour. When the convulsion came she lost her power of speech, her limbs got shrunk and contracted and she fell down senseless. No remedy gave her any relief. Some friend recommended Baba's Udi to her father and asked him to get it from Kakasaheb Dixit at Vile Parle (a suburb of Bombay). Then the Irani gentleman got the Udi and gave it mixed with water to his daughter daily for drinking. In the beginning the convulsions, which were coming on hourly, came every seven hours and after a few days the daughter recovered completely.

Harda Gentleman

An old gentleman of Harda (C.P) was suffering from a stone in his bladder. Such stones are generally removed by surgical operations and people recommended him to undergo one. He was old and weak, lacked strength of mind and could not think of submitting himself to surgical treatment. His suffering was soon to end in another way. The Inamdar (City Officer) of that town happened to come there at this time. He was a devotee of Baba and had always a stock of Udi with him. On the recommendation of friends, his son got some Udi from and mixing it with water, gave it to his old father to drink. Within five minutes the Udi was assimilated, the stone was dissolved and came out through his urine and old man was soon relieved.

Bombay Lady

A woman of the Kayastha Prabhu caste in Bombay always suffered terrible pain at her delivery. She was very much frightened each time she became pregnant and did not know what to do. Shri Rama-Maruti of Kalyan, who was a devotee of Baba, advised her husband to take her to Shirdi for a painless delivery. When she next became pregnant, both husband and wife came to Shirdi, stayed there for some months and worshipped Baba and got all the benefit of His company. After some time the hour of delivery came and as usual there was obstruction in the passage from the womb. She began to suffer labor pains, did not know what to do, but began to pray to Baba for relief. In the meantime, some neighboring women turned up and after invoking Baba's aid, gave her the Udi mixture to drink. In five minutes, the woman delivered safely and painlessly. The issue was still-born according to its fate; but the mother who got rid of the anxiety and pain, thanked Baba for the safe delivery and ever remained grateful to Him.

Bow to Shri Sai - Peace to be all

Chapter XXXV

Tested and Never Found Wanting
Kaka Mahajani's Friend and Master - Bandra Insomnia Case
Bala Patil Newaskar

This Chapter also continues the subject of the importance of the Udi; it also gives two cases in which Baba was tested and not found wanting. These cases will be taken up first.

Preliminary

In spiritual matters or endeavors, sectarianism is the greatest bar to our progress. Those, who believe the God is without form, are heard saying that to believe the God is with the form is an illusion and that the Saints are only human beings. Then why should they bend their heads before them and offer Dakshina? Persons belonging to other sects will also raise objections and say, "Why should they bow and offer allegiance to other Saints, leaving their Sadgurus?" Similar objections regarding Sai Baba were heard before and are heard even now. Some said that when they went to Shirdi, Baba asked for Dakshina from them. Is it good that Saints should collect money in this fashion? If they do so, where is their Sainthood? But there are many instances where men went to Shirdi to scoff; but remained there to pray. Two such instances are given below.

Kaka Mahajani's Friend

A friend of Kaka Mahajani was a worshipper of God without form and was averse to idolatry. Out of curiosity he agreed to go to Shirdi with Kaka Mahajani on two conditions, viz., (1) that he would neither bow to Baba, (2) nor pay Him any Dakshina. Kaka agreed to these conditions and they both left Bombay on a Saturday night and reached Shirdi the next morning. As soon as they put their feet on the steps of the Masjid, Baba, looking at the friend from a little distance, addressed him in sweet words as follows, "Oh, welcome sir". The tone that uttered these words was a very peculiar one. It exactly resembled the tone of the friend's father. It reminded him of his departed father and sent a thrill of joy through his body. What an enchanting power the tone had! Being surprised the friend said, "This is no doubt the voice of my father". Then he at once up and, forgetting his resolution, placed his head upon Baba's Feet.

Then Baba asked for Dakshina twice, once in the morning and again at noon at the time of their taking leave; but He asked it from Kaka only and not from the friend. The latter whispered to Kaka, "Baba asked for Dakshina from you twice. I am with you, why does He omit me?" You ask Baba Himself" was Kaka's reply. Baba asked Kaka what his friend was whispering, and then the friend asked Baba himself whether he should pay any Dakshina. Baba replied, "You had no mind to pay, so you were not asked; but if you want to pay now you may." Then the friend paid Rs.17 as Dakshina, the same amount that Kaka paid. Baba then addressed him a few words of advice, "You do away, destroy the Teli's wall (sense of difference) between us, so that we can see and meet each other face to face". Then Baba allowed them to depart. Thought the weather was cloudy and threatening, Baba assured them of their safe journey and both of them reached Bombay safely. When he reached home and opened the door and windows of his house, he found two sparrows fallen dead on the ground and one just flying out through a window. He thought that if he had left the windows open, two sparrows would have been saved, but thought again, that they had met their lot and that Baba had sent him back soon just to save the third sparrow.

Kaka Mahajani's Master

Kaka was the Manager in the firm of Thakkar Dharmasey Jethabhai, a solicitor of Bombay. Both the Master and the Manager were on intimate terms. Mr. Thakkar knew that Kaka was often going to Shirdi, staying there for some days and returning, when Baba permitted him. Out of curiosity and just to test Baba, Mr. Thakkar decided to go to Shirdi with Kaka during Shimga holidays. As Kaka's return was uncertain, he took another man with him as an associate. The three started together and Kaka bought two seers of raisins (dried grapes with seed) on the way for presentation to Baba. They reached Shirdi in due time, and went to the Masjid for darshan.

Babasaheb Tarkhad was there, Mr. Thakkar asked him why he came there. "For darshan", Tarkhad replied. Mr. Thakkar asked if miracles took place there. Tarkhad replied that it (to see miracles) was not his attitude, but the earnest intentions of the Bhaktas were satisfied here. Then Kaka prostrated himself before Baba and offered the raisins to Him. Baba ordered them to be distributed. Mr. Thakkar got a few of them. He did not like the raisins and he was advised by his doctor not to eat them without washing and cleaning them. So he was in a fix. He did not like to eat them, nor could he reject them. To keep up formalities, he put them into his mouth, but did not know what to do with the seeds. He could not spit them out on the floor of the Masjid, so he pocketed them against his wish. He then said in his mind that if Baba was a Saint, how could He be ignorant of his dislike for the raisins and could He force them on him. When this thought arose in his mind Baba again gave him some more raisins. He could not eat them, but held them in his hand. Then Baba asked him to eat them up. He obeyed and found, to his surprise, that they were all seedless. He wanted to see miracles and here was one. He knew that Baba read his thought; and as per his wish converted raisins (with seeds) into seedless grapes. What a wonderful power!

Again to test further he asked Tarkhad, who was sitting by and who also got some raisins, "What kind of grapes you got?" He replied "They variety with seeds." Mr. Thakkar was still more surprised to hear this. Then to confirm his growing faith Thakkar thought in his mind that if Baba was a real Saint, the raisins should be now given to Kaka first. Reading this thought also, Baba ordered that distribution should be commenced from Kaka. These proofs were sufficient for Thakkar.

Then Shama introduced Mr. Thakkar as the master of Kaka, upon which Baba said, "How could he be his master? He has got a different Master altogether". Kaka appreciated this reply. Forgetting his resolve, Thakkar saluted Baba and returned to the Wada.

After the noon-Arati was over, they all went to the Masjid for taking Baba's leave for their departure. Shama spoke for them. Baba then spoke as follows:

"There was a fickle-minded gentleman. He had health and

wealth and was free from both physical and mental afflictions, but he took on him needless anxieties and burdens and wandered hither and thither, thus losing his peace of mind. Sometimes he dropped the burdens and at other times carried them again. His mind knew no steadiness. Seeing his state, I took pity on him and said, "Now please keep your faith on any one place (point) you like, why roam like this? Stick quietly to one place".

Thakkar at once came to know that, that was an exact description of himself. He wished that Kaka should also return with him but no one expected that Kaka would be allowed to leave Shirdi so soon. Baba read also this thought to his and permitted Kaka to return with his master. Thakkar got one more proof of Baba's capacity to read another's mind. Then Baba asked Kaka for Rs. 15 as Dakshina and received it. To Kaka He said, "If I take one rupee as Dakshina from anybody I have to return it tenfold to him. I never take anything gratis. I never ask any one indiscriminately. I only ask and take from him whom the Fakir (My Guru) points out. If anyone is indebted formerly to the Fakir money is received from him. The donor gives, i.e. sows his seeds, only to reap a rich harvest in future. Wealth should be the means to work out Dharma. If it is used for personal enjoyment, it is wasted. Unless you have given it before, you do not get it now. So the best way to receive is to give. The giving of Dakshina advances Vairagya (Non-attachment) and thereby Bhakti and Jnana. Give one and receive tenfold".

On hearing these words Mr. Thakkar himself gave Rs.15 in Baba's hand, forgetting his resolve not to do so. He thought he did well in coming to Shirdi as all his doubts were solved and he learnt so much.

Baba's skill in handling such cases was unique. Though He did all those things He was totally non-attached to them. Whether anybody saluted Him or not, or whether anybody gave Him Dakshina or not, it was the same to Him. None He disrespected. He felt no pleasure because He was worshipped and no pain because He was disregarded. He transcended the pairs of opposites, viz. pleasure and pain, etc...

Insomnia Case

A Kayastha Prabhu gentleman of Bandra suffered from Insomnia for long. As soon as he laid himself down for sleep, his departed father appeared to him in his dream, and abused and scolded him severely. This broke his sleep and made him restless the whole night. Every night this went on and the man did not know what to do. One day he consulted a devotee of Baba in this respect. He recommended the Udi as the only infallible remedy he knew. He gave him some Udi and asked him to apply a little of it to his forehead before going to bed and keep the Udi-packet under the pillow. He tried this remedy, and found to his great surprise and joy, that he got sound sleep and that there was no disturbance of any kind. He continued the remedy and always remembered Sai. Then he got a picture of Sai Baba which he hung on the wall near his pillow and started worshipping it daily and on Thursdays, offering garland, naivedya etc... Then he got on well and forgot altogether his past trouble.

Balaji Patil Newaskar

This man was a great devotee of Baba. He rendered most excellent and disinterested service. Every day he swept and kept clean all the passages and streets in Shirdi through which Baba passed in His daily routine. This work was, after him, equally well-done by another female devotee named Rahda-Krishna-Mai, and after her by Abdoola. When Balaji reaped his corn every year, he brought the whole quantity and presented it to Baba. He returned with what Baba gave him and maintained himself and his family with it. This course was followed by him for many years and after him by his son.

Power and Efficacy of Udi

Once it happened that at Balaji's death anniversary day, a certain number of guests were invited and the dinner was prepared for them. But at the dinner-time it was found that thrice the number of people invited had turned up. Mrs. Newaskar was in a fix. She thought that the food would not suffice for the people assembled and that if it fell short, the honor of the family would be at stake. Her mother-in-law comforted her by saying, "Don't be afraid, it is not ours, but Sai's food; cover every vessel with cloth, putting some Udi in it, and serve from the same without opening it: Sai will save us from ignominy." She did as she was advised and it was found to their surprise and joy that not only did the food suffice for all, but plenty of it remained after serving. "As one feels intently, so he realizes accordingly" was proved in this case.

Sai Appearing as Serpent

Once Raghu Patil of Shirdi went to Balaji Patil at Newase, that evening he found that a serpent entered the cowshed hissing. All the cattle were afraid and began to move. The inmates of the house were frightened, but Balaji thought that it was Sai who appeared in his house as a serpent. Without being afraid in the least he brought a cup of milk and placing it before the serpent said, "Baba, why do you miss and make noise? Do you want to frighten us? Take this cup of milk and drink it with a calm mind". Saying this, he sat close by unperturbed. The other members were frightened and did not know what to do. In a short time the serpent disappeared. Nobody knew where it went. It was not found though a search was made in the cowshed.

Balaji had two wives and some children. They sometimes went to Shirdi from Newase for taking Baba's darshan. Then Baba bought saris and other clothes which were given to them with His blessings.

Bow to Shri Sai - peace be to all

Chapter XXXVI

Wonderful Stories of (1) Two Goa Gentleman And (2) Mrs. Aurangabadkar

This Chapter relates the wonderful stories of two gentlemen from Goa and Mrs. Aurangabadkar of Sholapur.

Two Gentlemen

Once two gentlemen came from Goa for taking darshan of Sai Baba, and prostrated themselves before him. Though both came together, Baba asked only one them to give Him Rs.15 as Dakshina which was paid willingly. The other man voluntarily offered Rs. 35. This sum was rejected by Baba to the astonishment of all. Shama, who was present, asked Baba, "What is this? Both came together, one's Dakshina you accept, the other, though voluntarily paid, you refuse. Why this distinction? Baba replied, "Shama, you know nothing. I take nothing from anybody. The Masjidmayi (The presiding Deity of the Masjid) calls for the debt; the donor pays it and becomes free. Have I any home, property or family to look after? I require nothing. I am ever free. Debt, enmity and murder have to be atoned for, there is not escape". Baba then continued in His characteristic way as follows:

As first he was poor and took a vow to his God that he would pay his first month's salary if he got an appointment. He got one on Rs.15 p.m. Then he steadily got promotions, from Rs.15 he got Rs. 30, 60, 100, 200 and ultimately Rs.700 per month. But in his prosperity he forgot clean the vow he took. The force of his karma has driven him here and I asked that amount (Rs.15) from him as Dakshina.

Another story, While wandering by the sea-side I came to a huge mansion and sat on its verandah. The owner gave me a good reception and fed me sumptuously. He showed me a neat and clean place near a cupboard for sleeping. I slept there. While I was sound asleep, the man removed a Laterite slab and broke the wall entered in and scissored off all the money from my pocket. When I woke up, I found that Rs.30,000 were stolen. I was

212

greatly distressed and sat weeping and moaning. The money was in currency notes and I thought that the Brahmin had stolen it. I lost all interest in food and drink and sat for a fortnight on the verandah, bemoaning my loss. After the fortnight was over, a passing fakir saw me crying, and made enquiries regarding the cause of my sorrow. I told him everything. He said, "If you act according to my bidding, you will recover your money; go to a fakir, I shall give his whereabouts, surrender yourself to him, he will get back your money; in the meanwhile give up your favorite food till you recover your money." I followed the fakir's advice and got my money. Then I left the Wada and went to the sea-shore. There was a steamer, but I could not get into it as it was crowded. There a good- natured peon interceded for me and I got in luckily. That brought me to another shore, where I caught a train and came to the Masjidmayi.

The story finished and Baba asked Shama to take the guests and arrange for their feeding. Then Shama took them home and fed them. At dinner, Shama said to the guests that Baba's story was rather mysterious, as He had never gone to the seaside, never had any money (Rs.30,000), never travelled, never lost any money and never recovered it, and enquired whether they under-stood it and caught its significance. The guests were deeply moved and were shedding tears. In a choking voice they said that Baba was omniscient, infinite, the One (Para Brahma) without a second. The story He gave out is exactly our story, What He spoke has already taken place in our case. How He knew this, is a won-der of wonders! We shall give all the details after the meals.

Then after the meals while they were chewing betel-leaves, the guests began to tell their stories. One of them said:

"A hill station on the ghats is my native place. I went to Goa to earn my living by securing a job. I took a vow to God Datta that if I got any service, I would offer Him my first month's sala-ry. By His grace I got an appointment of Rs.15 and then I got promotions as described by Baba. I did forget all about my vow. Baba has just reminded me of it in this way and recovered Rs. 15 from me. It is not Dakshina as one may think it to be, but a re-payment of an old debt and fulfillment of long forgotten vow".

Moral

Baba never, in fact, actually begged any money, nor allowed His Bhaktas to beg. He regarded money as a danger or bar to spiritual progress and did not allow His Bhaktas to fall into its clutches. Bhagat Mhalsapati is an instance on this point. He was very poor and could hardly make both ends meet. Baba never allowed him to make any money, nor gave him anything from the Dakshina amount. Once a kind and liberal merchant named Hansaraj gave a large amount of money to Mhalsapati in Baba's presence, but Baba did not allow him to accept it.

Then the second guest began his tale. "My Brahmin (cook) was serving me faithfully for 35 years. Unfortunately he fell into bad ways, his mind changed and he robbed me of my treasure. By removing a laterite slab from my wall where my cup-board is fixed, he came in while we were all asleep and carried away all my accumulated wealth, Rs. 30,000 in currency notes. I know not how Baba mentioned the exact amount. I sat crying day and night. My enquiries came to nothing. I spent a fortnight in great anxiety. As I sat on the verandah, sad and dejected, a passing fakir noted my condition and enquired of its cause, and I told him all about it. He told me that an Avalia by name Sai lives in Shirdi, Kopergaon Taluka. Make vow to Him and give up any food that you like best and say to Him mentally that 'I have given up eating that food till I take your darshan'. Then I took the vow and gave up eating rice and said, "Baba, I will eat it after recovering my property and after taking your darshan".

Fifteen days passed after this. The Brahmin, of his own accord, came to me, returned my money and apologized, saying, "I went mad and acted thus; I now place my head on your feet, please forgive me". Thus everything ended well. The fakir that met me and helped me was not seen again. An intensive desire to see Sai Baba, whom the fakir pointed out to me, arose in my mind. I thought that the fakir who came all the way to my house was no other than Sai Baba. Would He, who saw me and helped me to get my lost money ever covet to get Rs.35? On the contrary without expecting anything from us, He always tries His best to lead us on the path of spiritual progress.

I was overjoyed when I recovered my stolen property and being infatuated, I forgot all about my vow. Then when I was at Colaba, one night I saw Sai Baba in my dream. This reminded me of my promised visit to Shirdi. I went to Goa and from there wanted to start for Shirdi, by taking a steamer to Bombay, en route. But when I came to the harbor, I found that the steamer was crowded and there was no place. The captain did not allow me, but on the intercession of a peon, who was stranger to me, I was allowed to get into the steamer which brought me to Bombay. From there, I got in the train and came here. Surely I think that Baba is all-pervading and all-knowing. What are we and where is our home? How great our good fortune that Baba got back our money and drew us here to Himself? You Shirdi folk must be infinitely superior and more fortunate than we; for Baba has played, laughed, talked and lived with you for so many years. I think that your store of good merits must be infinite, for it attracted Baba into Shirdi. Sai is our Datta. He ordered the vow. He gave me a seat in the steamer and brought me here and thus gave proof of His omniscience and omnipotence".

Mrs. Aurangabadkar

A lady from Sholapur, wife of Sakharam Aurangabadkar had no issue during the long period of 27 years. She had made a number of vows of Gods and Goddesses for an issue, but was not successful. She then became almost hopeless. To make a last attempt in this matter, she came to Shirdi with her step-son Vishwanath and stayed there for two months, serving Baba. Whenever she went to the Masjid, she found it full and Baba surrounded by devotees. She wanted to see Baba alone, fall at His feet and open her heart and pray for an issue, but she got no suitable opportunity.

Ultimately she requested Shama to intercede with Baba for her when He was alone. Shama said to her that Baba's Darbar was open, still he would try for her and that the Lord might bless her. He asked her to sit ready with a cocoa-nut and joss-sticks on the open courtyard at the time of Baba's meals and that when he beckoned to her, she should come up. One day after dinner, Shama was rubbing Baba's wet hands with a towel when the latter pinched Shama's cheek. Shama feigning anger said, "Deva is it proper for you to pinch me like this? We don't want such a mischievous God who pinches us thus. Are we Your dependents, is this the fruit of our intimacy?" Baba replied, "Oh Shama, during the 72 generations that you were with me, I never pinched you till now and now you resent my touching you". Shama, "We want a God that will give us ever kisses and sweets to eat; we do not want any respect from You, or heaven, balloon etc... Let our faith unto Your Feet be ever wide-awake". Baba, "Yes, I have indeed come for that. I have been feeding and nursing you and have got love and affection for you".

Then Baba went up and took his seat. Shama beckoned to the lady. She came up, bowed and presented the cocoa-nut and joss-sticks. Baba shook the cocoa-nut which was dry. The Kernal within rolled and made a noise. Baba said, "Shama, this is rolling, see what it says". Shama, "The woman prays that a child might be similarly rolling and quickening in the womb. So give her the coconut with Your blessings".

Baba, "Will the coconut give her any issue? How people are foolish and fancy such things!"

Shama, "I know the power of Your word and blessing. Your word will give her a string or series of children. You are wrangling and not giving real blessing".

The parley went on for a while, Baba repeatedly ordering to break the coconut and Shama pleading for the gift of the unbroken fruit to the lady. Finally Baba yielded and said, "She will have an issue". "When?" asked Shama. "In 12 months" was the reply. The coconut was therefore broken into two part, one was eaten by the two, and the other was given to the lady.

The Shama turned up to the lady and said, "Dear madam, you are a witness to my words. If within twelve months you do not get any issue, I will break a coconut against this Deva's head and drive him out of this Masjid. If I fail in this, I will not call myself Madhav. You will soon realize what I say".

She delivered a son in one year's time and the son was brought to Baba in his fifth month. Both husband and wife prostrated themselves before Baba and the grateful father (Mr. Aurangabad-kar) paid a sum of Rs.500 which was spent in constructing a shed for Baba's house "Shyamakarna".

Bow to Shri Sai - Peace be to all

216

Chapter XXVII Chavadi Procession

In this chapter Hemadpant after making some preliminary observations on some points of Vedanta, describes the Chavadi procession.

Preliminary

Blessed is Sai's life, blessed is His daily routine. His ways and actions are indescribable. Sometimes He was intoxicated with Brahmanand (divine joy), and at other times content with Self-knowledge. Doing so many things sometimes, He was unconcerned with them. Though He seemed at times quite action-less (doing nothing) He was not idle or dozing; He always abided in His own Self. Though He looked calm and quiet as the placid sea, He was deep and unfathomable. Who can describe His ineffable nature? He regarded men as brothers, women as sisters and mothers. He was a perfect and perpetual celibate as everybody knows. May the understanding (knowledge), we got in His company, last long unto death. Let us ever serve Him with whole-hearted devotion to His feet. Let us see Him (God) in all beings and let us ever love His name.

Hemadpant, after making some lengthy dissertations on some topics of Vedanta, which he himself considers as a digression, goes on to describe the Chavadi procession.

Chavadi Procession

Baba's dormitory has been already described. One day He slept in the Masjid and on the next, in the Chavadi (a small building containing a room or two near the Masjid). This alternate sleeping in both these buildings went on till Baba's Mahasamadhi. From 10th December 1909 devotees began to offer regular worship to Baba in the Chavadi. This we will now describe with His grace. When the turn of retiring to the Chavadi came, people flocked to the Masjid and made bhajan in the mandap (courtyard) for a few hours. Behind them was a beautiful Ratha (small car), to the right a Tulsi Vrindavan (planter with holy Tulsi) and in front

217

Baba, and between these the devotees fond of bhajan.

Men and women who had a liking for the bhajan came in time. Some took Tal, Chiplis and Kartal, Mridang, Khanjiri and Ghol (all musical instruments) in their hands and conducted the bhajan. Sai Baba was the Magnet Who drew all the devotees to Him there. Outside in the open, some trimmed their divatyas, (torches), some decorated the palanquin, and some stood with cane-sticks in their hands and uttered cries of victory to Baba. The corner was decorated with buntings. Round about the Masjid, rows of burning lamps shed their light. Baba's horse 'Shyamakarna' stood fully decorated outside.

Then Tatya Patil came with a party of men to Baba and asked Him to be ready. Baba sat quiet in his place till Tatya came and helped Him to get up by putting his arm under Baba's armpit. Tatya called Baba by the name of Mama. Really their relationship was extremely intimate. Baba wore on his body the usual kafni, took His satka (short stick) under His arm-pit and after taking His chillum (a clay pipe used by sadhus for smoking cannabis) and cannabis and placing a cloth over His shoulder became ready to start. Then Tatya threw a golden embroidered beautiful Shela (Shawl) over His body.

After this, Baba then moved a little the bundle of fuel sticks lying behind with His right toe and then extinguishing the burning lamp with His right hand, started for the Chavadi. Then all sorts of musical instruments, tashe, band and horns and mridang, gave out their different sounds; and fireworks exhibited their different and various colored views. Men and women singing Baba's name started walking, singing bhajans to the accompaniment of mridang and veena. Some danced with joy and some carried various flags and standards. The Bhaldars announced Baba's name when He came on the steps of the Masjid.

On the two sides of Baba stood persons, who held chavaris (an ornate fan) and others who fanned Baba. On the way were spread folds of cloth on which Baba walked on, being supported by devotees' hands. Tatyaba held the left hand and Mhalasapati the right and Bapusaheb Jog held the chhatra (umbrella) over His head. In this fashion Baba marched on to the Chavadi. The fully decorated red horse, named Shyamakarna led the way and behind

218

him were all the carriers, waiters, musical players and the crowd of devotees. Hari-nama (the name of the Lord) chanted to the accompaniment of music rent the skies as also the name of Sai. In this manner the procession reached the corner when all the persons that joined this party seemed well pleased and delighted.

On coming to this corner Baba stood facing the Chavadi and shone with a peculiar lustre. It seemed, as if the face of Baba glittered like dawn, or like the glory of the rising sun. Baba stood there with a concentrated mind, facing the north, as if He was calling somebody. All the instruments played their music while Baba moved His right arm up and down for some time. Kakasaheb Dixit at this time came forward with a silver plate containing flowers besmeared with gulal (red powder) and threw them on Baba's body off and on. The musical instruments played their best at this juncture and Baba's face beamed with steady and added radiance and beauty, and all the persons drank this lustre to their hearts' content. Words fail to describe the scene and splendor of this occasion.

Some times Mhalasapati began to dance being possessed or obsessed by some deity, but all were surprised to see that Baba's concentration was not in the least disturbed. With a lantern in his hand Tatya Patil walked on Baba's left side and Bhagat Mhalasapati on the right, holding with his hand the hem of Baba's garment. What a beautiful procession and what an expression of devotion! To witness this, men and women, poor and rich, flocked together there. Baba walked very slow. Bhaktas followed on both sides with love and devotion. With joy pervading the whole atmosphere of the place, the procession reached the Chavadi. That scene and those days are gone now. Nobody can see them now or in the future; still remembering and visualizing that scene and sight, we can bring solace and comfort to our minds.

The Chavadi was also fully decorated with a good white ceiling, mirrors and many sorts of lamps. On reaching it Tatya went ahead and spread an asan (multi-layered mat or seat for a holy person) and placing a bolster, made Baba sit there and made Him wear good angaraksha (coat). Then the devotees worshipped Him in various ways. They put on His head a mugut (crown) with a tuft above, placed garlands of flowers and jewels round His neck and marking His forehead with musk-mixed vertical lines and a dot (as Vaishnava devotees do) they stared at Him for long to their hearts' content. They changed His head-dress now and then and held it aloft on the head, fearing that Baba might throw it away. Baba knew the heart of them all and meekly submitted to all their methods without objection. With these decorations He looked wonderfully beautiful.

Nanasaheb Nimonkar held the Chhatra (umbrella) with its beautiful pendants which moved in a circle with its supporting stick. Bapusaheb Jog washed the feet of Baba in a silver dish and offered 'arghya' and worship with due formalities, then besmeared His arms with sandal paste, and offered tambul (betel-leaves). Baba sat on the asan (gadi - cushion throne), while Tatya and others kept standing and falling at His feet. When Baba sat on the gadi supporting Himself against the bolster, devotees on both sides waved chamars and fans. Shama then prepared the chillum and handed it over to Tatyaba who drew a flame out of it by his breath and then gave it to Baba. After Baba had His smoke, it was given to Bhagat Mhalasapati and then it was passed round to all.

Blessed was the inanimate chillum. It had first to undergo many ordeals of penance, such as being treated by the clay pot-makers, dried in the open sun and burnt in fire and then it had the good fortune to get the contact of Baba's hand and His kiss. After this function was over, devotees put garlands of flowers on His neck and gave Him nosegays (small bouquets of flowers) and bunches of flowers for smelling. Baba who was dis-passion or non-attachment incarnate, cared a fig for all these necklaces of jewels, and garlands of flowers and other decorations; but out of real love to His devotees, He allowed them to have their own way and to please themselves. Finally Bapusaheb Jog waved the arati over Baba, observing all formalities, the musical instruments playing their auspicious tunes.

When this arati was over, the devotees returned home one by one saluting Baba and taking His leave. When Tatya Patil, after offering chillum, attar (scent) and rosewater, rose to depart, Baba said to him lovingly - "Guard Me, go if you like, but return sometimes at night and enquire after Me." Replying in the affirmative Tatyaba left the Chavadi and went home. Then Baba Himself prepared His bed. He arranged 50 or 60 sadha chadders (plain shawls made of fine white cashmere without any ornament) one upon another and thus making His bed, went to rest.

We shall also now take rest and close this chapter with a request to the readers that they should remember Sai Baba and His Chavadi procession daily before they retire and go to bed.

Bow to Shri Sai - Peace be to all

Chapter XXXVIII

Baba's Handi - Disrespect of Shrine - Kala or Hodge-Podge
& Cup of Butter-Milk

In the last chapter we described Baba's Chavadi procession. In
this we take up Baba's Handi (cooking pot) and some other
subjects.

Preliminary

Oh, blessed Sadguru Sai, we bow to You, Who have given
happiness to the whole world, accomplished the welfare of the
devotees and have removed the affliction of those who have resorted to Your Feet. Being very liberal and being the protector and
savior of the Bhaktas who surrender themselves to You, You
incarnate yourself in this world to oblige the people and do them
good. The liquid essence of Pure Self was poured into the mould
of Brahma and out of this has come out the crest-jewel of the
saints: Sai. This Sai is Atmarama Himself. He is the abode of
perfect divine bliss.

Having Himself attained all objects of life, He made His
devotees desire less and free.

Baba's Handi

Different sadhanas (means of accomplishments) are prescribed in our scriptures for different yugas (epoch or era within a
four age cycle). Tapas (Penance) is recommended for Krita or
Satya Yuga (Golden Age), Jnana (Knowledge) for Treta Yuga
(Silver Age), Yajna (Sacrifice) for Dwapara Yuga Bronze Age)
and Dana (Charity) for Kali Yuga (Iron Age - the present age on earth).
Of all the charities, giving food is the best one. We are much perturbed when we get no food at noon. Other beings feel similarly
under similar circumstances. Knowing this, he who gives food to
the poor and hungry, is the best donor or charitable person.

The Taittiriya Upanishad says that "Food is Brahma; from
food all the creatures are born and having been born, by food they
live, and having departed, into food again they enter." When an

Atithi (uninvited guest) comes to our door at noon, it is our duty to welcome him by giving him food. Other kinds of charities, viz., giving away wealth, property and clothes etc.., require some discrimination, but in the matter of food, no such consideration is necessary. Let anybody come to our door at noon, he should be served forthwith; and if lame, crippled, blind and diseased paupers come, they should be fed first and the able bodied persons and our relations afterwards. The merit of feeding the former is much greater than that of feeding the latter.

Other kinds of charities are imperfect without this Annadanam (giving of food) as stars are without the moon, a necklace without its central medal, a crown without pinnacle, a tank without a lotus, bhajan without love, a married lady without the kumkummark, singing without a sweet voice or butter-milk without salt. Just as varan (lentil or dal soup) excels all other dishes, Annadanam is the best of all merits. Now let us see how Baba prepared food and distributed it.

It has been stated before that Baba required very little food for Himself and what little He wanted, was obtained by begging from a few houses. But when He took it into His mind to distribute food to all, He made all preparations from beginning to end, Himself. He depended on nobody and troubled none in this matter. First He went to the bazaar and bought all the things, corn, flour, spices etc.., for cash. He did also the grinding. In the open courtyard of the Masjid, He arranged a big hearth and after lighting a fire underneath kept a Handi over it with a proper measure of water. There were two kinds of Handi, one small and the other big. The former provided food for 50 persons, the later for 100.

Sometimes He cooked 'Mitthe Chaval' (sweet rice), and at other times 'pulava' with meat. At times in the boiling varan (soup), He let in small balls of thick or flat breads of wheat flour. He pounded the spices on a stone slab, and put the thin pulverized spices into the cooking pot. He took all the pains to make the dishes very palatable. He prepared 'Ambil' by boiling jawari flour in water and mixing it with butter milk. With the food He distributed this Ambil to all alike.

To see whether the food was properly cooked or not, Baba rolled up the sleeve of His Kafni and put His bare arm in the boiling cauldron without the least fear, and churned (moved) the whole mass from side to side and up and down. There was no mark of burn on His arm, nor fear on His face. When the cooking was over, Baba got the pots in the Masjid, and had them duly consecrated by the Moulvi (Iman - Muslim leader).

First He sent part of the food as prasad to Mhalasapati and Tatya Patil and then He served the remaining contents with His own hand to all the poor and helpless people to their hearts' content. Really blessed and fortunate must be those people who got food prepared by Baba and served by Him.

Somebody may raise a doubt here and ask - "Did Baba distribute vegetable and animal food as prasad alike to all His devotees?" The answer is plain and simple. Those who were accustomed to eating animal food were given food from the Handi as prasad and those who were not so accustomed, were not allowed to touch it. He never created in them any wish or desire to indulge in this food.

There is a principle well established that when a Guru himself gives anything as prasad, the disciple who thinks and doubts whether it is acceptable or otherwise, goes to perdition. In order to see how any disciple has imbibed this principle, Baba at times proposed tests. For instance, on an Ekadashi day He gave some rupees to Dada Kelkar and asked him to go in person to Koralha to get mutton from there. This Dada Kelkar was an orthodox Brahmin and kept all orthodox manners in his life. He knew that offering wealth, grain and clothes etc.., to a Sadguru was not enough but that implicit obedience to and prompt compliance with His order was the real Dakshina that pleased Him most.

So Dada Kelkar dressed himself and started for the place. Then Baba called him back and said, "Don't go yourself, but send somebody." Then Dada sent his servant Pandu for the purpose. Seeing him starting, Baba asked Dada to call him back and cancelled that program. On another occasion Baba asked Dada just to see how the salted `Pulava' (mutton dish) was done. The latter said casually and formally that it was alright. Then Baba said to him - "Neither you have seen it with your eyes, nor tasted in with your tongue, then how could you say that it was good? Just take out the lid and see".

Saying this Baba caught his arm and thrust it into the pot and added, "Draw out your arm and taking a ladle, put some quantity in the dish without caring for your orthodoxy and without blustering." When a wave of real love rises in a mother's mind, she pinches her child with her hand and when it begins to cry and shout, she hugs it close to her bosom. Similarly Baba, in a true motherly way pinched Dada Kelkar in this fashion. Really no saint or guru will ever force his orthodox disciple to eat forbidden food and defile himself thereby.

The Handi business went on for some time till 1910 and was stopped thereafter. As stated before, Das Ganu spread the fame of Baba by his kirtans far and wide in the Bombay Presidency and people from that part of the country began to flock to Shirdi, which became in a few days a place of pilgrimage. The devotees brought with them various articles for presentation and offered various dishes of food as naivedya. The quantity of naivedya offered by them was so much that the fakirs and paupers could feed themselves to their hearts' content, leaving some surplus behind. Before stating how naivedya was distributed, we shall refer to Nanasaheb Chandorkar's story showing Baba's regard and respect for local Shrines and deities.

Nanasaheb's Disrespect of a Shrine

By drawing inferences or guessing in their own way some people said that Sai was a Brahmin, and some that He was a Muslim. Really He belonged to no caste. No one knew definitely when He was born and in what community and who were His parents. Then how could He be a Muslim or Brahmin? If He were a Muslim, how could He keep Dhuni fire ever burning in the Masjid, how could there be a Tulsi Vrindavan there, how could He allow the blowing of conches and ringing of bells and the playing of the musical instruments, how could He allow all the different forms of Hindu worship, there? Had He been a Muslim, could He have pierced ears and could He have been spent money from His pocket for repairing Hindu temples? On the contrary He never tolerated the slightest disrespect to Hindu Shrines and Deities.

Once Nanasaheb Chandorkar came to Shirdi with his 'Sadu' -

husband of his sister-in-law, Mr. Biniwalle, when they went to the Masjid and sat before Baba talking, the latter suddenly got angry with Nanasaheb and said - "You are so long in My company and how do you behave like this?" Nanasaheb then at first did not understand anything and humbly requested Baba to explain. Baba asked him when he came to Kopergaon and how he came to Shirdi from thence. Nanasaheb then at once realized his mistake. He usually worshipped the Shrine of Datta, on the banks of the Godavari at Kopergaon on his way to Shirdi, but this time he dissuaded his relation who was a Datta Bhakta from going to that Shrine, to avoid delay and drove straight. He confessed all this to Baba and told Him that while bathing in the Godavari, a big thorn went into his foot and gave him much trouble. Baba said that, that was the slight punishment be met and warned him to be more careful in future.

Kala (hodge-podge)

To revert to the distribution of the naivedya (food offered to God). - After the arati was over and after Baba sent away all the people with Udi and blessings, He went inside and sat with his back to the Nimbar for meals, with two rows of the Bhaktas, one on each side. The Bhaktas who brought naivedya thrust inside their dishes containing a variety of food such as Puris, Mande, Polis, Basundi, Sanza, fine rice etc.., and kept waiting outside for prasad consecrated by Baba. All the foods were mixed in a hotch-potch (stew of vegetables or meat) and placed before Baba. He offered it all to God and consecrated it. Then portions of the same were given to the persons waiting outside and the rest was served to the inner party with Baba at the center. The Bhaktas sitting in two rows then dined to their hearts' content. Baba asked Shama and Nanasaheb Nimonkar daily to serve the consecrated food to all the persons sitting inside and look to their individual needs and comforts. This they did very carefully and willingly. Every morsel of the food thus partaken gave them nutrition and satisfaction. Such sweet, lovely and consecrated food it was! Ever auspicious and every holy!

Cup of ButterMilk

Once Hemadpant had eaten his full in this company, when Baba offered him a cup of buttermilk (A fermented milk drink). Its white appearance pleased him, but he was afraid that there was no space inside for it. He, however, took a sip which proved very tasty. Seeing his faltering attitude, Baba said - "Drink it all, you won't get any such opportunity hereafter." He drank it off then, but found that Baba's words were prophetic, for He passed away soon.

Now, readers, we have certainly to thank Hemadpant. He drank the cup of buttermilk, but has supplied us with sufficient quantity of nectar in the form of Baba's Leelas. Let us drink cups and cups of this nectar and be satisfied and happy.

Bow to Shri Sai - Peace be to all

Chapter XXXIX & L
Baba's Knowledge of Sanskrit

His Interpretation of a Verse from Gita &
Construction of the Samadhi Mandir

This chapter (39) deals with Baba's interpretation of a verse from the Bradshaw-Gita. As some people believed that Baba knew not Sanskrit, and the interpretation was Nanasaheb Chandorkar's, Hemadpant wrote another chapter (50) refuting that objection. As the chapter No.50 deals with the same subject-matter, it is incorporated in this chapter.

Preliminary

Blessed is Shirdi and blessed is Dwarkamai where Shri Sai lived and moved until He took Mahasamadhi. Blessed are the people of Shirdi whom He obliged and for whom He came such long distance. Shirdi was a small village first, but it attained great importance, on account of His contact and became a Tirtha, holy place of pilgrimage. Equally blessed are the womenfolk of Shirdi, blessed is their whole and undivided faith in Him. They sang the glories of Baba while bathing, grinding, pounding corn and doing other house-hold work. Blessed is their love, for they sang sweet songs which calm and pacify the minds of the singers and listeners.

Baba's Interpretation

Nobody believed that Baba knew Sanskrit, one day He surprised all by giving a good interpretation of a verse from the Gita to Nanasaheb Chandorkar. A brief account about this matter was written by Mr. B.V. Deo, Retired Mamlatdar and published in Marathi in 'Shri Sai Leela' magazine, Vol. IV. Sphuta Vishaya, page 563. Short accounts of the same are also published in 'Sai Baba's Charters and Sayings' page 61 and in 'The Wondrous Saint Sai Baba', page 36 - both by Brother B.V.Narsimhaswami. Mr. B.V. Deo has also given an English version of this in his statement dated September 27th, 1936 and published on page 66 of

"Devotees' Experiences, Part III", published by the said Swami.
As Mr. Deo has got firsthand information about this Subject from
Nanasaheb himself we give below his version.

Nanasaheb Chandorkar was a good student of Vedanta. He
had read Gita with commentaries and prided himself on his
knowledge of all that. He fancied that Baba knew nothing of all
this or of Sanskrit. So, Baba one day pricked the bubble. These
were the days before crowds flocked to Baba, when Baba had
solitary talks at the Mosque with such devotees. Nana was sitting
near Baba and massaging His Legs and muttering something.

Baba - Nana, what are you mumbling yourself?

Nana - I am reciting shloka (verse) from Sanskrit.

Baba - What shloka?

Nana - From Aggravate-Gita

Baba - Utter it loudly.

Nana then recited B.G. IV-34 which is as follows:

'Tadviddhi Pranipatena Pariprashnena Sevaya, Upadekshyanti
Te Jnanam Jnaninastattwadarshinah'

Baba - Nana, do you understand it?

Nana - Yes.

Baba - If you do, then tell me.

Nana - It means this - "Making Sashtanga Namaskar, i.e.,
prostration, questioning the guru, serving him, learn what this
Jnana is. Then, those Jnanis that have attained the real knowledge
of the Sad-Vastu (Brahma) will give you upadesha (instruction) of
Jnana."

Baba - Nana, I do not want this sort of collected purport of the
whole stanza. Give me each word, its grammatical force and
meaning.

Then Nana explained it word by word.

Baba - Nana, is it enough to make prostration merely?

Nana - I do not know any other meaning for the word 'pranipata' than 'making prostration'.

Baba - What is 'pariprashna'?

Nana - Asking questions.

Baba - What does 'Prashna' mean?

Nana - The same (questioning).

229

Baba - If 'pariprashna' means the same as prashna (question), why did Vyasa add the prefix 'pari'? Was Vyasa off his head?

Nana - I do not know of any other meaning for the word 'pariprashna'.

Baba - 'Seva', what sort of 'seva' is meant?

Nana - Just what we are doing always

Baba - Is it enough to render such service?

Nana - I do not know what more is signified by the word 'seva'.

Baba - In the next line "upadekshyanti te jnanam", can you so read it as to read any other word in lieu of Jnanam?

Nana - Yes.

Baba - What word?

Nana - Ajnanam.

Baba - Taking that word (instead of Jnana) is any meaning made out of the verse?

Nana - No, Shankara Bhashya gives no such construction.

Baba - Never mind if it does not. Is there any objection to using the word "Ajnana" if it gives a better sense?

Nana - I do not understand how to construe by placing "Ajnana" in it.

Baba - Why does Krishna refer Arjuna to Jnanis or Tattwadarshis to do his prostration, interrogation and service? Was not Krishna a Tattwadarshi, in fact Jnana himself.

Nana - Yes He was. But I do not make out why he referred Arjuna to Jnanis?

Baba - Have you not understood this?

Nana was humiliated. His pride was knocked on the head. Then Baba began to explain -

(1)   It is not enough merely to prostrate before the Jnanis. We must make Sarvaswa Sharangati (complete surrender) to the Sadguru.

(2)   Mere questioning is not enough. The question must not be made with any improper motive or attitude or to trap the Guru and catch at mistakes in the answer, or out of idle curiosity. It must be serious and with a view to achieve moksha or spiritual

progress.

(3)   Seva is not rendering service, retaining still the feeling that one is free to offer or refuse service. One must feel that he is not the master of the body, that the body is Guru's and exists merely to render service to him.

If this is done, the Sadguru will show you what the Janna referred to in the previous stanza is. Nana did not understand what is meant by saying that a guru teaches ajnana.

Baba - How is Jnana Upadesh, i.e., imparting of realization to be effected? Destroying ignorance is Jnana. (cf. Verse-Ovi-1396 of Jnaneshwari commenting on Gita 18-66 says - "removal of ignorance is like this, Oh Arjuna, If dream and sleep disappear, you are yourself. It is like that." Also Ovi 83 on Gita V-16 says - "Is there anything different or independent in Jnana besides the destruction of ignorance?")* Expelling darkness means light. Destroying duality (dwaita) means non-duality (adwaita). Whenever we speak of destroying Dwaita, we speak of Adwaita. Whenever we talk of destroying darkness, we talk of light. If we have to realize the Adwaita state, the feeling of Dwaita in ourselves has to be removed. That is the realization of the Adwaita state. Who can speak of Adwaita while remaining in Dwaita? If one did, unless one gets into that state, how can one know it and realize it?

Again, the Shishya (disciple) like the Sadguru is really embodiment of Jnana. The difference between the two lies in the attitude, high realization, marvelous super-human Sattva and unrivalled capacity and Aishwarya Yoga (divine powers). The Sadguru is Nirguna, Sat-Chit-Ananda. He has indeed taken human form to elevate mankind and raise the world. But his real Nirguna nature is not destroyed thereby, even a bit. His beingness (or reality), divine power and wisdom remain undiminished. The disciple also is in fact of the same swarupa. But, it is overlaid by the effect of the samaskaras of innumerable births in the shape of ignorance, which hides from his view that he is Shuddha Chaitanya (see B.G. Ch. V- 15).

As stated therein, he gets the impressions - "I am Jiva, a

creature, humble and poor." The Guru has to root out these offshoots of ignorance and has to give upadesh or instruction. To the disciple, held spell-bound for endless generations by the ideas of his being a creature, humble and poor, the Guru imparts in hundreds of births the teaching - "You are God, you are mighty and opulent." Then, he realizes a bit that he is God really. The perpetual delusion under which the disciple is laboring, that he is the body, that he is a creature (jiva) or ego, that God (Paramatma) and the world are different from him, is an error inherited from innumerable past births. From actions based on it, he has derived his joy, sorrows and mixtures of both. To remove this delusion, this error, this root ignorance, he must start the inquiry. How did the ignorance arise? Where is it? And to show him this is called the Guru's upadesh. The following are the instances of Ajnana:

1. I am a Jiva (creature).
2. Body is the soul (I am the body).
3. God, world and Jiva are different.
4. I am not God. Not Knowing, that body is not the soul.
5. Not knowing that God, world and Jiva are one.

Unless these errors are exposed to his view, the disciple cannot learn what is God, jiva, world, body; how they are inter-related and whether they are different from each other, or are one and the same. To teach him these and destroy his ignorance is this instruction in Jnana or Ajnana. Why should Jnana be imparted to the jiva, (who is) a Jnanamurti? Upadesh is merely to show him his error and destroy his ignorance.

Baba added: (1) Pranipata implies surrender. (2) Surrender must be of body, mind and wealth; Re: (3) Why should Krishna refer Arjuna to other Jnanis?

Sadbhakta takes everything to be Devastate (Bhagavad Gita VII-19 i.e., any Guru will be Krishna to the devotee) and Guru takes disciple to be Devastate and Krishna treats both as his Prana and Atma (B.G.7-18, commentary of Jnanadev on this). As Shri Krishna knows that there are such Bhaktas and Gurus, He refers Arjuna to them so that their greatness may increase and be known.

Construction of the Samadhi-Mandir

Baba never talked, nor ever made any fuss about the things
which He wanted to accomplish, but He so skillfully arranged the
circumstances and surroundings that the people were surprised at
the slow but sure results attained. The construction of the
Samadhi-mandir is an instance in point. Shriman Bapusaheb
Booty, the famous multi-millionaire of Nagpur lived in Shirdi
with his family. Once an idea arose in his mind that he should
have a building of his own there. Sometimes after this, while he
was sleeping in Dixit's Wada, he got a vision. Bava appeared in
his dream and ordered him to build a Wada of his own with
temple. Shama, who was sleeping there, got also a similar vision.
When Bapusaheb was awakened, he saw Shama crying and asked
him why. The latter replied that in his vision Baba came close to
him and ordered distinctly, "Build the Wada with the temple. I
shall fulfill the desires of all. Hearing the sweet and loving words
of Baba, I was overpowered with emotion, my throat was choked,
my eyes were overflowing with tears, and I began to cry."

Bapusaheb was surprised to see that both their visions tallied.
Being a rich and capable man, he decided to build a Wada there
and drew up a plan with Madhavarao (Shama). Kakasaheb Dixit
also approved of it. And when it was placed before Baba, He also
sanctioned it immediately. Then the construction work was duly
started and under the supervision of Shama, the ground floor, the
cellar and the well were completed. Baba also on his way to and
from Lendi suggested certain improvements. Further work was
entrusted to Bapusaheb Jog and when it was going on, an idea
struck Bapusaheb Booty's mind that there should be an open room
or platform and in the center the image of Murlidhar (Lord
Krishna with the flute) be installed. He asked Shama to refer this
matter to Baba and get His consent.

The latter asked Baba about this when He was just passing by
the Wada. Hearing Shama, Baba gave His consent saying, " the
temple is complete I will come there to stay" and staring at the
Wada He added - "after the Wada is complete, we shall use it ourselves, we shall live, move and play there, embrace each other,
and be very happy." Then Shama asked Baba whether this was the

auspicious time to begin the foundation work of the central room of the Shrine. The latter answered in the affirmative. Shama got a coconut broke it and started the work. In due time the work was completed and an order was also given for making a good image of Murlidhar. But before it was ready, a new thing turned up. Baba became seriously ill and was about to pass away.

Bapusaheb became very sad and dejected, thinking that if Baba passed away, his Wada would not be consecrated by the holy touch of Baba's Feet, and all his money (about a lakh of rupees) would be wasted away. But the words, "Place or keep Me in the Wada" which came out of Baba's mouth just before His passing away, consoled not only Bapusaheb, but one and all. In due time Baba's holy body was placed and preserved in the central shrine meant or designed for Murlidhar and Baba Himself became Murlidhar and the Wada thus became the Samadhi Mandir of Sai Baba. His wonderful life is unfathomable.

Blessed and fortunate is Bapusaheb Booty in whose Wada lies the holy and the pure body of Baba.

Bow to Shri Sai - Peace be to all

Chapter XL Stories of Baba

(1) Attending Mrs. Deo's Udyapan Ceremony as a Sannyasi
with two Others (Trio)
(2) Hemadpant's House in the Form of His Picture.

In this chapter we give two stories; (1) How Baba attended the
Udyapan ceremony of Mr. B.V. Deo's mother at his house at
Dahanu and (2) How Baba attended the Shimga dinner-party
in Hemadpant's house at Bandra.

Preliminary

Blessed is Shri Sai Samartha who gives instructions in both
temporal and spiritual matters to His devotees and makes them
happy by enabling them to achieve the goal of their life, - Sai He
who when places His hand on their heads transfers His powers to
them and thus destroying the sense of differentiation, makes them
attain the Unattainable Thing. - He who embraces the Bhaktas
who prostrate themselves before Him with no sense of duality or
difference. He becomes one with the Bhaktas as the sea with the
rivers when they meet it in the rainy season and gives them His
power and position. It follows from this that he who sings the
Leelas of God's Bhaktas is equally or more dear to Him than one
who sings the Leelas of God only. Now we return to the stories of
this chapter.

Mrs. Deo's Udyapan Ceremony

Mr. B.V. Deo was a Mamlatdar at Dahanu (Thana District).
His mother had observed 25 or 30 different vows and a Udyapan
(concluding) ceremony in connection therewith was to be performed. This ceremony included the feeding of one hundred or
two hundred Brahmins. Mr. Deo fixed a date for the ceremony
and wrote a letter to Bapusaheb Jog asking him to request Sai
Baba on his behalf to attend the dinner of the ceremony, as without His attendance the ceremony would not be duly completed.
Bapusaheb Jog read out the letter to Baba. Baba noted carefully
the pure hearted invitation and said, "I always think of him who

remembers Me. I require no conveyance, carriage, tanga, nor train nor airplane. I run and manifest myself to him who lovingly calls me. Write to him a pleasing reply that three of us (the trio), Myself, yourself and a third will go and attend it." Mr. Jog informed Mr. Deo of what Baba said. The latter was much pleased, but he knew that Baba never went to any place except Rahata, Rui and Nimgaon in person. He also thought that nothing was impossible to Baba as He was all-pervading and that He might suddenly come, in any form He likes and fulfill His words.

A few days before this, a Sannyasi with Bengali dress and professing to work for the cause of the protection of the cows, came to the station-master at Dahanu to collect subscriptions. The latter told him to go into the town and see the Mamlatdar (Mr. Deo) and with his help collect funds. Just then the Mamlatdar happened to come there. The station master then introduced the Sannyasi to him. Both sat talking on the platform. Mr. Deo told him that a subscription list for some other charitable cause had already been opened by the leading citizen, Rao Saheb Narottam Shetti and so it was not good to start another subscription list and that it would be better if he would visit the place after two or four months. Hearing this, the Sannyasi left the place.

About a month afterwards, the Sannyasi came in a tanga and stopped in front of Mr. Deo's house at about ten a.m. Deo thought that he came for subscriptions. Seeing him busy with the preparations of the ceremony, the Sannyasi said that he had come not for money but for meals. Deo said, "Alright, very glad, you are welcome, the house is yours." The Sannyasi, "Two lads are with me." Deo, "Well, come with them." As there was time (two hours) for dinner, Deo enquired where he should send for them. He said that it was not necessary as he would come himself at the appointed time. Deo asked him to come at noon. Exactly at twelve noon, the Trio came and joined the dinner party and after feeding themselves went away.

After the ceremony was finished, Deo wrote a letter to Bapusaheb Jog complaining of Baba's breach of promise. Jog went to Baba with the letter, but before it was opened Baba spoke - "Ah, he says that I promised him to come but deceived him. Inform him that I did attend his dinner with two others, but he failed to recognize Me. Then why did he call me at all? Tell him that he thought that the Sannyasi came to ask for subscription money; did I not remove his doubt in that respect and did I not say that I would come with two others, and did not the Trio come in time and take their meals? See, to keep My words I would sacrifice my life, I would never be untrue to My words." This reply gladdened Jog's heart and he communicated the whole of the reply to Deo. As soon as he read it, he burst into tears of joy, but he took himself to task mentally for vainly blaming Baba. He wondered how he was deceived by the Sannyasi's prior visit and his coming to him for subscriptions, how he also failed to catch the significance of the Sannyasi's words that he would come with two others for meals.

This story clearly shows that when the devotees surrender themselves completely to their Sadguru, He sees that the religious functions in their houses are duly executed and complied with all the necessary formalities.

Hemadpant's Shimga Dinner

Now let us take another story which shows how Baba appeared in the form of His picture and fulfilled the desire of His devotee.

In 1917 on the full-moon morning, Hemadpant had a vision. Baba appeared to him in his dream in the form of a well-dressed Sannyasi, woke him up, and said that He would come to him for meals that day. This awakening constituted a part of the dream. When he fully awoke, he saw no Sai nor any Sannyasi. But when he began to recollect the dream, he remembered each and every word the Sannyasi uttered in his dream. Though he was in contact with Baba for seven years and though he always meditated on Baba, he never expected that Baba would come to his house for meals. However, being much pleased with Baba's words, he went to his wife and informed her that being the Holi day, a Sannyasi guest was coming for meals and that some more rice should be prepared. She enquired about the guest, who he was and whence he was coming. Then not to lead her astray and not to cause any misunderstanding he gave her the truth, i.e., told her about the dream. She doubtingly asked whether it was possible that Baba should come there (Bandra) from Shirdi, leaving the dainty dishes there for accepting their coarse food. Hemadpant then assured her that Baba might not come in person but He might attend in the form of a guest and that they would lose nothing if they cooked some more rice.

After this, preparations for the dinner went on and it was quite ready at noon. The Holika-worship was gone through and the leaves (dishes) were spread and arranged with 'Rangoli' marks around them. Two rows were put up with a central seat between them for the guest. All the members of the family - sons, grand-sons, daughters and sons-in-law etc.., came and occupied their proper seats and the serving of the various articles commenced. While this was being done, everybody was watching for the guest, but none turned up though it was past noon.

Then the door was closed and chained; the anna-shuddhi (ghee) was served. This was a signal to start eating. Formal offer-ing to the Vaishwadeva (Fire), and Naivedya to Shri Krishna were also over and the members were about to begin, when foot-steps in the staircase were distinctly heard. Hemadpant went immedi-ately and opened the door and saw two men there: Ali Mahomed and Moulana Ismu Mujavar, both who upon seeing that meals were ready and everyone else was about to begin eating, apolo-gized to Hemadpant and requested him to excuse their interfer-ence.

They said - "You left your seat and came running to us, others are waiting for you, so please take this your Thing and I shall re-late all the wonderful tale about it later on at your convenience." So saying he took out from his armpit a packet wrapped in an old newspaper cover and placed it on the table. Hemadpant uncov-ered the packet and saw, to his great wonder and surprise, a big nice picture of Sai Baba. Seeing it, he was much moved, tears ran from his eyes and hair stood on end all over his body, and he bent and placed his head on the feet of Baba in the picture. He thought that Baba had blessed him by this miracle or Leela. Out of curios-ity he asked Ali Mahomed whence he got this picture. He said that he bought it from a shop and that he would give all the details about it sometime afterwards and wished that as all the members were waiting for him, he should go and join them. Hemadpant thanked him, bade them goodbye and returned to the dining hall. The picture was placed on the central seat reserved for the guest and after the due offering of the Naivedya; the whole party commenced eating and finished it in proper time. Seeing the beautiful form in the picture everybody was extremely pleased and wondered how all this happened.

The is how Sai Baba kept up and fulfilled His words uttered by Him in the dream of Hemadpant. The story of the picture with all its details, viz., how Ali Mahomed got it, why he bought it and gave it to Hemadpant, is reserved for the next chapter.

Bow to Shri Sai - Peace be to all

Chapter XLI

Story of the Picture - Stealing the Rags and
Reading of Jnaneshwari.
As stated in the last chapter, we continue here the
story of the picture.

Nine years after the occurrence of the incident depicted in the
last chapter, Ali Mahomed saw Hemadpant and related to him
the following story:

One day while wandering in the streets of Bombay he bought
the picture from a street-hawker; then he framed and set it on a
wall in his house at Bandra (suburb of Bombay). As he loved
Baba, he daily took darshan of it. Three months before he gave
the picture to Hemadpant, he was suffering from an abscess or
swelling on his leg for which an operation was performed and he
was convalescing in the house of his brother-in-law, Mr. Noor-
Mahomed Peerbhoy in Bombay. For three months his house in
Bandra was closed; and nobody was living there. Only the
pictures of the famous Baba Abdul Rahiman, Moulanasaheb
Mahomed Hussain, Baba Sai, Baba Tajudin and other saints
(living) were there. The wheel of time did not even spare these.
He was lying sick and suffering in Bombay. Why should the pictures   suffer there (in Bandra)? It seems that they have also their
ins and outs (births and deaths). All the pictures met their fate, but
how Sai Baba's picture escaped it, nobody had been able to
explain to me up till now. It shows the all-pervasiveness,
omnipresence of Sai and His inscrutable power.

He got a small picture of Saint Baba Abdul Rahiman from
Mahomed Hussain Thariyatopan many years ago. He gave it to
his brother-in-law, Noor-Mahomed Peerbhoy and it was lying on
his table for eight years. Once the latter saw it, took it to a photog-
rapher and got it enlarged to life-size and distributed copies of the
same amongst his relations and friends, including Ali Mahomed
who fixed it up in his Bandra house. Noor-Mahomed was a
disciple of Saint Abdul Rahiman and when he went to present the

240

picture to his Guru in an open darbar held by him, the Guru got wild and ran to beat him, and drove him out. He felt very sorry and dejected. He thought that he lost so much of his money, and incurred his Guru's displeasure and anger.

As his Guru did not like image worship, he took the enlarged picture with him to the Appollo Bunder and, after hiring a boat, went in it and drowned it in the sea. He requested the friends and relations to return their copies and after getting them (six in all) back, had them thrown by a fisherman in the Bandra sea. At this time Ali Mahomed was in his brother-in-law's house. He was told by him that his suffering would come to an end if he would soon drown the pictures of the saints in the sea. Hearing this, Ali Mahomed sent his Mehta (Manager) to his Bandra house and got all the pictures of the saints in his house thrown into the sea.

When Ali Mahomed returned home after two months, he was surprised to find Baba's picture on the wall as before. He did not understand how his Mehta took away all the pictures except this. He immediately took it out and kept it in his cupboard, fearing that if his brother-in-law saw it, he would do away with it. While he was thanking how it should be disposed of, and who would keep it and guard it well, Sai Baba Himself as it were, suggested to him that he should see and consult Moulana Ismu Mujavar and abide by his opinion. He saw the Moulana and told him every-thing. After mature consideration they both decided that the picture should be presented to Annasaheb (Hemadpant) and that he would protect it well. Then they both went to Hemadpant and presented the picture in the nick of time.

This story shows how Baba knew all the past, present and future, and how skillfully He pulled the wires and fulfilled desired of His devotees. The following story shows that Baba liked very much those persons who took real interest in matters spiritual and that He removed all their difficulties and made them happy.

Stealing the Rags and Reading of Jnaneshwari

Mr. B.V. Deo who was Mamlatdar of Dahanu (Thana District) wished for a long time to read Jnaneshwari - (the well-known Marathi commentary on the Bhagavad Gita by Jnaneshwar), along with other scriptures. He could read daily one chapter of the

Bhagavad Gita and some portion of other books; but when he took Jnaneshwari in hand, some difficulties cropped up and he was precluded from reading it. He took three months' leave, went to Shirdi and thence to his home at Pound for rest. He could read there other books but when he opened Jnaneshwari, some evil or stray thoughts came crowding in his mind and stopped him in the effort.

Try however he might; he was not able to read even a few lines of the book with ease. So he resolved in his mind that when Baba would create love for the book and would order him to read it, he would begin and not till then. Then in the month of February 1914 he went with his family to Shirdi. There Jog asked him whether he daily read Jnaneshwari. Deo said that he was desirous of reading it, but he was not successful and that only when Baba would order him to read it, he would commence. Jog then advised him to take a copy of the book and present it to Baba and to start the reading after it was consecrated and returned by Him. Deo then replied that he did not want to resort to this device, as Baba knows his heart. Would He not know his desire and satisfy it by giving him a clear order to read?

Deo then saw Baba and offered one rupee as Dakshina. Baba asked for Rs. 20 which he gave. At night, he saw one Balakram and enquired how he secured Baba's devotion and grace. Balakram told him that he would communicate everything next day after arati. When Deo went for darshan next day, Baba asked for Rs.20 which he gave willingly. As the Masjid was crowded, Deo went aside and sat in a corner. Baba asked him to come close and sit with a calm mind, which Deo did.

Then after the noon-arati was over and after the men dispersed, Deo saw again Balakram and asked him his previous history, what Baba told him and how he was taught meditation. Balakram was going to reply when Baba sent one Chandru, a leper devotee to call Deo to Him. When Deo went to Baba, the latter asked him when and with whom and what he was talking. He said that he talked with Balakram and heard from him His fame. Then Baba asked again Rs.25 as Dakshina which Deo gladly gave.

Then Baba took him inside and sitting near the post charged

him saying - "You stole away My rags without My knowledge." Deo denied all knowledge of the rags, but Baba asked him to make a search. He searched but found none. Then Baba got angry and said - "There is nobody here, you are the only thief, so grey haired and old, you came here for stealing."

After this Baba lost His temper, got terribly wild, gave all sorts of abuses and scoldings. Deo remained silent and watching, and thought that he might get a beating also. After about an hour or so, Baba asked him to go to the Wada. He returned to the Wada and told Jog and Balakram all that had happened. Then in the afternoon Baba sent for all and Deo also, and said that His words might have pained the old man (Deo) but as he committed the theft, He could not but speak out.

Then Baba asked again for Rs. 12 Deo collected the amount, paid it and prostrated himself before Him. Then Baba said to him - "What are you doing?" "Nothing" replied Deo. Then Baba - "Go on daily reading the Pothi (Jnaneshwari), go and sit in the Wada, read something regularly every day and while reading, explain the portion read, to all with love and devotion. I am sitting here ready to give you the whole gold embroidered Shela (valuable cloth), then why go to others to steal rags, and why should you get into the habit of stealing?"

Deo was much pleased to hear the words of Baba, for He asked him to start reading Pothi (Jnaneshwari). He thought that he got what he wanted and that he could read the book with ease thenceforth. He again prostrated himself before Baba and said that he surrendered himself to Him and that he should be treated as a child and be helped in his reading. He realized then what Baba meant by 'stealing the rags'. What he asked Balakram constituted the 'rags' and Baba did not like his behavior in this respect. As He was ready to answer any question, He did not like him to ask others and make unnecessary enquiries and therefore He harassed and scolded him. Deo thought that He really did not 'harass and scold' him but taught that He was ready to fulfill his desires, and there was no use asking others in vain. Deo took these scoldings as flowers and blessings and went home satisfied and contented.

The matter did not end here. Baba did not stop with only issuing an order to read. Within a year He went to Deo and enquired about his progress. On 2nd April 1914, on Thursday morning, Baba gave him a dream vision. He sat on the upper floor and asked him whether he understood the Pothi. "No" answered Deo. Baba - "Then when are you going to understand?" Deo burst into tears and said, "Unless You shower Your grace, the reading is mere worry and the understanding is still more difficult. I say this definitely." Baba - "While reading you make haste, read it before Me, in My presence." Deo - "What shall I read?" Baba - "Read Adhyatma (spiritualism)." Deo went to bring the book when he opened his eyes and was awakened. We leave the readers to imagine what ineffable joy and bliss Deo felt after this vision.

Bow to Shri Sai - Peace be to all

Chapter XLII Baba's Passing Away

Previous Indication - Averting Death of Ramachandra Dada Patil
and Tatya Kote Patil - Charity to Laxmibai Shinde
Last Moment. This chapter describes the Passing away of Baba.

Preliminary

The stories given in the previous chapter have shown that the light of Guru's grace removes out fear of the mundane existence, opens the path of salvation and turns our misery into happiness. If we always remember the feet of the Sadguru, our troubles come to an end, death loses its sting and the misery of this mundane existence is obliterated. Therefore those who care for their welfare should carefully listen to these stories of Sai Samarth, which will purify their minds.

Here, Hemadpant dwells on Dr. Pandit's worship and his marking Baba's forehead with Tripundra, i.e., three horizontal lines; but as this has been already described in chapter XI, this has been omitted here.

Previous Indication

The readers up till now heard the stories of Baba's life. Let them now hear attentively Baba's Passing away. Baba got a slight attack of fever on 28th September, 1918. The fever lasted for two or three days, but afterwards Baba gave up his food and thereby He grew weaker and weaker. On the 17th day, i.e., Tuesday, the 15th October 1918, Baba left His mortal coil at about 2:30 p.m. (as per Professor G.G. Narke's letter, dated 5th November 1918, to Dadasaheb Khaparde, published in "Sai Leela" magazine, Page 78, first year). Two years before this, i.e., in 1916, Baba gave an indication of His Passing away, but nobody understood it then. It was as follows: - On the Vijayadashmi (Dasara) day Baba at once got into wild rage in the evening when people were returning from 'Seemollanghan' (crossing the border or limits of the village). Taking off His head-dress, kafni and langota etc.., He tore them and threw them in the Dhuni before Him. Fed by this offering, the fire in the Dhuni began to burn brighter and Baba shone still brighter. He stood there stark naked and with His burning red eyes shouted - "You fellows, now have a look and decide finally whether I am a Muslim or a Hindu." Everybody was trembling with fear and none dared to approach Baba. After some time Bhagoji Shinde, the leper devotee of Baba, went boldly near Him and succeeded in tying a langota (waist-band) round His waist and said - "Baba, what is all this? Today is the Seemollanghan, i.e., Dasara Holiday." Baba striking the ground with His satka said - This is my Seemollanghan (crossing the border)." Baba did not cool down till 11:00 p.m. and the people doubted whether the Chavadi procession would ever take place that night.

After an hour Baba resumed His normal condition and dressing Himself as usual attended the Chavadi procession as described before. By this incident Baba gave a suggestion that Dasara was the proper time for Him to cross the border of life, but none understood its meaning. Baba gave also another indication as follows:

Averting Death of Ramachandra and Tatya Patil

Sometime after this, Ramachandra Patil became seriously ill. He suffered a lot. He tried all remedies, but finding no relief, despaired of his life and was waiting for the last moment. The one midnight Baba suddenly stood near his pillow. Patil held His Feet and said - "I have lost all hopes of life; please tell me definitely when I shall die." Merciful Baba said - "Don't be anxious, your hundi (death-warrant) has been withdrawn and you will soon recover, but I am afraid of Tatya Patil. He will pass away on Vijayadashami of Shaka 1840 (1918 A.D.). Do not divulge this to anybody, nor to him, for he will be terribly frightened." Ramachandra Dada got well, but he felt nervous about Tatya's life, for he knew that Baba's word was unalterable, and that Tatya would breathe his last within two years. He kept this hint secret, told it to none but one Bala Shimpi (a tailor). Only these two persons - Ramachandra Dada and Bala Shimpi were in fear and suspense regarding Tatya's life.

Ramachandra Dada soon left his bed and was on his legs.

Time passed quickly. The month of Bhadrapad of Shaka 1840 (1918 A.D.) was ending and Ashwin was in sight. True to Baba's word, Tatya fell sick and was bedridden; and so he could not come for Baba's darshan. Baba was also down with fever. Tatya had full faith in Baba and Baba in Lord Hari, who was His Protector. Tatya's illness began to grow from bad to worse and he could not move at all but always remembered Baba. The predicament of Baba began to grow equally worse. The day predicted, i.e., Vijayadashami was impending and both Ramachandra Dada and Bala Shimpi were terribly frightened about Tatya and with their bodies trembling and perspiring with fear, thought that as predicted by Baba, Tatya's end was nigh. Vijayadashami dawned and Tatya's pulse began to beat very slow and he was expected to pass away shortly. But a curious thing happened. Tatya remained, his death was averted and Baba passed away in his stead. It seemed as if there was an exchange. People said that Baba gave up His life for Tatya; why He did so? He alone knows as His ways are inscrutable. It seems, however, that in this incident, Baba gave a hint of His passing away, substituting Tatya's name for His.

Next morning (16th October) Baba appeared to Das Ganu at Pandharpur in his dream and said to him - "The Masjid collapsed; all the oilmen and grocers of Shirdi teased me a lot, so I leave the place. I therefore came to inform you here, please go there quickly and cover me with 'Bhakkal' flowers." Das Ganu got the information also from Shirdi letters. So he came to Shirdi with his disciples and started bhajan and kirtan and sang the Lord's name, all through the day before Baba's samadhi. Himself weaving a beautiful garland of flowers studded with Lord Hari's name he placed it on Baba's samadhi and gave a mass-feeding in Baba's name.

Charity to Laxmibai

Dasara or Vijayadashami (festival of the victory of Ram over Ravan) is regarded by all the Hindus as the most auspicious time and it is befitting that Baba should choose this time for His crossing the border-line. He was ailing some days before this, but He was ever conscious internally. Just before the last movement He sat up erect without anybody's aid, and looked better. People thought that the danger had passed off and He was getting well. He knew that He was to pass away soon and therefore, He wanted to give some money as charity to Laxmibai Shinde.

Baba Pervading All Creatures

This Laxmibai Shinde was a good and well-to-do woman. She was working in the Masjid day and night. Except Bhagat Mhalasapati, Tatya and Laxmibai, none was allowed to step in the Masjid at night. Once while Baba was sitting in the Masjid with Tatya in the evening, Laxmibai came and saluted Baba. The latter said to her - "Oh Laxmi, I am very hungry." Off she went saying - "Baba, wait a bit, I return immediately with bread." She did return with bread and vegetables and placed the same before Baba. He took it up and gave it to a dog.

Laxmibai then asked - "What is this, Baba, I ran in haste, prepared bread with my own hands for You and You threw it to a dog without eating a morsel of it; You gave me trouble unnecessarily." Baba replied - "Why do you grieve for nothing? The appeasement of the dog's hunger is the same as Mine. The dog has got a soul; the creatures may be different, but the hunger of all is the same, though some speak and others are dumb. Know for certain, that he, who feeds the hungry, really serves Me with food. Regard this as an axiomatic Truth." This is an ordinary incident but Baba thereby propounded a great spiritual truth and showed its practical application in daily life without hurting anybody's feelings. From this time onward Laxmibai began to offer Him daily bread and milk with love and devotion. Baba accepted and ate it appreciatively. He took a part of this and sent the remainder with Laxmibai to Radha-Krishna-Mai who always relished and ate Baba's remnant prasad. This bread-story should not be considered as a digression; it shows how Sai Baba pervaded all the creatures and transcended them. He is omnipresent, birth-less, deathless and immortal.

Baba remembered Laxmibai's service. How could He forget her? Just before leaving the body, He put His hand in His pocket and gave her once five rupees and again four rupees, 9 rupee coins. This figure (9) is indicative of the nine types of devotion described in chapter 21 or it may be the Dakshina offered at the time of Seemollanghan. Laxmibai was a well-to-do woman and so she was not in want of any money. So Baba might have suggested to her and brought prominently to her notice the nine characteristics of a good disciple mentioned in the 6th verse of chapter ten, skandha eleven of the Bhagwat, wherein first five and then four characteristics are mentioned in the first and second couplets.* Baba followed the order, first paid Rs.5 and then Rs.4 in all Rs.9. Not only nine, but many times nine rupees passed through Laxmibai's hand, but Baba's this gift of Nine, she will ever remember.

Being so watchful and conscious, Baba also took other precautions in His last moment. In order that He should not be embroiled or entangled with love and affection for His devotees, He ordered them all to clear off. Kakasaheb Dixit, Bapusaheb Booty and others were in the Masjid anxiously waiting upon Baba, but He asked them to go to the Wada and return after meals. They could not leave Baba's presence, nor could they disobey Him. So with heavy hearts and heavy feet they went to the Wada. They knew that Baba's case was very serious and that they could not forget Him. They sat for meals, but their mind was elsewhere, it was with Baba.

Before they finished, news came to them of Baba's leaving the mortal coil. Leaving their dishes, they ran to the Masjid and found that Baba rested finally on Bayaji's lap. He did not fall down on the ground nor did He lie on His bed, but sitting quietly on His seat and doing charity with His own hand threw off the mortal coil. Saints embody themselves and come into this world with a definite mission and after that is fulfilled they pass away as quietly and easily as they came.

Bow to Shri Sai - Peace be to all

Chapters XLIII & XLIV Baba's Passing Away

Chapters 43 and 44 continue the story of Baba's Passing away, and therefore they are taken together.

Previous Preparation

It is the general practice amongst the Hindus that when a man is about to die, some good religious scripture is read out to him with the object that his mind should be withdrawn from worldly things and fixed in matters spiritual, so that his future progress should be natural and easy. Everybody knows that when King Parikshiti was cursed by the son of a Brahmin Rishi and was about to die after a week, the great sage Shuka expounded to him the famous Bahagwat Puran in that week. This practice is followed even now and Gita, Bhagawat and other sacred books are read out to dying persons.

Baba being an incarnation of God needed no such help, but just to set an example to the people, He followed this practice. When He knew that He was to pass away soon, He ordered one Mr. Vaze to read Ramavijaya to Him. Mr. Vaze read the book once in the week. Then Baba asked him to read the same again day and night and he finished the second reading in three days. Thus eleven days passed. Then again he read for three days and was exhausted. So Baba let him go and kept Himself quiet. He abided on His Self and was waiting for the last moment.

Two or three days previous, Baba had stopped His morning travels and begging rounds and sat in the Masjid. He was conscious to the last and was advising the devotees not to lose heart. He let nobody know the exact time of His departure. Kakasaheb Dixit and Shriman Booty were dining daily with Him in the Masjid. That day (15th October) after arati, He asked them to go to their residence for dining. Still a few, viz., Laxmibai Shinde, Bhagoji Shinde, Bayaji, Laxman Bala Shimpi and Nanasaheb Nimonkar remained there. Shama was sitting down on the steps. After giving Rs. 9 to Laxmibai Shinde, Baba said that He did not feel well there (in the Masjid) and that He should be taken to the Dagadi (stone) Wada of Booty, where He would be alright.

Saying these last words, He leaned on Bayaji's body and breathed His last. Bhagoji noticed that His breathing had stopped and he immediately told this to Nanasaheb Nimonkar who was sitting below. Nanasaheb brought some water and poured it in Baba's mouth. It came out. Then he cried out loudly 'Oh Deva.' Baba seemed just to open His eyes and say 'Ah' in a low tone. But it soon become evident that Baba had left His body for good.

The news of Baba's passing away spread like wildfire in the village of Shirdi and all people, men, women and children ran to the Masjid and began to mourn this loss in various ways. Some cried out loudly, some wallowed on in the streets and some fell down senseless. Tears ran down from the eyes of all and every one was smitten with sorrow.

Then the question arose - How to dispose of Baba's body? Some (Mohammedans) said that the body should be interred in an open space and a tomb built over it. Even Khushalchand and Amir Shakkar shared this opinion. But Ramachandra Patil, the village officer said to the villagers with a firm and determined voice, "Your thought is not acceptable to us. Baba's body should be no-where placed except in the Wada." Thus people were divided on this point and discussion regarding this point went on for 36 hours.

On Wednesday morning Baba appeared to Laxman Mama Joshi in his dream and drawing him by His hand said - "Get up soon; Bapusaheb thinks that I am dead and so he won't come; you do the worship and the Kakad (morning) arati." Laxman Mama was the village astrologer and was the maternal uncle of Shama. He was an orthodox Brahmin and daily first worshipped Baba in the morning and then all the village deities. He had full faith in Baba. After the vision he came with all the puja materials and not minding the protests of the moulvis, did the Poop and the Kakad arati with all due formalities and went away. Then at noon Bapusaheb Jog came with all others and went through the noon-arati ceremony as usual.

Paying due respect to Baba's words the people decided to place His body in the Wada and started digging the central portion there. In the evening of Tuesday the Sub-Inspector came from Rahata and others from other places turned up and they all agreed to the proposal. Next morning Amirbhai came from Bombay and the Mamlatdar from Kopergaon. The people seemed divided in their opinion. Some insisted on interring His body in the open field. The Mamlatdar therefore took a general plebiscite and found that the proposal to use the Wada secured double the number of votes. He, however, wanted to refer the matter to the Collector and Kakasaheb Dixit got himself ready to go to Ahmednagar. In the meanwhile, by Baba's inspiration there was a change in the opinion of the other people and all the people unanimously voted for the proposal. On Wednesday evening Baba's body was taken in procession and brought to the Wada and was interred there with due formalities in the garbha, i.e., the central portion reserved for Murlidhar. In fact Baba became the Murlidhar and the Wada became a temple and a holy shrine, where so many devotees went and are going now to find rest and peace. All the obsequies of Baba were duly performed by Balasaheb Bhate and Upasani, a great devotee of Baba.

Breaking of the Brick

Some days before Baba's departure, there occurred an ominous sign foreboding the event. There was, in the Masjid an old brick on which Baba rested His hand and sat. At night time He leaned against it and had His asan. This went on for many years.

One day, during Baba's absence, a boy who was sweeping the floor took it up in his hand, and unfortunately it slipped from thence fell down broken into two pieces.

When Baba came to know about this, He bemoaned its loss, crying - "It is not the brick but My fate that has been broken into pieces. It was My life-long companion, with it I always meditated on the Self, it was as dear to Me as My life, it has left Me today." Some may raise here a question - "Why should Baba express this sorrow for such an inanimate thing as a brick?" To this Hemadpant replies that saints incarnate in this world with the express mission of saving the poor helpless people, and when they embody themselves and mix and act with the people, they act like them, i.e., outwardly laugh, play and cry like all other people, but inwardly they are wide awake to their duties and mission.

72 Hours Samadhi

Thirty two years before this, i.e., in 1886, Baba made an attempt to cross the border line. On a Margashirsha Purnima (Full moon) day, Baba suffered from a severe attack of asthma. To get rid of it Baba decided to take His prana high up and go into samadhi. He said to Bhagat Mhalsapati - "Protect My body for three days. If I return, it will be alright; if I do not, bury My body in that open land (pointing to it) and fix two flags there as a mark." Saying this, Baba fell down at about 10 P.M. His breathing stopped, as well as His pulse. It seemed as if His prana left the body. All the people including the villagers came there and wanted to hold an inquest and bury the body in the place pointed by Baba. But Mhalasapati prevented this. With Baba's body on his lap he sat full three days guarding it. After three days passed, Baba showed signs of life at 3 A.M. His breathing commenced, the abdomen began to move. His eyes opened and stretching His limbs, Baba returned to consciousness (life) again.

From this and other accounts, let the readers consider whether Sai Baba was the three and a half cubits' body that He occupied for some years and that He left thereafter or He was the Self inside. The body, composed of the five elements is perishable and transient, but the Self within is the thing - Absolute Reality which is immortal and intransigent. The pure Being, Consciousness or Brahma, the Ruler and Controller of the senses and mind is the thing Sai. This pervades all things in the universe and there is no space without it. For fulfilling His mission He assumed the body and after it was fulfilled, He threw away the body (the finite aspect), and assumed His infinite aspect. Sai ever lives, as also the previous Incarnation of God Datta, Shri Narsimha Saraswati of Ganagapur. His Passing away is only an outward aspect, but really He pervades all animate and inanimate things and is their Inner Controller and Ruler. This can be, and is even now experienced by many who surrender themselves completely to Him and worship Him with wholehearted devotion.

Though it is not possible for us to see Baba's form now, still if we go to Shirdi, we shall find His beautiful life-like portrait adorning the masjid. This has been drawn by Shamrao Jaykar, a famous artist and well-known devotee of Baba. To an imaginative and devout spectator this portrait can give even today the satisfaction of taking Baba's darshan. Though Baba has no body now, He lives there and everywhere, and will affect the welfare of the devotees even now as He was doing before when He was embodied. Saints like Baba never die, though they look like men, they are in reality God Himself.

Bapusaheb Jog's Sannyas

Hemadpant closes this chapter with the account of Jog's sannyas. Sakharam Hari alias Bapusaheb Jog was the uncle of the famous Varkari Vishnubuva Jog of Poona. After his retirement from Government Service (He was a Supervisor in the Public Works Department) in 1909, he came and lived in Shirdi with his wife. He had no issue. Both husband and wife loved Baba and spent all their time in worshipping and serving Baba. After Megha's death, Bapusaheb daily did the arati ceremony in the Masjid and Chavadi till Baba's maha-samadhi. He was also entrusted with the work of reading and explaining Jnaneshwari and Ekanathm Bhagawat in Sathe's Wada to the audience. After serving for many years, Jog asked Baba - "I have served you so long; my mind is not yet calm and composed, how is it that my contact with Saints has not improved me? When will You bless me?" - Hearing the Bhakta's prayer Baba replied - "In due time your bad actions (their fruit or result) will be destroyed, your merits and demerits will be reduced to ashes, and I shall consider you blessed, when you will renounce all attachments, conquer lust and palate, and getting rid of all impediments, serve God wholeheartedly and resort to the begging bowl (accept sannyas)." After some time, Baba's words came true. His wife predeceased him and as he had no other attachment, he became free and accepted sannyas before his death and realized the goal of his life.

Baba's Nectar-like words

The kind and merciful Sai Baba said many a time the following sweet words in the Masjid - "He who loves Me most, always sees Me. The whole world is desolate to him without Me, he tells no stories but Mine. He ceaselessly meditates upon Me and always chants My name. I feel indebted to him who surrenders himself completely to Me and ever remembers Me. I shall repay his debt by giving him salvation (self-realization). I am dependent on him who thinks and hungers after Me and who does not eat anything without first offering it to Me. He, who thus comes to Me, becomes one with Me, just as a river gets to the sea and becomes merged (one) with it. So leaving out pride and egoism and with no trace of them, you should surrender yourself to Me Who am seated in your heart."

Who is this ME?

Sai Baba expounded many a time Who this ME (or I) is. He said, "You need not go far or anywhere in search of Me. Barring your name and form, there exists in you, as well as in all beings, a sense of Being or Consciousness of Existence. That is Myself. Knowing this, you see Me inside yourself, as well as in all beings. If you practice this, you will realize all-pervasiveness, and thus attain oneness with Me."

Hemadpant, therefore, makes a bow to the readers and requests them humbly and lovingly that they should love and respect all Gods, saints and devotees. Has not Baba often said, "He who carps and cavils at others, pierces Me in the heart and injures Me, but he that suffers and endures, pleases Me most." Baba thus pervades all beings and creatures and besets them on all sides. He likes nothing but love to all beings.

Such nectar, pure auspicious ambrosia always flowed from Baba's lips. He therefore, concludes - Those who lovingly sing Baba's fame and those who hear the same with devotion, both become one with Sai.

Bow to Sri Sai - Peace be to all

Chapter XLV

Kakasaheb's Doubt and Anandrao's Vision - Wooden Plank Baba's bedstead and not Bhagat's.

Preliminary

We have described in the last three chapters Baba's Passing away. His physical or finite form has no doubt disappeared from our view; but the infinite or spiritual form (Spirit of Baba) ever lives. The Leelas which occurred during His lifetime have been dwelt upon at great length up till now. Ever since His passing away, fresh Leelas have taken place and are even now happening. This clearly shows that Baba is ever-living and helping His devotees as before.

The people, who got the contact of Baba when He was living, were indeed very fortunate, but if any of them did not get a dispassion for the things and enjoyments of the world and had not their minds turned to the Lord, it was purely their ill-luck. What was then wanted and is now wanted is the whole-hearted devotion to Baba. All our senses, organs, and mind should cooperate in worshipping and serving Baba. It is no use in engaging some organs in the worship and deflecting others. If a thing like worship or meditation is to be done, it ought to be done with all our mind and soul.

The love that a chaste woman bears to her husband is sometimes compared to that which a disciple bears to his master (Guru). Yet the former falls far short of the latter, which is incomparable. No one, whether he be father, mother, brother or any other relation, comes to our aid in attaining the goal of life (self-realization). We have to chalk out and traverse the path of self-realization ourselves. We have to discriminate between the Unreal and the Real, renounce the things and enjoyments of this world and the next, control our senses and mind, and aspire for liberation only. Instead of depending upon others, we should have full faith in ourselves. When we begin to practice discrimination, we come to know, that the world is transient and unreal and our passion for worldly things becomes less and less, and ultimately we get dis-passion or non-attachment for them. Then we know that the Brahma which is no other than our Guru is the sole reality and as It transcends and besets the seeming universe, we begin to worship It in all creatures. This is the unitive Bhajan or worship. When we thus worship the Brahma or Guru wholeheartedly, we become one with Him and attain self-realization. In short, always chanting the name of the Guru, and meditating on Him enables us to see Him in all beings, and confers eternal bliss on us. The following story will illustrate this.

Kakasaheb's Doubt and Anandrao's Vision

It is well-known, that Sai Baba had enjoined Kakasaheb Dixit to read daily two works of Shri Ekanath: (1) Bhagawat and (2) Bhawartha Ramayan. Kakasaheb read these daily while Baba was living and he followed the practice even after Baba's passing away. Once in Kaka Mahajani's house in Choupati, Bombay, Kakasaheb was reading Ekanathi Bhagawat in the morning. Madhavarao Deshpande alias Shama and Kaka Mahajani were then present and listened attentively to the portion read, viz., the 2nd Chapter, 11th skandha of the book. Therein the nine Nathas or Siddhas of the Rishabha family, viz., Kavi, Hari, Antariksha, Prabuddha, Pippalayan, Avirhotra, Drumil, Chamas and Karabha-jan expounded the principles of the Bhagawat Dharma to King Janak. The latter asked all the nine Nathas most important questions and each of them answered them satisfactorily.

The first, i.e., Kavi explained what is Bhagawat Dharma; Hari, the characteristics of a Bhakta (devotee); Antariksha, what is Maya; Prabuddha, how to cross Maya; Pippalayan, what is Para-Brahma; Avirhotra, what is Karma; Drumil, the incarnations of God and their deeds; Chamas, how a non-devotee fares after death; Karabhajan, the different modes of worship of God in different ages. The substance of all the exposition was that in this Kali age, the only means of liberation was the remembrance of Hari's (Lord's) or Guru's feet.

After the reading was over, Kakasaheb said in a despondent tone to Madhavarao and others - "How wonderful is the discourse of the nine Nathas on Bhakti or devotion. But at the same time how difficult it is to put it into practice! The Nathas were perfect, but is it possible for fools like us to attain the devotion as deline-ated by them? we won't get it even after several births, then how are we to get salvation? It seems that there is no hope for us." Madhavarao did not like this pessimistic attitude of Kakasaheb. He said - "It is a pity that one who by his good luck got such a jewel (Guru) as Baba, should cry out so disparagingly; If he has unwavering faith in Baba, why should he feel restless? The Bhakti of the Nathas may be strong and wonderful, but is not ours' loving and affectionate? And has not Baba told us authoritatively that remembering and chanting Hari's and Guru's name confers salvation? Then where is the cause for fear and anxiety? Kakasaheb was not satisfied with Madhavarao's explanation. He continued to be anxious and restless, the whole day, thinking and brooding over how to get the powerful Bhakti of the Nathas. Next morning, the following miracle took place.

One gentleman, named Anandrao Pakhade came there in search of Madhavarao. The reading of the Bhagawat was then going on. Mr. Pakhade sat near Madhavarao and was whispering something to him. He was mentioning in low tone his dream-vision. As there was some interruption in the reading by this whispering, Kakasaheb stopped the reading, and asked Madhava-rao what the matter was. The latter said - "Yesterday you expressed your doubt, now here is the explanation of it; hear Mr. Pakhade's vision which Baba gave him, explaining the character-istic of 'saving' devotion and showing that the devotion in the form of bow to, or worship of, Guru's feet is sufficient." All were anxious to hear the vision specially Kakasaheb. At their suggestion Mr. Pakhade began to relate the vision as follows.

I was standing in a deep sea in waist-deep water. There I saw Sai Baba all of a sudden. He was sitting on a beautiful throne studded with diamonds, with His Feet in water. I was most pleased and satisfied with the Form of Baba. The vision was so realistic that I never thought that it was a dream. Curiously enough Madhavarao was also standing there. He said to me feel-ingly - 'Anandrao, fall at Baba's Feet.' I rejoined "I also wish to do so, but His Feet are in water, how can I place my head on them? I am helpless." Hearing this he said to Baba - "Oh Deva, take out Your Feet which are under water." Then Baba immediately took out His feet. I caught them without delay and bowed to them. On seeing this Baba blessed me saying - Go now, you will attain your welfare, there is no cause for fear and anxiety. He also added - "Give a silk-bordered dhotar to my Shama, you will profit, thereby."

In compliance with Baba's order, Mr. Pakhade brought the dhotar and requested Kakasaheb to hand it over to Madhavarao; but the latter refused to accept it, saying that unless Baba gave a hint or suggestion for acceptance, he would not accept it. Then after some discussion Kakasaheb decided to cast lots. It was the invariable practice of Kakasaheb to cast lots in all dubious matters and to abide by the decision as shown by the picked up chit or lot. In this particular case two chits, on one of which was written 'To accept' and on another 'To reject', were placed at the feet of Baba's picture and an infant was asked to pick one of them. The 'To accept' chit was picked up and the dhotar was handed over to, and accepted by, Madhavarao. In this way both Anandrao and Madhavarao were satisfied and Kakasaheb's difficulty was solved.

This story exhorts us to give respect to the words of other saints, but at the same time asks us to have full faith in our Mother, i.e., the Guru, and abide by His instructions: for he knows our welfare better than any other person. Carve out on your heart, the following words of Baba - "There are innumerable saints in this world, but 'Our father' (Guru) is the Father (Real Guru). Others might say many good things, but we should never forget our Guru's words. In short, love your Guru whole-heartedly, surrender to Him completely and prostrate yourselves before Him reverentially and then you will see that there is no sea of the mundane existence before you to cross, there is no darkness before the sun."

Wooden plank Baba's Bedstead and not Bhagat's

In His earlier days, Baba slept on a wooden plank, 4 arms in length and only a span in breadth with panatis (earthen lamps) burning at the four corners. Later on He broke the plank into pieces and threw it away (Vide Chapter X). Once Baba was describing the greatness or importance of this plank to Kakasaheb, hearing this the latter said to Baba - "If You still love the wooden plank, I will again suspend or hang up one in the Masjid again for You to sleep at ease." Baba replied - "I won't like to sleep up, leaving Mhalasapati down on the ground." Then Kakasaheb said - "I will provide another plank for Mhalasapati." Baba - "How can he sleep on the plank? It is not easy to sleep up on the plank. He who has many good qualities in him can do so. He who can sleep 'with his eyes wide open' can effect that. When I go to sleep I ask often Mhalasapati to sit by My side, place his hand on My heart and watch the 'chanting of the Lord's name' there, and if he finds Me sleepy, wake Me up. He can't do even this. He himself gets drowsy and begins to nod his head. When I feel his hand heavy as a stone on My heart and cry out - 'Oh Bhagat', he moves and opens his eyes. How can he, who can't sit and sleep well on the ground and whose asana (posture) is not steady and who is a slave to sleep, sleep high up on a plank? On many other occasions Baba said, out of love for His devotees - "What is ours is with us, and what is another's is with him."

Bow to Shri Sai - Peace be to all

Chapter XLVI

Baba's Gaya Trip - Story of Goats.

This Chapter describes Shama's strip to Kashi, Prayag and Ga-ya and how Baba (in the Form of His portrait) was there ahead of him; it also describes Baba's reminiscences of the past birth of two goats.

Preliminary

Blessed, Oh Sai, are Your Feet, blessed is Your remembrance and blessed is Your darshan which frees us from the bond of Karma. Though Your Form is invisible to us now, still if the devotees believe in You, they get living experiences from You. By an invisible and subtle thread You draw Your devotees from far and near to Your Feet and embrace them like a kind and loving mother. The devotees do not know where You are, but You so skillfully pull the wires that they ultimately realize that You are at their back to help and support them.

The intelligent, wise and learned folk fall into the pit of the samsar on account of their egoism, but You save, by Your power, the poor, simple and devout persons. Inwardly and invisibly you play all the game, but show that you are not concerned with it. You do things and pose yourself as a non-doer. Nobody ever knows Your life. The best course therefore for us is to surrender our body, speech and mind to Your Feet and always chant Your name for destroying our sins. You fulfill the wishes of the devotees and to those who are without any desire You give bliss supreme. Chanting Your sweet name is the easiest sadhana for devotees. By this Saharan (means), our sins, Rajas and Tamas qualities will vanish, the Sattvic qualities and righteousness will gain predominance and along with this, discrimination, dis-passion and knowledge will follow.

Then we shall abide in our Self and our Guru (who are one and the same). This is what is called complete surrender to the Guru. The only sure sign of this is that our mind gets calm and peaceful. The greatness of this surrender, devotion and knowledge is unique; for peace, non-attachment, fame and salvation etc.., come in its train.

If Baba accepts a devotee, He follows him and stands by him, day and night, at his home or abroad. Let the devotee go anywhere he likes, Baba is there ahead of him in some form in an inconceivable manner. The following story illustrates this.

Sometime after Kakasaheb Dixit was introduced to Sai Baba, he decided to perform the thread (Upanayan) ceremony of his eldest son Babu at Nagpur. At about the same time Nanasaheb Chandorkar decided to perform the marriage ceremony of his eldest son at Gwalior. Both Dixit and Chandorkar came to Shirdi and lovingly invited Baba for these functions. Baba asked them to take Shama as His representative. When He was pressed to come in person, Baba told them to take Shama with them and that "after doing Benares and Prayag He would be ahead of Shama." Now mark these words for they show Baba's all-pervasiveness.

Taking the permission of Baba, Shama decided to go to Nagpur and Gwalior for these functions and ceremonies and thence to Kashi, Prayag and Gaya. Appa Kote made up his mind to accompany him. They both went first to Nagpur for the thread ceremony. Kakasaheb Dixit gave Shama Rs.200 for his expenses. Then they went to Gwalior for the marriage ceremony. There Nanasaheb Chandorkar gave Shama Rs.100 and his Vyahi (relation) Mr. Jather gave him also Rs.100.

Then Shama went to Kashi, and then to Ayodhya where he was well received in Jather's beautiful temple of Laxmi-Narayan at Kashi (Varanasi or Benares) and in the Rama-Mandir at Ayodhya by Jathar's manager. They (Shama and Kote) stayed for twenty-one days in Ayodhya and two months in Kashi (Benares).

They then left for Gaya. In the train they felt a little uneasy on hearing that plague was prevailing in Gaya. At night they alighted at Gaya station and stayed in the Dharmashala. In the morning the Gayawala (the Priest who arranges and provides for the lodging and boarding of the pilgrims) came there and aid - "The pilgrims have already started, you better make haste." Shama casually asked him whether there was plague in Gaya. "No" said the Gayawala. "Please come without any fear or anxiety and see yourself."

They went with him and stayed in his house which was a big and commodious Wada. Shama was pleased with the accommodation provided for him, but what pleased him most, was the beautiful big portrait of Baba fixed in the central and front portion of the building. Seeing this portrait Shama was overwhelmed with emotion. He remembered Baba's words, viz., "After doing Kashi and Prayag He would be ahead of Shama" and burst into tears. His hairs stood on end, his throat was choked and he began to sob.

The Gayawala thought that he was afraid of plague prevailing there and therefore was crying. But Shama enquired of him whence he got Baba's portrait there. He replied that he had two or three hundred agents working at Manmad and Punatambe for looking to the convenience of the pilgrims to Gaya and from them he heard about Baba's fame. Then about twelve years ago he went to Shirdi and took Baba's darshan. There he wanted Baba's portrait hung in Shama's house and with Baba's permission Shama gave it to him. This was the same portrait. Shama then remembered this former incident. The Gayawalas's joy knew no bounds when he learnt that the same Shama, who obliged him before, was his guest then. Then they both exchanged love and service and were most delighted and happy. The Gayawala gave him a right royal welcome. He was a very rich man. He sat in a palanquin and made Shama ride an elephant and attended to all his comforts and conveniences.

The moral of the story is this:
That Baba's words came out true to the letter and unbounded was His love towards the devotees. But leave this aside. He also loved all creatures equally, for He felt that He was one with them. The following story will illustrate this.

Two Goats

Baba was once returning from Lendi, when He saw a flock of goats. Two of them attracted His attention. He went to them, caressed and fondled them and bought them for Rs.32. The devotees were surprised at this conduct of Baba. They thought that Baba was duped in this bargain, as the goats would fetch Rs. two each, at the most Rs.3 or 4 each, i.e., Rs.8 for both. They began to take Baba to task for this, but Baba kept calm and cool. Shama and Tatya Kote asked Baba for an explanation. He said He should not store money as He had no home, and any family to look after. He asked them to purchase at His cost 4 seers of 'dal' (lentil) and feed the goats. After this was done, Baba returned the goats to the owner of the flock and gave out of the following reminiscences and story of the goats.

"Oh, Shama and Tatya, you think that I have been deceived in this bargain. No. Listen to their story. In their former birth they were human beings and had the good fortune to be My companions and sit by My side. They were brothers, sons of the same mother, loving each other at first, but later on, they became enemies. The elder brother was an idle fellow while the younger one was an active chap and earned a lot of money. The former became greedy and jealous and wanted to kill his brother and take away his money. They forgot their fraternal relations and began to quarrel with each other. The elder brother resorted to many devices to kill his younger brother, but all of his attempts failed. Thus they became deadly enemies and finally on one occasion the elder gave a deadly blow with a big stick on the latter's head while the latter struck the former with an axe, with the result that both fell dead on the spot. As the result of their actions, they were both born as goats. As they passed by me, I at once recognized them. I remembered their past history. Taking pity on them I wanted to feed them and give them rest and comfort and for this reason I spent all the money for which you reprove me. As you did not like My bargain I sent them back to their shepherd." Such was Sai's love for the goats!

Bow to Shri Sai - Peace be to all

Chapter XLVII Baba's Reminiscences

Story of Veerbhadrappa and Chenbassappa (Snake and Frog)

The last chapter described Baba's reminiscences about two goats.
This describes more such reminiscences and relates the story of
Veerbhadrappa and Chenbassappa.

Preliminary

Blessed is the face of Sai. If we cast a glance at Him for a
moment, He destroys the sorrow of many past births and confers
great bliss on us; and if He looks at us with grace, our bondage of
Karma is immediately snapped away and we are led to happiness.
The river Ganges washes away the dirt and sins of all people who
go to her for a bath; but she intently longs for the saints to come
to her and bless her with their feet and remove all the dirt (sins)
accumulated in her. She knows for certain that this accumulation
can only be removed by the holy feet of the saints. Sai is the crest-
jewel of the saints, and now hear from Him the following
purifying story.

The Snake and the Frog

Sai Baba said - "One morning after taking My breakfast I
strolled along till I came to a small river bank. As I was tired, I
rested there, washed My hands and feet and had a bath and felt
refreshed. There was a foot-path and a cart-track sheltered by
shady trees. The breeze was also blowing gently. As I was preparing to smoke chilli (His pipe), I heard the croaking of a frog. I was
striking the flint and lighting the fire, when a traveler turned up,
sat by My side, bowed to Me and politely invited Me to his house
for meals and rest. He lit up the pipe and handed it over to Me.
The croaking was heard again and he wanted to know what it
was. I told him that a frog was in trouble and was tasting the bitter
fruit of its own karma. We have to reap now the fruit of what we
sow (do) in our past life, and there is no use in crying about it.

Then he smoked and handed over the pipe to Me and said that
he would go there in person and see for himself. I told him that a

frog was caught by a big snake and was crying. Both were very wicked in their past life and were now reaping the fruit of their actions in these bodies. He went out and found that a huge black serpent was holding a big frog in its mouth.

He turned to Me and said that in about ten or twelve minutes the frog would be eaten up by the snake. I said, "No, this can't be. I am its father (protector) and I am here now. How shall I allow the snake to eat it up, am I here for nothing? Just see how I release it."

After smoking again, we walked on to the place. He was afraid and asked Me not to proceed further as the snake might attack us. Not minding him, I went ahead and addressed the creatures thus:

"Oh Veerbhadrappa, has not your enemy Bassappa yet repented though he has been born as a frog, and you too, though born as a serpent, still maintain bitter enmity against him? Curse upon you, be ashamed, give up your hatred now and rest in peace."

Hearing these words, the snake left the frog quickly and dove into the river and disappeared. The frog also jumped away and hid itself in the bushes.

The traveler was much surprised; he said that he could not understand how the snake dropped the frog and disappeared at the words uttered, who was Veerbhadrappa and who was Bassappa, and what was the cause of their enmity. I returned with him to the foot of the tree and after sharing a few puffs of smoke with him I explained the whole mystery to his as follows:

There was ancient holy place sanctified by a temple of Mahadev about four or five miles from My place. The temple was old and dilapidated. The residents of the place collected funds for its repairs. After a large amount was collected, arrangement for worship was made and plans with estimates for repairs were prepared. A rich local man was appointed the Treasurer and the whole work was entrusted to him. He was to keep regular accounts and be honest in all his dealings. He was a first class miser and spent very little for the repairs, which consequently made very little progress.

He spent all the funds, swallowed some amount himself and spent nothing from his pocket. He had a sweet tongue and was very clever in offering plausible explanations regarding the poor and tardy progress of the work. The people again went to him and said that unless he lent his helping hand and tried his best, the work would not be complete. They requested him to work out the scheme and again collected subscriptions and sent the amount to him. He received it, but sat as quiet as before without making any progress. After some days, God (Mahadev) appeared in his wife's dream and said to her - "You get up, build the dome of the temple, I will give you a hundred-fold of what you spend." She told this vision to her husband. He was afraid that it would involve him in some expenses and therefore laughed it out saying that it was a mere dream, a thing not to be relied and acted upon, or else why did not God appear to him and tell him? Was he far off from her? This looks like a bad dream, having for its object the creation of ill feeling between husband and wife. She had to remain quiet.

God does not like big subscriptions and donations collected against the wishes of the donors, but He likes ever trifling amounts given with love, devotion and appreciation. Some days after, God again appeared in her dream and said - "Do not bother yourself about your husband and the collections with him. Don't press him to spend any amount for the temple. What I want is feeling and devotion. So give, if you like, anything of your own."

She consulted her husband about this vision and decided to give God her ornaments given by her father. The miser felt disconcerted and decided to cheat even God in this item. He undervalued the ornaments at Rs.1,000 and bought them himself and in lieu of the amount gave a field to God as endowment or security. The wife agreed to this. The field or land was not his own, it belonged to one poor woman named Dubaki who mortgaged it to him for Rs.200. She was not able to redeem it for long. So the cunning miser cheated all, his wife, Dubaki and even God. The land was sterile, uncultivated and worth nothing and yielded nothing, even in best seasons.

Thus ended this transaction and the land was given in the possession of the poor priest who was pleased with the endowment. Sometime later on, strange things happened. There was a terrific storm and heavy downpour of rain; lightning struck the house of the miser, when he and his wife both died. Dubaki also breathed her last.

In the next life, the rich miser was born at Mathura in a Brahmin family and was named Veerbhadrappa. His devout wife was born as the daughter of the priest of the temple and was named Gouri. The woman Dubaki (the mortgagor) was born as a male in the family of the Gurav (attendant) of the temple and was named Chenbassappa. The priest was a friend of Mine; He often came to Me, chatted and smoked with Me. His daughter Gouri was also devoted to Me. She was growing fast and her father was seeking a good husband for her. I told him not to worry about this as the bridegroom himself would come seeking her. Then there came a poor boy named Veerbhadrappa of their caste, wandering and begging his bread to the priest's house. With My consent Gouri was given in marriage to him. He was also at first devoted to Me as I recommended his marriage with Gouri. Even in this new life he was hankering after money and asked Me to help him to get it as he was leading a married man's life.

Strange things happened. There was a sudden rise in prices. By Gouri's good luck, there was a great demand for land and the endowment land was sold for one lakh of rupees (100 times the worth of her ornaments). Half the amount was paid in cash and the remaining was to be paid in 25 installments of Rs. 2,000 each. All agreed to this transaction, but began to quarrel over the money. They came to Me for consultation. I told them that the property belonged to God and was vested in the priest and Gouri was his sole heiress and proprietress and no amount should be spent without her consent and that her husband had no right what-soever to the amount.

Hearing my opinion Veerbhadrappa was angry with Me and said that I wanted to establish Gouri's claim and embezzle her property. Hearing his words, I remembered God and kept quiet. Veerbhadrappa scolded his wife (Gouri) and she came to Me at noon and requested Me not to mind the words of others and not to discard her as she was My daughter. As she thus sought My protection I gave her a pledge that I would cross seven seas to help her. Then that night Gouri had a vision. Mahadev appeared in her dream and said - "The whole money is yours, do not give anything to anybody, spend some amount for temple purposes in consultation with Chenbassappa and if you want to use it for some other purpose, consult Baba in the Masjid (Myself)." Gouri told Me the vision and I gave her the proper advice in the matter. I told her to take the principal or capital amount to herself, give half the amount of interest to Chenbassappa and that Veerbhadrappa had nothing to do in the matter. While I was thus talking, both Veerbhadrappa and Chenbassappa came there quarrelling. I tried My best to appease them and told them God's vision to Gouri. Veerbhadrappa got wild and angry and threatened to kill Chenbassappa cutting him to pieces. The latter was timid; he caught my feet and sought my refuge. I pledged Myself to save him from the wrath of his foe.

Then after some time Veerbhadrappa died and was born as a snake and Chenbassappa died and was born as a frog. Hearing the croaking of Chenbassappa and remembering my pledge, I came here, saved him and kept My word. God runs to His devotees for help in times of danger. He saved Chenbassappa (the frog) by sending Me here. All this is God's Leela or sport."

The Moral

The moral of the story is that one has to reap what one sows, and there is no escape unless one suffers and squares up one's old debts and dealings with others, and that greed for money drags the greedy man to the lowest level and ultimately brings destruction on him and others.

Bow to Shri Sai - Peace be to all

Chapter XLVIII
Warding off Devotee's Calamities

Stories of (1) Shevade and (2) Sapatneker

At the commencement of this chapter, someone asked Hemadpant whether Sai Baba was a Guru or Sadguru. In order to answer the question Hemadpant describes the signs or marks of a Sadguru as follows: -

Signs of Sadguru

He who teaches us Veda and Vedanta or the six Shastras (systems), he who controls the breath, or brands his body with Mudras (metallic marks of Vishnu's weapons) or gives pleasing discourses regarding Brahma, he who gives mantras (sacred syllables) to the disciples and orders them to chant the same a certain number of times, but does not assure them any result in a definite time, he who by his spacious wordy knowledge explains beautifully the Ultimate Principle, but has himself got no experience or self-realization is not a Sadguru. But he, who by his discourse creates in us, a distaste for the enjoyments of this world and the next, and gives us a taste of self-realization, who is well versed in both the theoretical and practical knowledge (self-realization), deserves to be called a Sadguru. How can he, who is himself devoid of self-realization, give it to the disciples? A Sadguru does not, even in his dream, expect any service or profit from his disciples. On the contrary he wishes to serve them. He does not think that he is great and the disciple small. Not only he loves him as his son but regards him as equal to himself or as Brahma. The main characteristic of a Sadguru is that he is the abode of peace. He is never restless nor ruffled. He has no pride of his learning. The poor and the rich, the small and the great, are the same to him.

Hemadpant thinks that on account of the store or accumulation of merits in his past births, he had the good fortune of meeting and being blessed by such a Sadguru as Sai Baba. Even in full youth He hoarded nothing (expect perhaps chillum). He had no family, no friend, no home, nor any support. Since He was eighteen, His control of mind was perfect and extraordinary. He lived then fearless in a secluded place and always abided in His Self. Seeing the pure attachment of His devotees He always acted in their interests and hence He was in a way dependent on them.

What experiences He gave to His devotees while he was living in flesh, are even today, after His Mahasamadhi, obtained now by those who attach themselves to Him. What the devotees have to do is this - They have to trim their heart lamp of faith and devotion, and burn in it wicks of love, and when this is done, the flame of knowledge (self-realization) will be lit up and shine brighter. Mere knowledge without love is dry; nobody wants such knowledge. Without love there is no contentment; so we should have unbroken and unbounded love. How can we praise love? Everything is insignificant before it. Without love our reading, hearing and the study are of no avail. In the wake of love follow devotion, dis-passion, peace and liberation with all their treasures. We do not get love for anything unless we feel earnestly about it. So where there is real yearning and feeling, God manifests Himself. It includes love and is the means of liberation.

Now let us revert to the main story of this chapter. Let a man go to a true Saint with a pure mind, otherwise (fraudulently) and hold his feet; ultimately he is sure to be saved. This is illustrated by the following stories.

Mr. Shevade

Mr. Sapatneker of Akkalkot (Sholapur District) was studying for law. A fellow student Mr. Shevade met him. Other fellow students also gathered together and compared notes of their study. It was found by the questions and answers amongst themselves, that Mr. Shevade was the least prepared of all for the examination, and therefore all the students derided him. But he said that though he was not prepared, he was sure to pass the examination, as his Sai Baba was there to get him through it successfully. Mr. Sapatnekar was surprised at this remark. He took Mr. Shevade aside and asked him who this Sai Baba was whom he extolled so high. He replied - "There lives in a Masjid in Shirdi (Ahmednagar District) a fakir. He is a great Sat-purusha. There may be other saints, but this is unique. Unless there is a great store of merits on one's account, one can't see Him. I fully believe in Him, and what He says will be never untrue. He has assured me that I will pass definitely next year and I am confident that I will get through the final examination also with His grace." Mr. Sapatneker laughed at his friend's confidence and jeered at him and Baba.

Sapatnekars

Mr. Sapatnekar passed his examination, settled at Akkalkot and practiced as a lawyer there. Ten years after this, i.e., in 1913 he lost his only son on account of a throat disease. This broke his heart. He sought relief by making a pilgrimage to Pandharpur, Ganagapur and other holy places. He got no peace of mind. Then he read Vedanta, which also did not help him. In the meanwhile he remembered Mr. Shevade's remarks and his faith in Baba, and he thought that he too should go to Shirdi and see Baba. He went to Shirdi with his younger brother Panditrao and was much pleased to see Baba from a distance.

When he went near and prostrated himself and placed a coconut before Baba with pure feeling (devotion), the latter at once cried out, "Get away." Saptnekar hung down his head, moved back and sat aside. He wanted to consult somebody who would advise him how to proceed. Somebody mentioned Bala Shimpi's name. Sapatnekar saw him and sought his help.

They bought Baba's photos and came with them to the Masjid. Baba Shimpi took a photo in his hand, gave it to Baba and asked him whose photo it was. Baba said that this photo was the 'Yara' (Lover) of him, pointing to Sapatnekar. Saying this Baba laughed and all others joined. Bala asked Baba the significance of the laugh and beckoned Sapatnekar to come forward and take darshan. When Saptnakar began to prostrate himself, Baba again cried "Get out." Sapatnekar did not know what to do. Then they both joined their hands and sat before Baba, praying. Baba finally ordered Sapatnekar to clear out immediately. Both were sad and dejected. As Baba's order had to be obeyed, Sapatnekar left Shirdi with a heavy heart praying that he should be allowed to take darshan next time.

272

Mrs. Sapatnekar

One year elapsed. Still his mind was not at peace. He went to Gangapur, where he felt more restless. Then he went to Madhegaon for rest and finally decided to go to Kashi.

Two days before starting, his wife got a vision. In her dream she was going with a pitcher to Lakadsha's well. There a fakir with a piece of cloth round his head, who was sitting at the foot of the Neem tree, came close to her and said - "My dear lassie, why get exhausted for nothing? I get your pitcher filled with pure water." She was afraid of the fakir and hastened back with the empty pitcher. The fakir followed her. At this she was awakened and opened her eyes. She told this vision to her husband. They thought that this was an auspicious sign and they both left for Shirdi.

When they reached the Masjid, Baba was absent. He had gone to Lendi. They waited till His return. When He returned, she was surprised to see that the fakir she saw in her vision resembled exactly Baba. She reverentially prostrated herself before Baba and sat looking at him. Seeing her humility Baba was much pleased and began to tell a story in his peculiar characteristic fashion to a third party. He said - "My arms, abdomen and waist are paining for a long time. I took many medicines, the pains did not abate. I got sick of the medicines as they gave me no relief, but I am surprised to see now that all the pains have disappeared at once." Though no name was mentioned it was the story of Mrs. Sapatnekar herself. Her pains, as described by Baba, left her soon and she was happy.

Then Mr. Sapatnekar went ahead to take darshan. He was again welcomed with the former, "Get out." This time he was more penitent and persevering. He said that Baba's displeasure was due to his past deeds and resolved to make amends for the same. He determined to see Baba alone and ask his pardon for his past actions. This he did. He placed his head on Baba's feet and Baba placed His hand on it and Sapatnekar sat stroking Baba's leg. Then a shepherdess came and sat massaging Baba's waist. Baba in his characteristic way began to tell the story of a bania. He related the various vicissitudes of all his life, including the death of his only son.

Sapatnekar was surprised to see that the story which Baba related was his own, and he wondered how Baba knew every detail of it. He came to know that He was omniscient and knew the hearts of all. When this thought crossed his mind, Baba still addressing the shepherdess and pointing to Sapatnekar said - "This fellow blames Me and charges Me with killing his son. Do I kill people's children? Why does this fellow come to the Masjid and cry? Now I will do this I will again bring that very child back in his wife's womb." With these words He placed His blessing and on his head and comforted him saying - "These feet are old and holy, you are carefree now; place entire faith in Me and you will soon get your object." Sapatnekar was much moved with emotion, he bathed Baba's feet with his tears and then returned to his residence.

Then he made preparations of worship and naivedya and came with his wife to the Masjid. He offered all this to Baba daily and accepted prasad from Him. There was a crowd in the Masjid and Sapatnekar went there and saluted Baba again and again.

Seeing heads clashing against heads Baba said to Sapatnekar - "Oh, why do you prostrate yourself now and then? The one Namaskar offered with love and humility is enough." Then Sapatnekar witnessed that night the Chavadi procession described before. In that procession Baba looked like a veritable Pandurang (Vithal).

At parting next day, Sapatnekar thought that he should first pay one rupee as dakshina and if Baba asked again, instead of saying no, he should pay one more, reserving with him sufficient amount as expenses for the journey. When he went to the Masjid and offered one rupee, Baba asked for another as per his intention and when it was paid, Baba blessed him saying - "Take the coconut, put it in your wife's oti (upper fold of her sari), and go away at ease without the least anxiety." He did so, and within a year a son was born to him and with an infant of eight months the pair came to Shirdi, placed it at Baba's feet and prayed thus - "Oh, Sainath, we do not know how to redeem Your obligations, therefore we prostrate ourselves before You, bless us poor helpless fellows, henceforth let Your holy feet be our sole refuge. Many thoughts and ideas trouble us in waking and dream states, so turn away our minds from them to Your bhajan and bless us."

The son was named Murlidhar. Two others (Bhaskar and Dinkar) were born afterwards. The Sapatnekar pair thus realized that Baba's words were never untrue and unfulfilled, but turned out literally true.

Bow to Shri Sai - Peace be to all

Chapter XLIX

Stories of (1) Hari Kanoba - (2) Somadeva Swami
(3) Nanasaheb Chandorkar.

Preliminary

The Vedas and the Puranas cannot sufficiently praise (describe) Brahma or Sadguru; then how can we, who are ignorant, describe our Sadguru Shri Sai Baba? We think that it is better for us to keep quiet in this matter. In reality the observance of the vow of silence is the best way of praising the Sadguru; but the good qualities of Sai Baba make us forget our vow of silence and inspire us to open our mouth. Good dishes taste flat if there be no company of friends and relations to partake of the dishes with us, but when they join us, the dishes acquire additional flavor. The same is the case with the Sai Leelamrit - the nectar in the form of Sai's leelas. This nectar we cannot partake alone. Friends and brothers have to join us - the more the better.

It is Sai Baba Himself that inspires these stories and gets them written as He desires. Our duty is to surrender completely to Him and meditate on Him. Practising penance is better than pilgrimage, vow, sacrifice, and charity. Worshipping Hari (Lord) is better than penance, and meditation on the Sadguru is the best of all. We have, therefore, to chant Sai's name by mouth, think over His sayings in our mind, meditate on His form, feel real love for Him in our heart and do all our actions for His sake.

There is no better means than this for snapping the bondage of samsar. If we can do our duty on our part as stated above, Sai is bound to help and liberate us. Now we revert to the stories of this chapter.

Hari Kanoba

A gentleman of Bombay named Hari Kanoba heard from his friends and relations many Leelas of Baba. He did not believe in them as he was a doubting Thomas. He wanted to test Baba himself. So he came to Shirdi with some Bombay friends. He wore a lace-bordered turban on his head and a new pair of sandals on his

276

feet. Seeing Baba from a distance he thought of going to Him and prostrating himself before Him. He did not know what to do with his new sandals. Still going to some corner outside in the open courtyard, he placed them there and went in the Masjid and took Baba's darshan. He made a reverential bow to Baba, took udi and prasad from Baba and returned. When he reached the corner he found that his sandals had disappeared. He searched for them in vain and returned to his lodging very much dejected.

He bathed, offered worship and naivedya and sat for meals, but all the while he was thinking about nothing but his sandals. After finishing his meals, he came out to wash his hands when he saw a Maratha boy coming towards him. He had in his hand a stick, on the top of which was suspended a pair of new sandals. He said to the men who had come out to wash their hands that Baba sent him with this stick in hand and asked him to go on the streets crying - "Hari Ka Beta. Jari Ka Pheta" and told him that "If anybody claims these sandals, first assure yourself that his name is Hari and that he is the son of Ka, i.e., Kanoba, and that he wears a lace-bordered turban and then give them to him." Hearing this, Hari Kanoba was pleasantly surprised. He went ahead to the boy and claimed the sandals as his own. He said to the boy that his name was Hari and that he was the son of Ka (Kanoba) and showed him his lace-bordered turban. The boy was satisfied and returned the sandals to him. Hari Kanoba wondered in his mind saying that his lace-bordered turban was visible to all and Baba might have seen it, but how could he know his name Hari and that he was the son of Kanoba, as this was his first trip to Shirdi. He came there with the sole object of testing Baba and with no other motive. He came to know by this incident that Baba was a great Satpurush. He got what he wanted and returned home well pleased.

Somadeva Swami

Now hear the story of another man who came to try Baba. Bhaiji, brother of Kakasaheb Dixit was staying at Nagpur. When he had gone to the Himalayas in 1906, he made an acquaintance with one Somadeva Swami of Hardwar at Uttarkashi down the Gangotri Valley. Both took down each other's names in their diaries. Five years afterwards Somadeva Swami came to Nagpur and was Bhaiji's guest. There he was pleased to hear the Leelas of Baba and a strong desire arose in his mind to go to Shirdi and see Him. He got a letter of introduction from Bhaiji and left for Shirdi.

After passing Manmad and Kopergaon, he took a tanga and drove to Shirdi. As he came near Shirdi he saw two high flags floating over the Masjid in Shirdi. Generally we find different ways of behavior, different modes of living and different outward paraphernalia with different Saints. But these outward signs should never be our standards to judge the worth of the Saints. But with Somadeva Swami it was different. As soon as he saw the flags flying, he thought - "Why should a Saint take a liking for the flags, does this denote Sainthood? It implies the Saint's hankering after fame." Thinking thus he wished to cancel his Shirdi trip and said to his fellow travelers that he would go back. They said to him - "Then why did you come so long? If your mind gets restless by the sight of the flags, how much more agitated would you be on seeing in Shirdi the Ratha (car), the palanquin, the horse and all other paraphernalia?" The Swami got more confounded and said - "Not a few such Sadhus, with horses, palanquins and tom-toms have I seen and it is better for me to return than see such Sadhus." Saying this he started to return. The fellow travelers pressed him not to do so, but to proceed. They asked him to stop his crooked way of thinking and told him that the Sadhu, i.e., Baba did not care a bit for the flags and other paraphernalia, nor for fame. It was the people, His devotees that kept up all this paraphernalia out of love and devotion to Him.

Finally he was persuaded to continue his journey, go to Shirdi and see Baba. When he went and saw Baba from the courtyard, he was melted inside, his eyes were full of tears, his throat was choked and all his evil and crooked thoughts vanished. He re-membered his Guru's saying that - 'that is our abode and place of rest where the mind is most pleased and charmed.' He wished to roll himself in the dust of Baba's Feet and when he approached Baba, the latter got wild and cried aloud - "Let all our humbug (paraphernalia) be with us, you go back to your home, beware if you come back to this Masjid. Why take the darshan of one who

flies a flag over his Masjid? Is this a sign of sainthood? Remain
here not a moment." The Swami was taken aback by surprise. He
realized that Baba read his heart and spoke it out. How omniscient
He was! He knew that he was least intelligent and that Baba was
noble and pure. He saw Baba embracing somebody, touching
someone with his hand, comforting others, staring kindly at some,
laughing at others, giving udi prasad to some and thus pleasing
and satisfying all. Why should he alone be dealt with so harshly?
Thinking seriously he came to realize that Baba's conduct responded exactly to his inner thought and that he should take a lesson from this and improve; and that Baba's wrath was a blessing
in disguise. It is needless to say that later on, his faith in Baba was
confirmed and he became a staunch devotee of Baba.

Nanasaheb Chandorkar

Hemadpant concludes this chapter with a story of Nanasaheb
Chandorkar. When Nanasaheb was once sitting in the Masjid with
Mhalasapati and others, a Mohammedan gentleman from Bijapur
came with his family to see Baba. Seeing gosha (veiled) ladies
with him, Nanasaheb wanted to go away, but Baba prevented him
from doing so. The ladies came and took the darshan of Baba.
When one of the ladies removed her veil in saluting Baba's feet
and then resumed it again, Nanasaheb, who saw her face, was so
much smitten with her rare beauty that he wished to see her face
again.

Knowing Nana's restlessness of mind, Baba spoke to him after
the lady had left the place as follows - "Nana, why are you getting
agitated in vain? Let the senses do their allotted work, or duty, we
should not meddle with their work. God has created this beautiful
world and it is our duty to appreciate its beauty. The mind will get
steady and calm slowly and gradually. When the front door was
open, why go by the back one? When the heart is pure, there is no
difficulty, whatsoever. Why should one be afraid of any one if
there be no evil thought in us? The eyes may do their work, why
should you feel shy and tottering?"

Shama was there and he could not follow the meaning of what
Baba said. So he asked Nana about this on their way home. Nana
told him about his restlessness at the sight of the beautiful lady,

how Baba knew it and advised him about it. Nana explained Baba's meaning as follows - "That our mind is fickle by nature, it should not be allowed to get wild. The senses may get restless, the body, however, should be held in check and not allowed to be impatient. Senses run after objects, but we should not follow them and crave for their objects. By slow and gradual practice, restlessness can be conquered. We should not be swayed by the senses, but they cannot be completely controlled. We should curb them rightly and properly according to the need of the occasion. Beauty is the subject of sight; we should fearlessly look at the beauty of objects. There is no room for shyness or fear. Only we should never entertain evil thoughts. Making the mind desire-less, observe God's works of beauty. In this way the senses will be easily and naturally controlled and even in enjoying objects you will be reminded of God. If the outer senses are not held in check and if the mind be allowed to run after objects and be attached to them, our cycle of births and deaths will not come to an end. Objects of sense are things harmful. With Viveka (discrimination) as our charioteer, we will control the mind and will not allow the senses to go astray. With such a charioteer we reach the Vishnu-pada, the final abode, our real Home from which there is no return."

Bow to Shri Sai - Peace be to all

Chapter L

Chapter 50 of the original Satcharita has been incorporated in Chapter 39, as it dealt with the same subject matter. Now, Chapter 51 of the Satcharita has been treated here as Chapter 50. This Chapter gives the stories of (1) Kakasaheb Dixit (2) Shri Tembye Swami (3) Balaram Dhurandhar.

Preliminary

Victory be unto Sai Who is the main stay of the Bhaktas, Who is our Sadguru, Who expounds the meaning of the Gita and Who gives us all powers. Oh Sai, look favorably on us and bless us all.

The sandalwood trees grow on the Malaya mountains and ward off heat. The clouds, pour their rainwater and thereby, cool and refresh all the people. The flowers, blossom in the spring and, enable us to worship God, therewith. So the stories of Sai Baba come forth, in order to give solace and comfort to the readers. Both, those, who tell; and those who hear the stories of Baba, are blessed and holy, as also the mouths of the former and the ears of the latter.

It is well-established fact, that though we try hundreds of means or sadhanas, we do not attain the spiritual goal of life, unless a Sadguru blesses us with his grace. Hear the following story in illustration of this statement

Kakasaheb Dixit (1864-1926)

Mr. Hari Sitaram alias Kakasaheb Dixit was born in 1864, in a Vadnagara Nagar-Brahmin family, at Khandwa. His primary education was done at Khandwa, Hinganghat, and secondary education at Nagpur. He came to Bombay for higher education and studied first in the Wilson College and then in the Elphinstone College. After graduation in 1883, he passed his LL.B. and solicitor's examination; and then served in the firm of the Government Solicitors, Messrs.' Little and Co., and then, after sometime started a solicitors' firm of his own.

Before 1909, Sai Baba's name was not familiar to Kakasaheb, but after that he soon becomes His great devotees. While he was staying at Lonavla, he happened to see his old friend. Mr. Nanasaheb Chandorkar. Both spent some time, in talking about many things. Kakasaheb described to him, how when he was boarding a train in London, he met with an accident, in which his foot slipped and was injured. Hundreds of remedies gave him no relief. Nanasaheb then told him that if he wished to get rid of the pain and lameness of his leg, he should go to his Sadguru, Sai Baba. He also gave him all the particulars of Sai Baba and mentioned to him Sai Baba's dictum "I draw to Me My man from far off, or even across the seven seas, like a sparrow with a string fastened to its feet." He also made it clear to him that if he be not Baba's man, he would not be attracted to Him and given a darshan. Kakasaheb was pleased to hear all this, and said to Nanasaheb that he would go to Baba, see Him and pray to Him to cure not so much his lame leg, but bring round his lame, fickle mind and give him eternal Bliss.

Sometime after, Kakasaheb went to Ahmednagar; and stayed with sirdar Kakasaheb Mirikar in connection with securing votes for a seat, in the Bombay Legislative Council. Mr. Balasaheb Mirikar, son of Kakasaheb Mirikar, who was a Mamalatdar of Kopergaon, also came at that time to Ahmendnagar in connection with a Horse Exhibition there. After the election business was over, Kakasaheb Dixit wanted to go to Shirdi and both the Mirikars, father and son were also thinking in their house about a fit and proper person, as a guide, with whom he should be sent there. There Sai Baba was arranging things for his reception. Shama got a telegram from his father-in-law at Ahemdnagar, stating that his wife was seriously ill, and that he should come to see her with his wife. Shama with Baba's permission went there, and saw his mother-in-law and found her improving and better. Nanasaheb Panshe and Appasaheb Gadre happened to see Shama, on their way to the Exhibition Dixit there and take him to Shirdi along with him. Kakasaheb Dixit and the Mirikars were also informed of Shama's arrival. In the evening Shama came to Mirikars, who introduced him to Kakasaheb. They arranged that Shama should leave for Kopergaon with Kakasaheb by the Ten O'clock night train. After this was settled, a curious thing happened.

Balasaheb Mirikar threw aside the veil or covering on Baba's big portrait and showed the same to Kakasaheb. He was surprised to see that He, Whom he was going to meet at Shirdi, was already there in the form of His portrait to greet him, at this juncture.

He was much moved and made his prostration before the portrait. This portrait belonged to Megha. The glass over it was broken and it was sent to Mirikars for repairs. The necessary repairs had been already made; and it was decided to return the portrait with Kakasaheb and Shama.

Before ten O'clock, they went to the station and booked their passage; but when the train arrived, they found that the Second Class was overcrowded; and then there was no room for them. Fortunately, the guard of the train turned out to be an acquaintance of Kakasaheb; and he put them up in the First Class. Thus they travelled comfortably and alighted at Kopergaon. Their joy knew no bounds when they saw there Nanasaheb Chandorkar, who was also bound for Shirdi. Kakasaheb and Nanasaheb embraced each other, and then after bathing in the sacred Godavari river they started for Shirdi. After coming there and getting Baba's darshan, Kakasaheb's mind was melted, his eyes were full of tears and he was overflowing with joy. Baba said to him, that he also was waiting for him; and had sent Shama ahead to receive him.

Kakasaheb then passed many happy years in Baba's company. He built a Wada in Shirdi which he made as his, more or less, permanent home. The experiences he got from Baba are so manifold, that it is not possible to relate them all here. The readers are advised to read a special (Kakasaheb Dixit) No. of 'Shri Sai Leela' magazine, Vol. 12, No. 6-9. we close this account with the mention of one fact only. Baba had comforted him by saying that in the end, "He will take him in air coach (Viman)", (i.e., secure him a happy death). This came out true. On the 5th of July 1926, he was travelling in the train with Hemadpant and talking about Sai Baba. He seemed deeply engrossed in Sai Baba. All of a sudden he threw his neck on Hemadpant's shoulder, and breathed his last with no trace of pain and uneasiness.

Shri Tembye Swami

We come to the next story, which shows how Saints love each other with fraternal affection. Once Shri Vasudevanand Saraswati, known as Shri Tembye Swami encamped, at Rajamahendri (Andhra Country), on the banks of Godavari. He was a devout, orthodox, Jnani and Yogi Bhakta of the God Dattatreya. One, a Mr. Pundalikrao, lawyer of Nanded (Nizam State) went to see him with some friends. While they were talking with him, the names of Shirdi and Sai Baba were casually mentioned.

Hearing Baba's name, the Swami bowed with his hands; and taking a coconut gave it to Pundalikrao, and said to him, "Offer this to my brother Sai, with my pranam and request Him not to forget me, but ever love me." He also added that the Swamis do not generally bow to others, but in this case an exception had to be made. Mr. Pundalikrao consented to take the fruit and his message to Baba. The Swami was right in calling Baba a brother, for as he maintained an Agnihotra (Sacred fire) day and night, in his orthodox fashion; Baba too kept His Agnihotra, i.e., Dhuni ever burning in the Masjid.

After one month Pundalikrao and others left for Shirdi with the coconut, and reached Manmad, and as they felt thirsty they went to a rivulet for drinking water. As water should not be drunk on an empty stomach, they took out some refreshments, i.e., Chivda (flattened rice mixed with spice). The Chivda tasted pungent and in order to soften it, someone suggested and broke the coconut and mixed its scrapings with it. Thus they made the Chivda mare tasty and palatable. Unfortunately the fruit broken, turned out to be the same that was entrusted to Pundalikrao. As they neared Shirdi, Pundalikrao remembered the trust, i.e., the coconut and was very sorry to learn that it was broken and utilized. Fearing and trembling, he came to Shirdi and saw Baba.

Baba had already received a wireless message, regarding the coconut, from the Tembye Swami, and Himself asked Pundalikrao first to give the things sent by His brother. He held fast Baba's Feet, confessed his guilt and negligence, repented and asked for Baba's pardon. He offered to give another fruit as a substitute, but Baba refused to accept it saying that the worth of that coconut was by far, many times more, than an ordinary one and that it could not be replaced by another one. Baba also added- "Now you need not worry yourself any more about the matter. It was on account of my wish that the coconut was entrusted to you, and ultimately broken on the way; why should you take the responsibility of the actions on you? Do not entertain the sense of doer-ship in doing good, as well as for bad deeds; be entirely pride-less and ego-less in all things and thus your spiritual progress will be rapid." What a beautiful spiritual instruction Baba gave!

Balaram Dhurandhar (1878-1925)

Mr. Balaram Dhurandhar belonged to the Pathari Prabhu community, of Santacruz, Bombay. He was an advocate of the Bombay High Court and sometime Principal of the Government Law School, Bombay. The whole Dhurandhar family was pious and religious. Mr. Balaram served his community, and wrote and published an account of it. He then turned his attention to spiritual and religious matters. He studied carefully Gita, and its commentary Jnaneshwari; and other philosophical and other metaphysical works. He was a devotee of Vithoba of Pandharpur and he came in contact with Sai Baba in 1912.

Six months previous, his brothers Babulji and Vamanrao came to Shirdi and took Baba's darshan. They returned home, and mentioned their sweet experiences to Balaram and other members. Then they all decided to see Sai Baba. Before they came to Shirdi, Baba declared openly that - "Today many of my Darbar people are coming." The Dhurandhar brothers were astonished to hear this remark of Baba, from others; as they had not given any previous intimation of their trip. All the other people prostrated themselves before Baba, and sat talking to Him. Baba said to them- "These are my Darbar people to whom I referred before" and said to the Dhurandhar brothers- "We are acquainted with each other for the last sixty generations." All the brothers were meek and modest; they stood with joined hands, staring at Baba's Feet.

All the Sattvic emotions such as tears, hairs on the neck standing up, choking, etc.., moved them and they were all happy.

Then they went to their lodging, took their meals and after taking a little rest again came to the Masjid. Balaram sat near Baba, massaging His Legs.

Baba Who was smoking a chillum advanced it towards him and beckoned him to smoke it. Balaram was not accustomed to smoking, still he accepted the pipe, smoked it with great difficulty; and returned it reverentially with a bow. This was the most auspicious moment for Balaram. He was suffering from Asthma for six years. This smoke completely cured him of the disease, which never troubled him again. Some six years later, on a particular day, he again got an attack of Asthma. This was precisely the time when Baba took his Mahasamadhi.

The day of this visit was a Thursday; and the Dhurandhar brothers had the good fortune of witnessing the Chavadi, Balaram saw the lustre of Pandurang on Baba's face and next morning at the Kakad-Arati time, the same phenomenon - the same lustre of his Beloved Deity- Pandurang was visible again on Baba's face.

Mr. Balaram Dhurandhar wrote, in Marathi, the life of the Maharashtra Saint Tukaram, but did not survive to see its publication. It was published, later on, by his brothers in 1928. In a short note on Balaram's life given in the beginning of the book, the above account of Balaram's visit has been fully corroborated therein.

Bow to Shri Sai - Peace be to all

Epilogue

We are done with Chapter 51 and now we come to the last Chapter (No. 52 in the original). In this Hemadpant gave his concluding remarks and promised to give an index, giving the contents of all the Chapters in verse as is given in Marathi sacred books, but unfortunately that index was not found in Hemadpant papers. It was therefore, composed and supplied by an able and worthy devotee of Sai Baba, Mr. B.V. Deo (Retired Mamlatdar) of Thana. As we give in English books an index in the beginning and contents of each Chapter at its top, we need not consider the last index Chapter here; and so we consider this Chapter as the Epilogue. Unfortunately Hemadpant did not survive to revise the manuscript of this Chapter and make it ready for the printing press. When it was sent to the press Mr. Deo found it to be incomplete and unintelligible in certain places; but it had to be published as it was found. The chief topics dealt therein are briefly given below.

Greatness of Sadguru Sai

We prostrate ourselves before and take refuge in that Sai Samarth Who besets all animate and inanimate things in the universe, from a post to God Brahma, pots, houses, mansions and even sky, Who pervades all creatures equally without any differentiation, to Whom all devotees are alike; and Who knows not honor and dishonor, like or dislike. If we remember Him and surrender to Him, He fulfills all our desires and makes us attain the goal of life.

This ocean of mundane existence is very hard to cross. Waves of infatuation beat high there against the bank of bad thoughts and break down trees of fortitude. The breeze of egoism blows forcibly and makes the ocean rough and agitated. Crocodiles in the form of anger and hatred move there fearlessly. Eddies in the form of the idea "I and Mine" and other doubts whirl there incessantly and innumerable fishes in the form of censure, hate and jealousy play there, Though this ocean is so fierce and

287

terrible, Sadguru Sai is its Agasti (Destroyer) and the devotees of Sai have not the least to fear of it. Our Sadguru is the boat, which will safety take us across this ocean.

Prayer

Now fall flat before Sai Baba and holding His Feet make the following prayer for the public:

Let not our mind wander and desire anything except Thee. Let this work (Satcharita) be in every house and let it be studied daily. Ward off the calamities of those who study it regularly.

Fala-Shruti (Reward of Study)

Now a few words about the reward you get, from a study of this work.

After bathing in the sacred Godavari and after taking the darshan of the Samadhi in the Samadhi Mandir in Shirdi, you should read or hear the Satcharita; if you do this all your threefold afflictions will vanish. Casually thinking about the stories of Sai, you will get unconsciously interested in spiritual life and if you then go on through the work with love, all your sins will be destroyed.

If you wish to get rid of the cycle of births and deaths, read Sai's stories and remember Him always; and get yourself attached (devoted) to His Feet. If you dive into the sea of Sai's stories, and then give them out to others, you will get an ever new flavor of them and save the hearers from perdition. If you go on meditating on Sai's Form, it will in course of time disappear and lead you into self-realization. It is very hard to know or realize the nature of Self or Brahma, but if you approach through the Sugun Brahma (Sai's Form) your progress will be easy.

If the devotee completely surrenders himself to Him, he will lose his individuality and be merged in Him and be one with Him, as the river in the sea. If you thus become merged with Him in any of the three states, viz., waking, dream and sleep, you get rid of the bond of samsara. If anybody after bathing reads this with love and faith, and completes it within a week, his calamities will disappear; or if he hears or reads it daily and regularly all his dangers will be warded off.

By its study, a man wishing for wealth will get it and a pure trader, success in his life. He will get the reward according to his faith and devotion. Without these, there will be no experience of any kind. If you read this respectfully, Sai will be pleased, and removing your ignorance and poverty, He will give you knowledge, wealth and prosperity.

With concentrated mind, if you read a Chapter daily, it will give you unbounded happiness. One, who has his welfare at heart, should study it carefully and then he will ever remember Sai gratefully and joyfully in birth after birth.

This work should be read at home specially on Guru Purnima (Ashadha full-moon day), Gokul-Ashtami, Rama-Navami and Dasara (Baba's anniversary day). If you study this one book carefully, all your desires will be satisfied and if you always remember Sai's Feet in your heart, you will easily cross the Bhava (Samara) sagar. By its study, the diseased and sick will get health, the poor wealth, the mean and afflicted prosperity, and the mind will get rid of all ideas and get steadiness.

Dear good and devoted readers and listeners, we also make our bow to you all, and make you a special request. Never forget Him whose stories you have read day by day or month by month. The more fervently you read or listen to these stories, the more encouragement Sai gives us to serve you and be of use to you. Both the author and the readers must cooperate in this work, help each other and be happy.

Prasad-Yachana

We close the with prayer to the Almighty for the following Prasad of favor:

May the readers and devotees get complete and wholehearted devotion to Sai's Feet. May His Form be ever fixed in their eyes and may they see Sai (the Lord) in all beings. Amen!

Bow to Shri Sai - Peace be to all

Arati to Shirdi Sai Baba

Oh Sai Baba, we wave lights before You, the bestower of happiness to the Jivas.

Give us - Your servants and devotees rest under the dust of Your feet.

Burning (destroying) desire, You remain absorbed in Your Self and show the Lord (God) to the aspirants.

As one feels intently, You give him experiences or realizations accordingly.

Oh kind-hearted, Your power is such!

Meditation on Your name removes our fear of the samsar.

Your method of work is really unfathomable as You always help the poor and helpless.

In this Kali Yuga, You - the all-pervasive Datta, have really incarnated as Saguna Brahma.

Ward off the fear of samsar of the devotees who come to You every Thursday so as to enable them to see the feet of the Lord.

Oh! God of Gods, I pray that let my treasure be the service of Your feet. Feed Madhav and *(devotee should substitute their name here)* with happiness as the cloud feeds the Chatak bird with pure water and thus keep up Your Word.

Amen!

Glossary

A

Abhangs - devotional songs in verses in specified meter
Abhishek - ritualistic holy bath
Acharya - a spiritual teacher
Adharma - irreligious
Adhibhautik - primordial materialism
Adhidaivik - primordial & godly
Adhyatma - see adhyatma ramayan
Adhyatmik - spiritual
Adhyatma Ramayan - esoteric version of Ram's story
Adi Maya - primordial illusions
Advaita - doctrine of identity of human soul and divine essence
Agarbattis - perfumed incense sticks
Agnihotri - brahmin who maintains a perpetual sacred fire
Agninarayan - divinity presiding over fire
Agyan - ignorance
Ahutis - offerings put into the sacred fire
Akshata - consecrated rice
Allah Malik - God is all powerful
Allah Miya - endearing name of 'Allah'
Amalak - Indian Gooseberry in English, a powerful ayurvedic fruit
Amavas/Amavasya - dark night prior to the new moon
Ambemohar - fragrant variety of rice grown on the hills of Western Maharashtra in India
Ambika - Goddess Durga
Ambil - a thin sour gruel
Amra - mango
Anandashram - a place of boarding & lodging named as such
Angarkha - long coat / cloak
Aṇimā - reducing one's body even to the size of an atom
Ankush - goad
Annas - old Indian coin; sixteen annas to a rupee
Anna-shuddhi - ghee i.e. clarified butter added to food for purification

Anushthan - practice of religious austerity

Anusmruti - one of the five jewels from the Mahabharata

Apar Brahma - Sagun (manifest) Brahma

Aratis - circulatory waving of wick lights along with singing of praises of deity/guru

Archana - a ritual of performing worship

Arghya - oblation of water to God

Artha - meaning

Arvachin - modern or recent

Asan - seat

Asat - untruth/illusory

Ashadi Ekadashi - 11th day of 4th month of Hindu calendar

Ashram - hermitage; four stages of life

Ashta Latvia bhava - the eight forms of spiritual changes/ecstasies

Ashtami - 8th day of Hindu calendar

Ashtang - the eight parts of the body: hands, thighs, breast, eyes, forehead etc....

Ashwatha - peepal tree, holy fig tree

Ashwin - 7th month of Hindu calendar around October

Atal - one of the seven hells - refer saptapatals

Atithi - guest

Atma/Atman - soul

Atmaram - one rejoicing in knowledge of the self

Atma-tatva - essence of the Supreme Spirit

Attar - perfume

Attithi Yagna - offering food to the uninvited guest who may come to the door step

Augusti - a sage

Aulia - Muslim saint

Aum/Aumkar - a symbol of Parabrahma to be meditated upon and worshipped

Avatar - an incarnation of God

Avyakrit - unmanifested

293

B

Bairagi - an ascetic
Balgopals - children of God; also childhood of Lord Krishna
Barat - marriage procession
Barfi - Indian sweet made of milk & sugar
Basundi - Indian sweet
Batasas - Indian sweet made of sugar
Beeba - myrobalan - marking nut
Bel - aegle marmelos or cratoeva religiosa, a tree sacred to Shiva
Bhadrapad - 6th month of Hindu calendar - Bhadon (August - September)
Bhagat - a devotee; a nickname given to Mhalsapati
Bhagvan - God
Bhagvat Dharma - ancient Hindu religious philosophy
Bhagvat Gita - preachings of Lord Krishna
Bhajan - devotional songs
Bhajan Mala - a garland of devotional songs
Bhajis - gram flour preparation, which is fried
Bhakri - thick bread of jowar (sorghum), bajri (millet) flour
Bhakta - a devotee
Bhakta Leelamrut - a sacred book written by Das Ganu
Bhakti - devotion
Bharits - brinjals seasoned with curds
Bharta - curry made from roasted brinjals
Bhat - plain rice
Bhavarth Ramayan - holy book
Bhavartha Dipika - Hindu sacred book
Bhavishyottar Puran - book predicting future events.
Bhikshu - one who solicits alms
Bhishma Stavaraj - one of the five jewels from the Maharajah
Bhoota Yagna - refer pancha maha yagnas
Bhu - dearer than life (part of Gayatri Mantra)
Bhuva - destroyer of sorrows (part of Gayatri Mantra)
Bhuvarlok - region between the sun & the earth
Bidi - hand rolled tobacco leaf indigenous cigarette

Brahma Gñyan - divine knowledge
Brahma Yagna - refer pancha maha yagnas
Brahmachari - a person vowed to celibacy
Brahmacharya - celibate
Brahmadev - Brahma, supreme Hindu deity, the creator
Brahmaiva - one who has no desires and has no fruits thereof. So he is not re-born. Therefore, there is no departure of his vital life force. In this world, such a person is Brahma and attains Brahman
Brahmalok - abode of Brahma, one of the heavens
Brahmananda - divine bliss
Brahmanic - one with the Brahma, the creator
Brahmaroop - embodiment of Brahma
Brahmarthi - seeker of Brahma
Buka - fragrant dark powder
Burfi - dense milk based sweet

C

Chaitra - first month of Hindu calender
Chakor - a partridge said to subsist on moon beams and to drink water from the clouds, native to Asia, including Israel, Lebanon, Turkey, Iran, Afghanistan, Pakistan and India
Chakravati - emperor
Chamar - the tail of Bos grunniens, used to whisk off flies
Chandi - another name of Goddess Durga
Chandogya Upanishad - one of the ancient and longest Upanishads
Chandrakant - a fabulous gem
Chandrayan - religious observation or penance
Changbada - traditional musical instruments
Chapatis - round unleavened flatbread
Charanatirtha - holy water obtained after washing Lord's feet
Charan - sacred feet of the deity
Chatak - Pied Cuckoo / Papiha that lives only on rain drops
Chaturai - cleverness
Chavadi - meeting place of the villagers, the office of the Kulkarni and where Baba slept on alternate nights
Chela - disciple
Chhapi - a piece of cloth placed around the chillum
Chillum - clay pipe for smoking - typically used by Sadhus with Cannabis
Chintamani - a jewel which grants a desired object
Chiplis - wooden sticks which are beaten to a rhythm
Chitnis - patwari - the village revenue officer
Chopdar - mace bearer
Chulli - a mud hearth (refer panch soonas)
Chuna - lime
Chutneys - a paste with seasoning, chillies, coriander leaves, lemon juice, etc..

D

Dadana - charity
Dada - respectful addressing of elder
Dakshina - offering of money as gift to God/sage
Dakshinayan - the half year in which the sun is said to move from north to south
Dal - pulses such as lentils
Dama - control of body & senses
Dana - charity
Dand - punishment
Danda - baton
Danta - to have restraint
Darshan - divine vision - to receive a transfer of Divinity when in the presence of a Holy person or object
Darshan yatra - pilgrimage for divine vision
Dashavatar - the ten incarnations of Vishnu as Fish, Tortoise, Boar,
Man-Lion, Vaman the Dwarf, Parshuram, Ram, Krishna, Buddha and Kalki yet to manifest
Dashmi - 10th day of Hindu calendar
Dasara - see Vijayadashmi
Daya - kindness
Dev Yagna - refer panch maha yagnas
Deva - endearing way of addressing Baba or any Hindu Saint
Devastate - Lord Krishna
Devasthan - holy place
Dhangar - shepherd woman
Dhanteras - 13th day of dark half of the month of Kartik, two days before Diwali
Dharamshala - a building for stay of pilgrims
Dharma - religious & social obligations which a Hindu devout has to adhere to
Dhoti/Dhotar - a piece of cloth worn round the lower body
Dhoti-poti - yogic practice of cleaning of internal organs
Dhuni - sacred fire

Dhwaja - flag
Dhyana - meditation
Digambar - naked pious sage, anger personified, descendent of Bhrigu, follower of Parashuram
Dñyaneshwar - Hindu saint
Dñyaneshwari - Hindu sacred book written by Dñyaneshwar
Dñyanoba Maharaj - sage Dñyaneshwar
Dugdugas - those who imitate the sound of a rickety, shaking article
Durbar - gathering of devotees around Baba
Durga - principal form of the Goddess
Dwaravati - Lord Krishna's Dwarka
Dwarka Mayi - the mosque in Shirdi which was used as a dwelling by Sai Baba

E, F & G

Eid - Muslim festival that marks the end of the month of Ramadan

Ekadashi - 11th day of a lunar fortnight

Eknath Bhagvat - holy book composed by Sant Eknath in 1570 AD

Fateha - Muslim way of offering food

Feni - preparation like 'sevain', made out of wheat or rice

Gadi - seat with bolster, usually made for a holy person

Gajendra Moksha - one of the five jewels from the Maharajah

Gandh/Gandha - sandalwood paste

Gandharva - celestial chorister

Ganga/Gangas - holy Indian river

Garima - refer to anima-garima-laghima

Gayatri Mantra - a sacred & powerful mantra from the Vedas

Gharba-avasta - being pregnant

Gharge - fried pat of wheat or rice, boiled with sugar

Ghats - banks of the rivers, canals, ponds, etc....

Ghee - clarified butter

Ghol - ring with bits of iron loosely attached and fastened to the top of a staff

Girija - Parvathi, consort of Lord Shiva

Gita Rahasya - Tilak's commentary on the Gita in Marathi

Gnyani - learned one

Godavari - a river of Western India

Gokul Ashtami - Lord Krishna's birthday

Gondhalis - musicians and singers and makers of gondhal/noise

Gopal Kala - feasting and merriment, following the breaking of the mud pot, filled with curds, parched rice, coins etc.... The pot is hung high and reached by the formation of human pyramids by the merrymakers

Grinati - one who teaches or gives sermon i.e. the guru

Guavas - Indian fruit

Gulal - coloured powder

Gulpapdi - cake made by frying wheat flour & adding it to jaggery

Gulvadi - wadis made out of jaggery

299

Gunas - the constituent qualities of nature
Gurav - a caste
Guru Bandhu - disciples of the same guru
Guru Charitra - the story of Narasimha Saraswati Swamiji, avatar of Dutta. Its reading is said to destroy all evils & grants salvation
Gurudev/Gururaya - guru, revered mentor, spiritual teacher
Gururaj - respectful address of a guru
Gurumaya - guru, the mother
Gurupurnima - annual full moon night for worship of guru
Guruputra - disciple
Gyan - knowledge

H, I & J

Hakim - learned in herbal medicines
Halal - slaughter of an animal in accordance with Islamic law
Handi - round vessel to cook food
Harijans - Hindu out-caste
Hatha Yoga - one of the yogic practices
Hiranyagarbha - the golden egg of the Brahman from which comes the earth, its seven islands and nine continents, the seven heavens and the seven nether lands
Holi - festival of colours
Holika - a deity, worshipped during Holi
Homa - havan
Idgah - a place for Muslim prayers
Indra - Vedic God of Weather and War, leader of the Gods
Ishavasya Bhavartha Bodhini - holy book
Ishavasya Upanishad - holy book
Ishta Devta - favourite deity
Jamadagni - pious sage, anger personified, descendent of Bhrigu, follower of Parashuram
Janalok - abode of sons of Brahma
Janmotsav - birthday celebration
Japa - the meditative repetition of a mantra or a divine name
Jari - see zari
Jeshth - 3rd month of Hindu calendar
Jhanj - musical instrument
Jholi - a bag for alms hanging from the shoulder
Jiresal - excellent variety of rice
Jiva/Jeeva - soul - atman - individual
Jñyana - knowledge
Jowar - sorghum grain

K - L

Kacharya - delicacy of sliced brinjals fried crisp & brown
Kadva - bitter
Kafni - long, ankle length shirt like robe
Kakad arati - early morning prayer
Kaliyug or Kaliyuga - the 4th age of the world, the iron age or that of vice.
Kalpataru/Kalpavraksh - wish fulfilling tree
Kamadhenu - cow that fulfils all desires
Kandani - refer panch soonas
Kans - Lord Krishna's maternal uncle, who tried to kill Krishna
Karmas - law of retribution / cause and effect
Karmath - one who takes to the path of knowledge
Kashi - Banaras, one of the holy places
Kasturi - musk
Kaustubh - one of the fourteen precious things obtained from churning of the ocean
Ketaki - pandanus odoratissimus - ,a type of flowering tree
Ketu - Shadow Planet in Hindu Astrology
Khanda-yoga - Yogic practice of severing & reassembling limbs of the body
Khanjari - small tambourine
Kheer - rice, milk and sugar dish
Kitchari - staple comfort food of India, revered for its easy digestibility and cleansing nature, it is a bland dish often fed to babies and the elderly in India, a mixture of rice and pulses
Kirtans - singing the God's praises to the accompaniment of music
Kolamba - the mud pot into which all offerings of food including Baba's alms were put
Kolhatinis - rope dancers
Konkan - new land created by Parashuram by forcing the waters of the ocean in the western ghats of India
Koran - a sacred book of the Muslims
Koshimbiri - raw fruit or vegetables pickled or preserved
Koss or Kos - measurement of distance - approx. 2 miles equal a koss

Kruttika Nakshatra - third of lunar mansions
Kuber - treasurer of the heavens
Kulkarani - patwari, a village officer
Kumar - vermillion
Kurdiyas - preparation of rice flour, fried in circular swirls
Laghima - becoming almost weightless
Lakh or Lac - is a unit in the Indian numbering system equal to one hundred thousand
Lalaji - a term of respectful address
Langoti - a loin cloth
Leelas - divine sport
Lendi - stream on the outskirts of Shirdi village
Long Maharaj - long snake
Lota - tumbler

M

Maha Bhagvat - holy book
Mahasamadhi - leaving the mortal coil, for a Saint or Divine Soul
Mahalok - sphere of sun and luminaries
Mahanaivedya - offerings of variety of delicious foods to a deity
Mahanirvan - refer to mahasamadhi
Mahar - refer to Harijan
Maharaj - respectful way of addressing Baba/emperor
Mahatal - one of the seven hells
Mahatma - high soul of noble nature
Mahattva - the 2nd of the twenty-five principles of samkhyas, one of the six Shastras
Mahendra - Indra, God of rain
Maheshwar - Lord Shiva
Mahima - expanding one's body to an infinitely large size
Mahoday Parva - 1. a festival of joy. 2. a good action that confers special merit upon the performance
Mahurat - auspicious time
Mala - garland
Mama - maternal uncle
Mamlatdar - a revenue official
Mandes - preparation of wheat flour, a very thin chappati slightly sweet
Mangal Ghat - banks on river Ganga in Kashi
Mantra - sacred verse or text from Vedas
Margashirsh Purnima - full moon night of 11th month of Hindu calender around December
Marjani - refer pancha soonas
Marwadi - Hindu community hailing from Marwar - Rajasthan (India)
Masjid - mosque
Masjidmai - mosque where Baba lived & named it Dwarkamai
Math - religious establishment
Maulana - title given to a learned Muslim
Maulvi - Muslim priest

Mavashibai - aunt / mother's sister

Maya - the invisible, illusory or unmanifest and also the material world

Mimansa - ancient Hindu philosophy

Moksha - salvation, release from cycle of existence

Moong Vadis - small, flatish cakes made from moong pulse

Moulvis - Muslim priest

Mridang - drum

Muga vadi - small, flatish cakes made from phaseolusmango

Muhurat - auspicious time

Muhurram/Moharram - 1st month of Mohammedan year; fast observed in memory of killing of Hasan & Hussein (grandsons of prophet Muhammad)

Mujawar - a devotee who tends the tomb of a saint

Mukti - liberation; four fold mukti means absorption into the essence of Brahman

Mullah - Muslim theologian

Munim - clerk

Munis - sages

Munshi - clerk

Munsif - civil judge

Muttal - one of the seven hells; refer saptapatals

N - O

Naivedya - food offering to the deity
Nakshatra - asterism in the moon's path
Namaaz - prayer offered by the Muslims
Namaskar - respectful salutations
Nanda-deep - light kept burning before a deity, day & night
Nandi - bull God, vehicle of Lord Shiva
Narada - the most enlightened of enlightened sages - son of Brahma
Naradiya Bhakti - way of worship as per the sage Narad
Narasimha - a fierce avatar of Lord Vishnu
Nath Bhagvat - sacred book
Nautanki - street play
Navachandi Havan - oblations to the fire with recitations of hymns in praise of Goddess Durga
Navrathra - 1st nine days of the light half of the month of Ashwin during which Durga is worshipped
Neelkanth - Lord Shiva
Neem - margosa
Nidhis - nine treasures of the God Kuber
Nimbar - niche in the western wall of the mosque where the sandalwood etc.... is applied
Nirakar - that which is without form
Niranjan - the lamp
Nirayan - leaving mortal coil
Nirgun - unmanifest, formless (abstract)
Nirvan - see mahasamadhi
Nirvikalpa - state of samadhi & complete peace
Oti - portion of the sari touching the lap
Ovi - verse

P

Pada-puja - worshipping of Lord's feet
Padukas - holy feet/shoes of the Lord
Palkhi - palanquin
Pan - betel leaf
Panch soonas - five sins i.e. " kandani" – pestle, " chulli " –
lighting the hearth fire, " u dkumbhi " – water pots; " peshani " –
grinding, " m arjani " – sweeping
Pancha - poor-man's dhoti which is short - also used as towel
Panchamrut - a blend of curd, milk, sugar, honey etc...
Panchang - a calendar which deals with five things, such as the
lunar date, the day of the week, planets' conjunction and half
lunar day
Panchmaha yagnas - five yagnas i.e. Brahma Yagna is reciting
of Vedas;
Pitru Yagna – offering food by encircling with water;
Dev Yagna – offering food to the deities; Bhoota Yagna –
offering food to all creatures. Attithi Yagna – offering food to the
uninvited guest who may come to the doorstep
Panchikaran - combining amicably together of the five elemen-
tary substances
Panch-pran - five vital airs i.e. prana, apana, samana, udana,
vayana
Panchratani Gita - a compilation of five jewels from the
Maharajah namely a) Srimad Bhagvat Gita, b) Sree Vishnu
Saharsranam Stotra, c) Bhishma Stavaraj, d) Anusmruti,
e) Gajendra Moksha
Pandits - one well versed in shastras
Panga - dough spread over a leaf, rolled and baked over fire
Panja - a hand, which symbolises the five great saints of the
Muslims
Pan-vida - rolled betel leaf with areca nut & other ingredients
Papad - thin, crisp cake of urad - black lentils
Parabrahma - nirguna Brahman, Brahman without qualities
Pārāyan - religious observances - regular reading of sacred
books / texts
Parees - a stone which can turn ordinary stone into gold

Parijat - flower
Parmarth - ultimate spiritual goal
Parmatma - the God
Patal - one of the seven hells
Pativrata - faithful & devoted wife
Payalu - child born with legs first
Payas - sweet made of milk, sugar & rice
Pedas - sweetmeat made of milk & sugar
Pehran - long shirt
Peshani - refer panch soonas
Phalgun Shud - 2nd fortnight of 12th month of Hindu calendar
Pheta - cloth headdress
Pie - coin of small denominational value of British India
Pilaf - rice cooked with other ingredients
Pind - symbolic representation of Shiva / food offerings to the departed soul
Pir - Muslim saint
Pitamber - a dhoti of yellow silk
Pitru Yagna - refer panch maha yagnas
Polis - refer puran poli
Pothi - sacred text
Prabhuraya - respectful address of the God
Pradakshina - circumambulation of an idol by way of reverence
Prajapati - the creator
Prakrithi - the nature
Pralay - deluge
Pran-ahuti - oblation to the five pranas done at the beginning of meals
Prarabdha - previous karma; actions of past life
Prasad - sanctified food offerings
Prathnasamajist - one who does not worship image
Prayag - confluence of three rivers
Puja - worship
Pujari - priest
Puja-thali - a round tray containing articles for worship of a deity
Punya - merit
Punyatitthi - auspicious day of any saint leaving mortal coil

Puran/Puranas - ancient Sanskrit Hindu mythology
Puranika - a Brahmin well versed in the puran (Hindu sacred text)
Puranpoli - a wheat cake with stuffing of bengal gram cooked with jaggery
Purdah - veil
Puris - thin puffed wheat cakes
Purnima - full moon night
Purush - the supreme soul
Pushpanjali - offering of flowers

R

Rahu - shadow planet in Hindu Astrology

Rajaram - Lord Ram, the king

Rajas - passion, one of the three gunas

Rakshas or Rakshasa - a demonic being in Hinduism

Ram Raksha Stotra - hymn of praise to Lord Ram

Ramnavami - birth day of Lord Ram

Ramvijay - holy book

Rangoli - design drawn with lime/coloured powder

Rasatal - one of the seven hells; refer saptapatals

Rashi - the 12 signs of the zodiac

Rath - chariot

Ravan - Ravan was the King of Lanka, who kidnapped Sita and was the enemy of Ram

Rishi - Seer or Saint

Rogda - puffed mass of dough baked on embers

Rudra - Lord Shiva

Rudraksha - seed of the Elaeocarpus ganitrus, a large evergreen broad-leaved tree whose seed is traditionally used for prayer beads in Hinduism and Buddhism. The seeds are known as rudraksha, or rudraksh. They are considered the "Tears of Lord Shiva" - Rudra.

S

Sabha-mandap - courtyard of Dwarkamai
Sachidananda - person pure in mind & body
Sadgati - liberation
Sadguru - realised teacher and avatar - an incarnation
Sadgurunatha - respectful address
Sadgururaya - respectful address of Sadguru
Sadhak - disciple
Sadhana - devoted striving
Sadhu - ascetic, holy man
Sagun - manifest, virtuous
Saimauli - Mother Sai
Sai Prabha - a magazine published by Sai devotees
Sairaya - respectful address of Sai Baba
Samadhan - quintessence of the mind
Samadhi - profound meditation; complete burial or entombment of a saint
Samadhi Mandir - temple where mortal remains of a saint are buried
Samarth - competent & powerful
Samara - the world
Sandhya - religious meditation and repetition of mantras in the mornings/evenings
Sanjoriya - stuffed cake made out of sheera
Sansthan - Sai Baba Sansthan of Shirdi / any organization
Sant Leelamrut - a sacred book written by Das Ganu
Sant Vijaya - a sacred book written by Mahapati
Sanyas - a stage of reclusion
Sanza - wheat pudding
Sapta Shringi - carved image of the Goddess near Vani (Nasik)
Saptapatals - netherworlds; seven hells - atal, vittal, muttal, tal-atal, mahatal, rasatal, patal
Saptashati - collection of seven hundred verses in praise of Durga in Markandaya Puran
Sardar - head of a group

Sari - dress worn by Indian women

Sarkar - master

Sarodes - those who play the seven-stringed instrument and constantly practise the prediction of good fortune to the lower caste.

Sat - truth / real

Satcharita - life & teachings of Sai Baba / any great person

Sat-chit-ananda - truth, consciousness & bliss

Satka - black wood baton about 2 1/2 feet long

Satsang - association with virtuous people

Satva - harmony, goodness, one of the three gunas

Satvaguna - righteousness

Satyalok - heaven of Brahma and rishis

Satya Sai Katha - reading of 3 chapter relating to Sai Nath from Das Ganu's Arvachin Bhakta Leelamrut

Satya Sai Vrat - Sai puja after bath and being abstemious

Satyanarayan puja - worship of Lord Satyanarayan

Seemolanghan - the crossing of the border in pompous procession on the festival of Dassera

Seer - unit of weight in India - approx. 2 kilos. However there were many local variants of the seer in India and South Asia.

Sesh/Sheshnag - a legendary 1000 headed serpent

Shake - Hindu calendar / commencement of an era

Shakti - primordial cosmic energy that represents the dynamic forces that are thought to move through the entire universe. The personification of divine feminine creative power.

Shakti–pata - transference of power from the guru to the disciple, which is effected by touch, words or even a mere glance

Shama - mental restraint

Shastras - Hindu religious literature

Shastris - well versed in shastras

Sheera - cream of wheat with sugar/jaggery and ghee

Sheera-puri - cream of wheat with sugar/jaggery and ghee and puffed wheat cake fried in oil

Shehnai - traditional Indian musical instrument played on auspicious occasions

Shethji - a term of respectful address

Shidha - rice, dal, flour and ghee

Shikharini - sweet dish made of ripe plantains in milk & sugar
Shiva-ling - the phallus or emblematic representation of Shiva
Shivaratri - name of a festival in honour of Lord Shiva
Shlokas - spiritual verses
Shradha - faith in the guru
Shravan - 5th month of Hindu calendar
Shrirang - Lord Shriranga
Shruti - Vedas severally or collectively
Siddha - a person who abides within the perpetual bliss of self realization i.e. a semi divine person - usually possessing miraculous powers
Siddha-rana - one who has acquired all the eight siddhis
Siddhi - miraculous powers
Skanda - sections of a holy book
Smaran - meditating on the Supreme Being
Smritis - The Vedas
Somakant - jewel which starts oozing water when the rays of the moon fall on it
Sovala - state of purity
Stambha - all space
Stotra/Stotras - hymns - religious couplets
Sudarshan Chakra - the discus of Vishnu, a flaming weapon
Sudras - fourth and lowest of the traditional varnas, or social classes, of India, traditionally artisans and labourers
Sunthwada - sweetmeat with ginger
Supari - areca nut
Surma - antimony black powder applied to the eyes
Sutak - thirteen days after death when a household is deemed to be impure and during which no religious rites are performed
Swami - respected Hindu guru
Swarlok - region between sun and polarstar

T

Tabut - see tazia
Takia/Takiya - resting place for Muslim fakirs
Tal - pair of cymbals
Talatal - one of the seven hells; refer saptapatals
Taluka - a division of the district
Tamas - inertia, darkness, one of the three gunas
Tamasha - a show
Tamburi - a small Turkish guitar with four strings
Tantras - a system of techniques
Tapa - ascetic fervour or practice
Tapasvis - ascetic engaged in penance
Tapolok - heaven of the tapasvis
Taptamudra - impressions on the skins made by hot stamping
Tarak mantra - hymn for crossing the ocean of existence
Tathastuta - be it as you wish
Taziya - the bier supposed to be symbolically, the tombs of Hassan and Hussein carried in procession during the Muslim time of Muhurram
Teli - oilman
Thali - platter
Tilak - circular auspicious mark on the forehead
Tirth - sacred water
Tirtha - holy place of pilgrimage
Tithi - Hindu calendar date
Titiksha - forbearance, bearing the opposites
Tonga - a small carriage drawn by horse / horses
Tongawallah - driver of the horse carriage
Tripundra - three horizontal lines drawn on the forehead by applying sandalwood paste, turmeric or kumkum, particularly to Lord Shiva or self
Trishanku - person left hanging between heaven & earth
Trishudhi - corporal, oral & mental purification
Tulsi - sacred basil plant
Tumrel - tin pot used by Baba for collecting food
Turban - head dress made of cloth
Tuvar - pulse (dal)

U

Uddhava Gita - 11th chapter of the Bhagavad Gita
Udi - holy ash from Baba's sacred fire known as dhuni
Udkumbhi - refer to panch soonas
Udyapan - the concluding ceremony for religious observance
Ukkal - pot where the grains are crushed to remove chaff
Uma - Parvathi, consort of Lord Shiva
Upadesh - sermon / advice
Uparna - small cloth worn loosely over the shoulders
Upasana - worship
Urus - in South India, a Muslim festival to commemorate the death anniversary of a Sufi Saint

V

Vades - cake made of pulses, ground spiced and fried
Vadranal - the fire under the ocean
Vaid / Vaidyas - learned in herbal medicines
Vairagi - an ascetic
Vairagya - a state of sainthood/asceticism
Vaishnav - devotee of Lord Vishnu
Vaishwadev - fire
Vajra - thunder bolt
Valpapdi - wax beans
Vanaprashthachari - 4th stage of life when those renouncing
society are taken to the forest
Vanjari - a trader who knows the paths in the forest
Varan - highly tasteful dish made of pulses
Varun - God of water
Vasanas - desires
Vayu - wind
Vedangas - shastras
Vedant/Vedanta - system of Hindu philosophy
Ved - ancient holy scripture
Vedic Mantras - Holy sounds delineated in the Vedas
Vedis - 1. brahmin well versed in Vedas; 2. an altar prepared for
sacrifice
Veena - Indian lute
Venkatesh Stotra - hymn to Vishnu
Vibhuti - see Udi
Vichar Sagar - Hindi version of 'Panchadasi'
Vijayadashmi - the 10th day of the light half of the Hindu
month Ashwin and the festival celebrating the victory of Ram
over Ravan
Viraja - state of desirelessness
Vishnu - Hindu God regarded as supreme deity (maintainer) &
second member of triad i.e. Brahma, Vishnu, Shiva
Vishnu Sahasranama - thousand names of Lord Vishnu
Vishnupad - the image of Vishnu's feet at Gaya

Vittal - one of the seven hells; refer saptapatals
Vivek Sindhu - written by Mukundraj in 1188, i.e. more than 100 years before Dñyaneshwari, on Adwait, in Marathi
Vrat - religious ritual for observance of vow
Vrindavan - tulsi (sacred basil) plant holder
Vrittis - way of behaviour

W, X, Y & Z

Wada - a dwelling
Yada Panchavatishthante - when all the five senses & the intellect become steady, considered the highest state of yoga
Yagnas/Yagya - sacrificial act or rite
Yajñya - effort
Yavan - Muslim
Yoga - Hindu system of philosophical meditation & asceticism for effecting re-union with the universal spirit
Yoga Agni - sacred fire
Yogacharaya - spiritual teacher for philosophical meditation

Author Biographies

Original Author

Annasahab Dabholkar (or) Hemadpant

Annasaheb Dabholkar or simply Dabholkar or Hemadpant as he was called by Sai Baba, was born in 1859 into a poor Brahmin family in Thana district, near Mumbai. His father and grandfather were religious and devout persons. His father died at an early age, and as such the family was very poor. Dabholkar completed his Middle School English education at Poona, but because his adverse financial circumstances he could not continue his education. He then was appointed a school-master in his home town, and married his wife, Rukhmabai, soon after.

Eventually, Dabholkar was appointed "Talati" (village-officer), and afterwards as Head Clerk in the Mamlatdar's office, (a kind of revenue / government high official in India). Next he was appointed as a Forest Settlement Officer and then as a Director of Famine Relief Work at Gujarat State. In 1901 he was appointed as the Mamlatdar of Shahapur in Thana district and in 1903 as a Magistrate.

In 1909, a friend of his, Dixit, went to Shirdi and had darshan of Baba and was convinced that Baba was a Saint Divine, a God in human form. Dixit immediately wrote to Dabholkar, by then the Magistrate at Anand, and told him that he met a Saint who was a walking God in Shirdi. Dabholkar first visited Shirdi in 1910 where he too had the good fortune to have darshan of Sai Baba.

After great inspiration from Sai Baba, Dabholkar began work in 1917 on the Shri Sai Satcharita, Baba's Life History. Dabholkar's work is thus treated as the first authoritative foundation of all writings on Baba's life and His mission. In writing this book, Hemadpant enlisted the cooperation of all Baba's devotees to share their experiences with him. Hemadpant completed the Satcharita in 1929, in his native language Marathi.

Baba called him "Hemadpant" after the name of Hemadri, the famous and learned court-poet of the Yadava kings in the 13th century. It was a tribute given by Baba to Dabholkar as it signified the poetic talent in him and his capacity in rational thinking.

After his retirement he served Sai Baba till Baba's Mahasamadhi in 1918 and afterwards managed very skillfully and efficiently Sai Baba's Shirdi Sansthan till his own death in 1929. He left behind him his wife, Rukhmabai, one son and 5 daughters.

~

English Translator

Nagash Devastate Gunaji

Sri N. V. Gunaji wrote or translated over twenty-eight books in his life. Born in Belgaum in July 1873, he studied in the Government Law College in Mumbai and returned to Belgaum to take up the practice of law. After practising law for several years Shri N.V. Gunaji was appointed CEO of the Belgaum Municipality. Mr. Gunaji also published two books on Naturopathy: "Scientific and Efficient Breathing" and "Anti T. B. & Anti Heart Failure". He treated patients through naturopathy and scientific massage.

Shri N. V. Gunaji passed away in 1963 a few months before his ninetieth year.

~

Editor this Edition

Evan Rofheart

Evan Rofheart is an Internationally known energy healer who specializes in holistic and spiritual principles and practices that heal and balance the body, mind and spirit.

Evan has been on a spiritual path since he was fifteen years old, he was initiated into the technique of Transcendental Meditation in 1973; he became a teacher of TM a few years later when he was eighteen. Evan was fortunate to attend some of the early TM Siddhi - Levitation courses in Europe, in the latter part of the 1970s.

In the early 1980s Evan founded Rofheart International Oil, in Houston, Texas, a company and business model which revolution-ized the Oil Trading and Oil Brokerage business. After leaving the oil business, Evan founded numerous other businesses; he has sold and leased jet aircraft throughout the world, run a successful restaurant, started and operated a chain of magazine stores in the New York Metropolitan area, and he even spent a few years in the motion picture industry.

By the latter part of the 1990s, after attending Drexel Univer-sity in Philadelphia, Evan realized his life-long dream of working in architecture; he has successfully designed and managed major projects for film director Steven Spielberg, the gallery owner-Larry Gagosian and many other clients in New York's Hamptons.

It was after reaching a high level of success in architecture that the Divine, in the person of Shirdi Sai Baba, pulled Evan back forcefully into Spirituality. Since that time, Evan has been a devotee of Shirdi Sai Baba, visiting India numerous times and being blessed to spend over a week in Shirdi, at Baba's Mahasamadhi.

Since 2007 Evan has been working full time as a spiritual healer and teacher, making his services available through his website www.evananda.net

Evan may be contacted at evananda@gmail.com

In 2016 Evan founded Enlightenment Press (http://enlightenment-press.com) to make spiritual books and publications available through various eBook platforms.

ENLIGHTMENT PRESS
Spirituality in ebooks today!

Enlightenment Press
makes spiritual books and publications available
through every book platform

Like us on Facebook
www.facebook.com/EnlightenmentPress

enlightenment-press.com

Made in the USA
Columbia, SC
05 March 2018